THE SECRETS OF CHINESE MEDITATION

By the same author

CH'AN AND ZEN TEACHING

Series I

Series II

Series III

The body of Ch'an Master Wen Yen, founder of the Yun Men sect at Yun Men monastery, Kwangtung province, China. (Died in 949)

THE SECRETS OF CHINESE MEDITATION

Self-cultivation by Mind Control
as taught in the Ch'an, Mayahana
and Taoist schools in China.

LU K'UAN YÜ
(CHARLES LUK)

Samuel Weiser, Inc.
York Beach, Maine

First published in England by Rider & Co. 1964
First American edition 1969 by
Samuel Weiser, Inc.
Box 612
York Beach, Maine 03910

This Weiser Classics Series Edition 1984

ISBN 0-87728-066-5

Printed in the United States by
Mitchell-Shear, Inc.
Ann Arbor, MI.

To the memory of
CARL GUSTAV JUNG and LOBZANG JIVAKA
whose encouragement has sustained my humble
efforts to present to Western Buddhists the
Dharma as taught in my country

CONTENTS

ILLUSTRATIONS

PREFACE

We take refuge in the Buddha,
We take refuge in the Dharma,
We take refuge in the Saṅgha,
We take refuge in the Triple Gem within ourselves.

THE Buddha Dharma is useless if it is not put into actual practice because if we do not have personal experience of it, it will be alien to us and we will never awaken to it in spite of our book-learning. An ancient said:

Self-cultivation has no other method,
It requires but knowledge of the way.
If the way only can be known,
Birth and death at once will end.

Therefore, in our self-cultivation, we should first know the way, and the Buddhas and great masters have taught us the appropriate methods in the sūtras and treatises. The purpose of this volume is to acquaint readers with various methods of meditation as practised in China so that they can choose any one of them for their self-cultivation.

At first we hesitated to present versions of Chinese texts on successful practices and on experiences of dhyāna as we have been criticized for being unduly optimistic about the future of the Buddha Dharma in the West. Fortunately, a learned reader of ours, Mr. Terence Gray, who recently paid a short visit to the Far East, has written us: 'I myself believe that even if it were true that the East is weary after a thousand years of efforts, those of the West are as fresh today as were the disciples of Hui Neng.' He has also kindly sent us a copy of Mr. D. E. Harding's little book entitled *On having no Head*[1] in which the author relates his personal experience of dhyāna. We are grateful to Mr. Gray for the encouraging news and to Mr. Harding for his book and have thus been emboldened to present in this volume different methods of meditation with the accounts of satisfactory results achieved by some practisers.

The Buddha Dharma has no room for race and nationality and nothing is more misleading than the groundless contention that Westerners are not fit to achieve enlightenment. In their former lives many were virtuous men and women who practised the Buddha's Teaching but failed to attain enlightenment; their good karmas have caused them to be reborn in countries where propitious conditions prevail so that they can resume their self-cultivation. Those who have been reborn in the West are capable of understanding the holy Teaching and will certainly achieve satisfactory results in their present life. Therefore, racial discrimination should be cast away for Lin Chi said: 'There is not a living being who cannot be liberated.'[2]

Buddhism is in decline in the East because of the division of the Dharma into different schools contradictory and hostile to each other. There are people who, instead of practising the methods taught in the sūtras and treatises, indulge in endless discussions which are empty and give no practical results. Others only learn to recite the sūtras by heart without striving to understand their profound meanings. Many are those who worship the Buddha, recite sūtras and repeat mantras in the

1. The Buddhist Society, London, 1961.
2. See *Ch'an and Zen Teaching*, Second Series, Rider (1961), p. 113.

hope of reaping merits for themselves and their families, without knowing that the World Honoured One teaches us to keep from illusions but not to cling to merits which are also illusory. We are urged by Him to forsake the cult of ego, then what merit do we earn when we cease to be selfish? What merit can a thief win when he stops stealing? There are also those who, in their study of Sanskrit and Tibetan, pass their precious time in practising the correct pronunciation either by pressing down the tongue or by putting it up against the palate or between the teeth, not realizing that philology has nothing to do with self-cultivation. Our modern students of sūtras and treatises, instead of studying their profound meanings, seem to be more interested in obtaining historical, linguistic and geographical data which have nothing to do with the Buddha Dharma which is beyond space and time.

During the last few years, in spite of my secluded life, I have met some of my readers in the West and have received very encouraging letters from others, and I have come to the conclusion that many Occidentals are now mature and digest quite well the Mahāyāna and Ch'an Teachings. At least half a dozen of them have related their personal experience of the state of dhyāna, amongst whom are two British readers in America. My optimism about the future of the Dharma in the West is, therefore, not groundless.

To prevent disbelief in the involuntary movements described in Chapters 6 and 7, I have given a sixty-five-minute demonstration of them to two British Bhikkhus, the Ven. Khema and the Ven. Aruno who are graduates of Oxford and Cambridge respectively and who happened to be in Hong Kong. The Ven. Aruno is Mr. Harding's son. Before their arrival, I gave the same demonstration to Mr. Hugh Ripman, a British banker, Mr. Paul H. Beidler, an American engineer, Dr. Huston Smith, professor of philosophy, Massachusetts Institute of Technology, Mr. Holmes Welch, author of *The Parting of the Way*, Madame Maurice Lebovich, a French painter, and a few well-known Chinese Buddhists, including

Mr. K. S. Fung, chief delegate of the Chinese Buddhists of the Hong Kong-Macao area at the Sixth Congress of the World Fellowship of Buddhists at Pnompenh, Cambodia, in 1961.

All brackets are mine.

UPĀSAKA LU K'UAN YÜ

Hong Kong.

THE SECRETS OF CHINESE MEDITATION

I

SELF-CULTIVATION AS TAUGHT IN THE ŚŪRAṄGAMA SŪTRA

ACCORDING to the Buddha, we all have inherent in ourselves the Tathāgata's wisdom which is unknown to us and which we cannot use because of our ignorance. We are also taught how to control our wandering minds so that our self-nature can return to its normal condition by which is meant a passionless, still and imperturbable state, free from all external influences, in which our immanent wisdom can manifest and function in the normal way, that is the way of the absolute, beyond all relativities and contraries.

Therefore, when discussing self-cultivation, we cannot stray from the Buddha Dharma for the World Honoured One taught us how to get out of saṁsāra for ever, whereas the highest achievement by other religious doctrines is only a temporary transmigration to the happy realm of devas from which, when the benefit of our good karma has been enjoyed to the full, we will be sent down again to the lower worlds of existence. For this reason, Yung Chia urged us not to seek happiness in saṁsāra and wrote in his Song of Enlightenment:

With force expended, a spent arrow's bound to fall and cause
Distasteful things to follow in the next incarnation.
How can it then compare with the wu wei reality
Which ensures a leap straight to the Tathāgata's stage?[1]

1. See *Ch'an and Zen Teaching*, Third Series, Rider (1962), p. 127.

As regards self-cultivation, there are many methods of practice which are found in the Chinese sūtras and śāstras but it is a matter for regret that authentic versions in Western languages are not yet available. Although we Buddhists in the East have access to the Chinese Tripiṭaka, it is impossible for us to practise all the methods simultaneously or one after the other in our quest of enlightenment (bodhi). In China, many Buddhists fail in self-cultivation because they choose wrongly methods unsuitable for them. For this reason, the late Master Hsu Yun said at the Jade Buddha monastery at Shanghai a few years ago:

Self-cultivation has no other method;
It requires but knowledge of the way.[1]

Because of His great compassion for all living beings whom He vowed to save, and in anticipation of our present confusion and perplexity in this Dharma ending age, the Buddha commanded twenty-five great Bodhisattvas and Arhats who were present in the Śūraṅgama assembly to speak of their methods of practice and of their personal experiences.

The Śūraṅgama Sūtra lists twenty-five ways of controlling the mind by meditation on the six sense data, six sense organs, six consciousnesses and seven elements—earth, water, fire, wind, space, sense-perception and consciousness. After each of the twenty-five great ones had related his personal experience and achievement, the Buddha ordered Mañjuśrī to compare their methods and to indicate the one most suitable for the benefit of Ānanda and those in the Dharma ending period, that is ourselves.

After rejecting the twenty-four methods which were not suitable for untrained minds, Mañjuśrī chose the one followed by Avalokiteśvara, which he praised as the most convenient for people on this earth. It consisted in disengaging the organ of hearing from its object, sound, and then directing that

1. See *Ch'an and Zen Teaching*, First Series, Rider (1960), p. 62.

Śākyamuni Buddha

organ into the stream of concentration. When the conception of both sound and stream-entry had been successfully wiped out, the duality of disturbance and stillness became illusory and non-existent. By advancing step by step, the subjective hearing and objective sound also vanished completely. This was where many meditators lost their way and were turned back to the realm of birth and death, but Avalokiteśvara said he did not stop there but strove to advance further. When the subjective awareness of this state and its object, that is the state itself, were perceived as illusory and non-existent, the awareness of voidness became all-embracing. However, the finest duality of subject and object, in other words the subtle view of ego and things (dharma), mentioned in the Diamond Sūtra, still remained and when this also was eliminated, this Bodhisattva reached the absolute state wherein all pairs of opposites, such as birth and death, creation and annihilation, beginning and end, ignorance and enlightenment, Buddhas and living beings, etc., have no room. Then the condition of nirvāṇa appeared, followed by a sudden leap over both the mundane and supramundane for realizing Absolute Universal Enlightenment (for the self) and Wonderful Englightenment (for others).[1]

Here are the relative passages in the Śūraṅgama Sūtra:

'The World Honoured One said to the great Bodhisattvas and chief Arhats in the assembly: "I want now to ask you, Bodhisattvas and arhats who have practised my Dharma and have reached the state beyond study,[2] this question: When you developed your minds for awakening to the eighteen realms of sense (dhātu),[3] which one did you regard as the best means of perfection and by what methods did you enter the state of samādhi?'[4]

1. Respectively the fifty-first and fifty-second stages of a Bodhisattva's development into a Buddha.

2. Aśaikṣa in Sanskrit; no longer learning, beyond study, the state of arhatship, the fourth of the śrāvaka stages; the preceding three stages requiring study. When an arhat is free from all illusions, he has nothing more to study.

3. Realms of sense, i.e. the six organs, their objects and their perceptions.

4. Internal state of imperturbability, exempt from all external sensations.

A. MEDITATION ON THE SIX SENSE DATA

1. Meditation on sound

'(Thereupon), Kauṇḍinya (one of) the first five bhikṣus, rose from his seat, prostrated himself with his head at the feet of the Buddha and declared: "When, soon after His enlightenment, we met the Tathāgata in the Mṛgadāva and Kukkuṭa parks, I heard His voice, understood His teaching and awakened to the Four Noble Truths.[1] When questioned by the Buddha, I interpreted them correctly and the Tathāgata sealed my awakening by naming me Ājñāta (Thorough Knowledge). As His wonderful voice was mysteriously all-embracing, I attained arhatship by means of sound. As the Buddha now asks about the best means of perfection, to me sound is the best according to my personal experience." '

2. Meditation on form

'Upaniṣad then rose from his seat, prostrated himself with his head at the feet of the Buddha and declared: "I also met the Buddha soon after His enlightenment. After meditating on impurity which I found repulsive and from which I kept, I awakened to the underlying nature of all forms. I realized that (even our) bleached bones which came from impurity would be reduced to dust and would finally return to the void. As both form and the void were perceived as non-existent, I achieved the state beyond study. The Tathāgata sealed my understanding and named me Niṣad.[2] After eradicating (relative) form, wonderful form (surūpa) appeared mysteriously all-embracing. Thus I attained arhatship through meditation on form. As the Buddha now asks about the best means of perfection, to me form is the best according to my personal experience." '

3. Meditation on smell

'A son of Buddha (kumāra)[3] named "Fragrance Adorned" then rose from his seat, prostrated himself with his head at the feet of the Buddha and declared: "After the Tathāgata had taught me to look into all worldly phenomena, I left Him and retired to set my mind at rest. While observing the rules of pure living, I saw bhikṣus burning sandal incense. In the stillness, its fragrance entered my nostrils. I enquired into this smell which was

1. Catvāriārya-satyāni, the four dogmas which are: suffering (duḥkha), its cause (samudaya), its ending (nirodha) and the way thereto (mārga). They are the doctrine first preached by the Buddha to his five former ascetic companions, and also those who accepted them in the śrāvaka stage.

2. Niṣad: going to the source of the phenomenal.

3. Kumāra: a Bodhisattva as son of the Tathāgata; a son of Buddha.

neither sandalwood nor voidness, and neither smoke nor fire and which had neither whence to come nor whither to go; thereby my intellect (manas) vanished and I achieved the state beyond the stream of transmigration (anāsrava).[1] The Tathāgata sealed my awakening and named me 'Fragrance Adorned'. After the sudden elimination of (relative) smell, wonderful fragrance became mysteriously all-embracing. Thus I attained arhatship by means of smell. As the Buddha now asks about the best means of perfection, to me smell is the best according to my personal experience." '

4. Meditation on taste

'The two sons of the Dharmarāja[2] called Bhaiṣajya-rāja and Bhaiṣajya-samudgata[3] who were present with five-hundred Brahma-devas,[4] then rose from their seats, prostrated themselves with their heads at the feet of the Buddha and declared: "Since the time without beginning, we have been skilful physicians in this world and have tasted with our own mouths herbs, plants and all kinds of mineral and stone found in the world, numbering 108,000 in all;[5] as a result we know perfectly their tastes, whether bitter, sour, salt, insipid, sweet or acrid, etc., their natural, changing or harmonizing properties, and whether they are cooling, heating, poisonous or wholesome. We received instruction from the Tathāgata and clearly knew that taste was neither existing nor non-existent, was neither body nor mind and did not exist apart from them. Since we could discern the cause of taste, we achieved our awakening which was sealed by the Buddha who then named us Bhaiṣajya-rāja and Bhaiṣajya- samudgata. We are now ranked among the 'sons of the Dharma king' in this assembly and because of our enlightenment by means of taste, we have attained the Bodhisattva stage. As the Buddha now asks about the best means of perfection, to us taste is the best according to our personal experience." '

5. Meditation on touch

'Bhadrapāla who was with sixteen companions who were all great Bodhisattvas, rose from his seat, prostrated himself with his head at the feet of the Buddha and declared: "When the Buddha with awe inspiring voice

1. Anāsrava: no leak; outside the passion-stream as contrasted with āsrava, 'leaking' or worldly cause.

2. Dharmarāja: the King of the Law, Buddha; a son of the Dharmarāja is a Bodhisattva.

3. The two Bodhisattvas of medicine, whose office is to heal the sick.

4. Brahma-devas: the gods of the Brahma heavens.

5. 108,000: the ten evils which are killing, stealing, carnality, lying, double-tongue, coarse speech, filthy language, covetousness, anger and wrong views; and their opposites in the eightfold path: correct view, correct thought, correct speech, correct deed, correct livelihood, correct zeal, correct remembrance and correct meditation. These ten and eight are the characteristics of living beings on this earth.

(Bhīśma-garjita-ghoṣa-svara-rāja) appeared in the world, I heard of the Dharma and left home. At the time of bathing, I followed the rules and entered the bathroom. Suddenly, I awakened to the causal water which cleanses neither dirt nor body; thereby I felt at ease and realized the state of nothingness. As I had not forgotten my former practice, when I left home to follow the Buddha in my present life, I achieved the state beyond study. That Buddha named me Bhadrapāla because of my awakening to wonderful touch and my realization of the rank of a son of Buddha. As the Buddha now asks about the best means of perfection, to me touch is the best according to my personal experience." '

6. Meditation on things (dharma)

'Mahākāśyapa who was present with the bhikṣuṇī "Golden Light" and others (of his group) then rose from his seat, prostrated himself with his head at the feet of the Buddha and declared: "In a former aeon, when Candra-sūrya-pradīpa Buddha appeared in this world, I had a chance of following him and of hearing the Dharma which I practised. After he had passed away, I revered his relics, lit lamps to perpetuate his Light and decorated his statue with pure gold powder. Since then, in every subsequent reincarnation, my body has been radiant with perfect golden light. This bhikṣuṇī 'Golden Light' and the others who are with her, are my retinue because we developed the same mind at the same time. I looked into the six changing sense data which can be reduced to complete extinction only through the state of nirvāṇa.[1] Thus my body and mind were able to pass through hundreds and thousands of aeons in a finger-snap. By eliminating all things (dharma), I realized arhatship and the World Honoured One declared that I was the foremost disciplinarian (dhūta).[2] I awakened to wonderful dharmas, thereby putting an end to the stream of transmigration (āsrava). As the Buddha now asks about the best means of perfection, to me things (dharma) are the best according to my personal experience." '

B. MEDITATION ON THE FIVE SENSE ORGANS

7. Meditation on the organ of sight

'Aniruddha then rose from his seat, prostrated himself with his head at the feet of the Buddha and declared: "After I left home, I was always very

1. Nirvāṇa: complete extinction of worldly feelings and passions, thereby ending all return to reincarnation with its concomitant suffering for entry into the transcendental realm of absolute eternity, bliss, self and purity.

2. Dhūta: an ascetic who succeeds in removing the trials of life and attains nirvāṇa.

fond of sleep and the Tathāgata scolded me, saying that I was like an animal. After this severe reprimand, I wept bitterly and blamed myself. Because of my sadness, I did not sleep for seven successive nights and went completely blind. Then the World Honoured One taught me how to take delight in the Enlightening Vajra samādhi which enabled me to perceive, not with my eyes (but with my mind), the Pure Truth pervading the ten directions, very clearly perceptible, as easy to see as a mango held in my own hand. The Tathāgata sealed my attainment of arhatship. As He now asks about the best means of perfection, to me seeing is, according to my personal experience, the best which is made possible by turning the organ of sight back to its source." '

8. Meditation on the organ of smell

'Kṣudrapanthaka then rose from his seat, prostrated himself with his head at the feet of the Buddha and declared: "I did not know much (about the Dharma) for lack of reading and reciting (the Scriptures). When I first met the Buddha, I heard of the Dharma and then left home. I tried to memorize a line of His gāthā but failed for a hundred days, because as soon as I could retain its first words, I forgot the last ones, and when I could remember the last words, I forgot the first ones. The Buddha took pity on my stupidity and taught me how to live in a quiet retreat and to regularize my breathing. At the time, I looked exhaustively into each in and out breath, and realized that its rise, stay, change and end lasted only an instant (kṣaṇa);[1] thereby my mind became clear and unhindered until I stepped out of the stream of transmigration and finally attained arhatship. I came to stay with the Buddha who sealed my realization of the state beyond study. As He now asks about the best means of perfection, to me breathing is the best according to my personal experience in turning the breath back to the condition of nothingness." '

9. Meditation on the organ of taste

'Gavāṁpati then rose from his seat, prostrated himself with his head at the feet of the Buddha and declared: "Because of my verbal sin when I trifled with monks in a former aeon, in every succeeding reincarnation, I have been born with a mouth that always chews the cud like a cow. The Tathāgata taught me the pure and clean doctrine of One Mind[2] which enabled me to eliminate the conception of mind for my entry into the state of samādhi. I looked into taste, realized that it was neither (a subjective) substance nor (an objective) thing and leaped beyond the stream of

1. Kṣaṇa: the shortest measure of time; sixty kṣaṇas equal one finger-snap, ninety a thought, 4,500 a minute.

2. Lit. One-flavoured Mind-ground Dharma-door to enlightenment.

transmigration; I thereby disengaged myself from both the inner body and mind and the outer universe, and was released from the three worlds of existence.[1] I was like a bird escaping from its cage, thus avoiding impurities and defilements. With my Dharma eye[2] now pure and clean, I attained arhatship and the Tathāgata personally sealed my realization of the stage beyond study. As the Buddha now asks about the best means of perfection, to me the turning of taste back to its knower is the best according to my personal experience." '

10. Meditation on the body

'Pilindavatsa then rose from his seat, prostrated himself with his head at the feet of the Buddha and declared: "When I first followed the Buddha to enter upon the Path, very often I heard the Tathāgata speak about the worldly which could not give joy and happiness. (One day) I went to town to beg for food, and as I was thinking about His teaching, I stepped inadvertently on a poisonous thorn that pierced my foot and caused me to feel pain all over my body. I thought of my body which knew and felt this great pain. Although there was this feeling, I looked into my pure and clean mind which no pain could affect. I also thought, 'How can this one body of mine have two kinds of feeling?', and after a short (mental) concentration on this, all of a sudden, my body and mind seemed to be non-existent and three weeks later, I achieved the stage beyond the stream of transmigration and thereby attained arhatship. The Buddha personally sealed my realization of the stage beyond study. As He now asks about the best means of perfection, to me the pure awareness that wipes out the (conception of) body is the best according to my personal experience." '

11. Meditation on the intellect (manas)

'Subhūti then rose from his seat, prostrated himself with his head at the feet of the Buddha and declared: "As my mind was already free from all hindrances in former aeons, I can now remember my previous incarnations as countless as the sands in the Ganges. Even when I was a foetus in my mother's womb, I was already awakened to the condition of still voidness which subsequently expanded to fill all the ten directions and which enabled me to teach living beings how to awaken to their absolute nature. Thanks to the Tathāgata, I realized the absolute voidness of self-natured awareness, and with the perfection of my immaterial nature, I attained arhatship, thereby entering suddenly into the Tathāgata's Precious Brightness which was as immense as space and the ocean, wherein I partially

1. The three states of mortal existence: world of desire, of form and beyond form.

2. Dharma eye which is able to penetrate all things, to see the truth that releases one from reincarnation.

achieved Buddha knowledge. The Buddha sealed my attainment of the stage beyond study; I am therefore regarded as the foremost disciple because of my understanding of immaterial self-nature. As the Buddha now asks about the best means of perfection, according to my personal experience, the best consists in perceiving the unreality of all phenomena, with the elimination of even this unreality, in order to reduce all things to nothingness." '

C. MEDITATION ON THE SIX CONSCIOUSNESSES

12. Meditation on sight perception

'Śāriputra then rose from his seat, prostrated himself with his head at the feet of the Buddha and declared: "In former aeons, the sight perception of my mind was already pure and clean, and in subsequent incarnations as countless as the sands in the Ganges, I could see without hindrance through all things either on a worldly or supramundane plane. (One day), I met on the road the two brothers Kāśyapa who were both preaching the doctrine of causality,[1] and after listening to them, my mind awakened to the truth and thereby became extensive and boundless. I then left home to follow the Buddha and achieved perfect sight perception thereby acquiring fearlessness (abhaya), attaining arhatship and qualifying as the Buddha's 'Elder Son'—'born from the Buddha's mouth and by transformation of the Dharma'. As the Buddha now asks about the best means of perfection, according to my personal experience, the best consists in realizing the most illuminating knowledge by means of the mind's radiant sight perception." '

13. Meditation on ear perception

'Samantabhadra Bodhisattva then rose from his seat, prostrated himself with his head at the feet of the Buddha and declared: "I was already a son of the Dharma king when formerly I was with the Tathāgatas who were countless as the sands in the Ganges. All the Buddhas in the ten directions who teach their disciples to plant Bodhisattva roots, urge them to practise Samantabhadra deeds, which are called after my name. World Honoured One, I always use my mind to hear in order to distinguish the variety of views held by living beings. If in a place, separated from here by a number of worlds as countless as the sands in the Ganges, a living being practises Samantabhadra deeds, I mount at once a six tusked elephant and reproduce myself in a hundred and a thousand apparitions to come to his aid. Even, if he is unable to see me because of his great karmic obstruction, I secretly lay my hand on his head to protect and comfort him so that he can succeed.

1. i.e. the Four Noble Truths that put an end to birth and death.

As the Buddha now asks about the best means of perfection, according to my personal experience, the best consists in hearing with the mind, which leads to non-discriminating discernment." '

14. Meditation on smell perception

'Sundarananda then rose from his seat, prostrated himself with his head at the feet of the Buddha and declared: "When I left home to follow the Buddha, although fully ordained I failed to realize the state of Samādhi because my mind was always unsettled; I was, therefore, unable to reach the condition beyond the stream of transmigration. The World Honoured One then taught me and Kauṣṭhila to fix the mind on the tip of the nose. I started this meditation and some three weeks later, I saw that the breath that went in and out of my nostrils was like smoke; inwardly both body and mind were clear and I looked through the (external) world which became a pure emptiness like crystal everywhere. The smoke gradually disappeared and my breath became white. As my mind opened I achieved the state beyond the stream of transmigration. Both my in and out breaths, now bright, illumined the ten directions so that I attained the arhat stage. The World Honoured One prophesied that I would win enlightenment. As He now asks abouts the best means of perfection, according to my personal experience, the best is to eliminate breath which will then turn radiant, ensuring attainment of the stage of perfection beyond the stream of transmigration." '

15. Meditation on tongue perception

'Pūrṇamaitrāyaṇīputra then rose from his seat, prostrated himself with his head at the feet of the Buddha and declared: "In former aeons, my power of speech was unhindered and I preached the (doctrine of) misery and unreality, thereby penetrating deep into absolute reality. I (also) expounded in the assembly the Tathāgata's Dharma doors to enlightenment as uncountable as the sands in the Ganges, and thereby won fearlessness (abhaya).[1] The World Honoured One knew that I had acquired the great power of speech, and taught me how to carry out the Buddha work by preaching. Therefore, in His presence, I assisted Him in turning the Wheel of the Law and since I could give the lion's roar,[2] I attained arhatship. He sealed my

1. There are two groups of fearlessness when expounding the Dharma to convert deluded living beings: (1) the four kinds of Bodhisattva fearlessness which arise from his power (a) of memorizing the Dharma to preach it to others; (b) of moral diagnosis and application of the appropriate remedy in each case; (c) of ratiocination overcoming all obstruction; and (d) of cutting off all doubts harboured by listeners; and (2) the four kinds of Buddha fearlessness which arise from (a) his omniscience; (b) perfection of character; (c) ability to overcome all opposition; and (d) to end all suffering.

2. To expound the Buddha Dharma without fear of men and things.

unexcelled skill in expounding the Dharma. As He now asks about the best means of perfection, according to my opinion, the best consists in employing the Dharma voice to subdue the enmity of Māra[1] and to stop the stream of transmigration." '

16. Meditation on the perception of objects of touch

'Upāli then rose from his seat, prostrated himself with his head at the feet of the Buddha and declared: "I personally accompanied the Buddha, and we climbed the city wall to flee from home. With my own eyes, I saw how He endured hardship in His practice during the first years of ascetic life, subdued all demons, overcame heretics and freed Himself from worldly desires and all impure efflux (āsrava) from the mind. He personally taught me discipline, including the three thousand regulations[2] and eighty thousand lines of conduct[3] which purified all my innate and conventional subtle karmas.[4] As my body and mind were in the nirvāṇic state, I attained arhatship and the Tathāgata sealed my mind because of my strict observance of discipline and control of body. I am now a pillar of discipline in this assembly and am regarded as the foremost disciple. As the Buddha now asks about the best means of perfection, in my opinion, the best consists in disciplining the body so that it can free itself from all restraints and then in disciplining the mind so that it can be all-pervading, which results in the freedom of both body and mind." '

17. Meditation on the faculty of mind (mano-vijñāna)

'Mahā-Maudgalyāyana then rose from his seat, prostrated himself with his head at the feet of the Buddha and declared: "One day as I was begging for food in the street, I met the three Kāśyapa brothers—Uruvilvā, Gayā and Nadī—who preached the profound doctrine of causality[5] taught by the Tathāgata. Suddenly my mind opened and became all-pervading. Then,

1. Māra is the enemy of Buddha.

2. A monk's regulations amount to 250; these are multiplied by four for the conditions of walking, standing, sitting and reclining and thus make 1,000; again multiplied by three for past, present and future, they become 3,000 regulations.

3. An abbrevation for 84,000. A monk's regulations amount to 3,000 (see note 2), these are multiplied by the seven spreading branches, i.e. three sins of body (killing, robbing, carnality) and four of speech (lying, slander, abuse, double-tongue), they make 21,000; again multiplied by four, i.e. the three poisons (desire, anger and stupidity) plus the ego idea, they make 84,000 in all. According to the Ch'an interpretation, the digits eight and four stand for the eighth consciousness and the four elements that make the body and mind, i.e. space, while the three zeros stand for time. These 84,000 lines of conduct serve to wipe out space and time.

4. Karma against natural law, e.g. stealing, and karma against conventional rules, e.g. for a monk to eat meat.

5. The doctrine of causality that reveals the uncreate.

the Tathāgata gave me a monk's robe (kaṣāya) and when I wore it, my hair and beard fell out. I rambled in the ten directions and met no obstruction. I thus acquired transcendental power which proved the foremost and led to my attainment of arhatship. Not only the World Honoured One, but all the Tathāgatas in the ten directions, praised my supernatural powers which were perfect, pure, sovereign and fearless. As the Buddha now asks about the best means of perfection, in my opinion, it consists of returning to stillness to allow the light of the mind to appear, just as muddy water by settling becomes pure and clean as crystal." '

D. MEDITATION ON THE SEVEN ELEMENTS[1]

18. Meditation on the element fire

'Ucchusma[2] then came forward in front of the Tathāgata, joined the palms of his two hands, prostrated himself with his head at the feet of the Buddha and declared: "I can still remember that in a very remote aeon I was filled with sensual desire. At the time a Buddha called 'The King of Immateriality' appeared in the world. According to him, those having lustful desires, increased their own hell fires. He then taught me to meditate on the bones in my body, on my four limbs and on my warm and cold breaths. So by turning inward the spiritual light for pointed concentration, my lustful mind turned into the fire of wisdom. Since then, I have been called 'Fire Head' by all the Buddhas. Because of my powerful Firelight samādhi, I attained arhatship. Then I took my great vow to become a demigod (vīra) so that when all Buddhas were about to attain enlightenment, I would personally help them to overcome the enmity of Māra.[3] As the Buddha now asks about the best means of perfection, according to my opinion, the best consists in looking into the non-existent heat in my body and mind in order to remove all hindrances thereto and to put an end to the stream of transmigration so that the great Precious Light can appear and lead to the realization of Supreme Bodhi." '

19. Meditation on the element earth

'Dharaṇiṁdhara Bodhisattva[4] then rose from his seat, prostrated himself with his head at the feet of the Buddha and declared: "I still remember that formerly when the Buddha of Universal Light appeared in the world, I was

1. The seven elements of the universe: fire, earth, water, wind, space, perception and consciousness.
2. i.e. Fire-head.
3. See p. 25, note 1.
4. Ruler of the earth.

a bhikṣu who used to level all obstacles, build bridges and carry sand and earth to improve the main roads, ferries, rice-fields and dangerous passes which were in bad condition or impassable to horses and carts. Thus I continued to toil for a long time in which an uncountable number of Buddhas appeared in the world. If someone made a purchase in the market-place and required another to carry it home for him, I did so without charge. When Viśvabhū Buddha[1] appeared in the world and famine was frequent, I became a carrier charging only one coin no matter whether the distance was long or short. If an ox cart could not move in a bog, I used my supernatural power to push its wheels free. One day, the king invited that Buddha to a feast; as the road was bad, I levelled it for him. The Tathāgata Viśvabhū placed his hand on my head and said: 'You should level your mind-ground (then), all things in the world will be on the same level.'[2] (Upon hearing this), my mind opened and I perceived that the molecules of my body did not differ from those of which the world is made. These molecules were such that they did not touch one another and could not be touched even by sharp weapons. I then awakened to the patient endurance of the uncreate (anutpattika-dharma-kṣānti) and thereby attained arhatship. Then by turning my mind inwards, I realized the Bodhisattva stage and when I heard the Tathāgatas expound the Buddha's universal knowledge in the profound Lotus Sūtra, I was the first listener to be awakened to it and was made a leader of the assembly. As the Buddha now asks about the best means of perfection, in my opinion, the best consists in looking into the sameness of body and universe which are created by infection from falsehood arising from the Tathāgata store, until this defilement vanishes and is replaced by perfect wisdom which then leads to the realization of Supreme Bodhi." '

20. Meditation on the element water

'Candraprabha Bodhisattva then rose from his seat, prostrated himself with his head at the feet of the Buddha and declared: "I still remember that in the remotest of aeons countless as the sands in the Ganges, there was a Buddha, called Varuṇa, who appeared in the world and taught Bodhisattvas to contemplate the element water in order to enter into the state of samādhi.

' "This method consisted in looking into the body wherein all watery elements do not by nature suppress one another, using as subjects of meditation first tears and snot, and then saliva, secretions, blood, urine and excrement, and then reversing the order, thereby perceiving that this water element in the body does not differ from that of the fragrant oceans that surround the Pure Lands of Buddhas, situated beyond our world.

1. The third of the seven Buddhas of antiquity. See *Ch'an and Zen Teaching*, Second Series. Part One.

2. Viśvabhū Buddha taught him to develop a universal mind.

' "When I achieved this contemplation, I succeeded in realizing only the sameness of the element water (everywhere), but failed to relinquish (my view of) the body. I was then a bhikṣu practising dhyāna (abstract meditation) and when my disciple peeped into the room, he saw that it was filled entirely with clear water, without anything else. As he was an ignorant boy, he picked up a broken tile, threw it into the water with a splash, gazed curiously and left. When I came out of my dhyāna state, I suddenly felt pain in my heart[1] as if I had the same trouble which Śāriputra had with a wicked demon.[2] I thought, 'Since I have realized arhatship, I should be free from all causal ailments. Why today, all of a sudden, have I a pain in my heart; is it not a sign of backsliding?' When the boy returned and related (what he had seen and done during my meditation), I said: 'When next you see water in my room, open the door, enter the water and take away the broken tile.' The boy obeyed, for when I again entered the dhyāna state, he saw the same broken tile in the water. He then opened the door to remove the tile. When I came out of dhyāna, my pain had vanished. Later, I met countless Buddhas before I encountered Sārgara-varadhara-buddhi-vikrīḍitā-bhijña Buddha (under whose instruction) I succeeded in relinquishing (the conception of) body, thereby realizing perfect union of this body and the fragrant oceans in the ten directions with absolute voidness, without any further differentiation. This is why I was called a 'son of Buddha'[3] and was qualified to attend all Bodhisattva meetings.

' "As the Buddha now asks about the best means of perfection, in my opinion the best consists in achieving the unhindered universalizing pervasion of the element water, thereby experiencing the 'patient endurance of the uncreate' (anutpattika-dharma-kṣānti)[4] which ensures Complete Enlightenment." '

21. Meditation on the element wind

'The Bodhisattva of Crystal Light then rose from his seat, prostrated himself with his head at the feet of the Buddha and declared: "I remember that

1. Because of his attachment to the false notion of the reality of an ego existing in his body.

2. When Śāriputra practised dhyāna on the bank of the Ganges, due to an evi karma in his previous life, he was slapped by a demon and was in great pain. The Buddha said to him: 'Fortunately you were in a dhyāna state, otherwise your body would have been damaged and you would have perished.'

3. Lit. Child-nature of simplicity. The stage of youth in Buddhahood, or the eighth of the ten stages in Bodhisattva-wisdom.

4. Rest in the imperturbable reality which is beyond birth and death and which requires a very patient endurance. The Prajñā-pārmitā-śāstra defines it as the unflinching faith and unperturbed abiding in the underlying reality of all things, which is beyond creation and destruction. It must be realized before attainment of Buddhahood.

once, in the remotest of aeons countless as the sands in the Ganges, there was a Buddha called 'Infinite Voice' who appeared in the world to reveal to Bodhisattvas the profoundly enlightened fundamental awareness which, by looking into this world and the bodily forms of all living beings, could perceive that all were created by the power of the wind arising from illusory concurrent causes. At the time, I inquired into the (illusory) setting up of the world,[1] changing time, bodily motion and motionlessness, and stirring of mind, in other words all kinds of movement which were fundamentally the same and did not differ from one another. I then realized that these movements had neither whence to come nor whither to go and that all living beings in the ten directions, as uncountable as dust, came from the same falsehood. Likewise, all living beings in every small world of the great chiliocosm[2] were like mosquitoes in a trap in which they hummed aimlessly and created a mad tumult. Soon after meeting that Buddha, I realized the patient endurance of the uncreate. As my mind opened, I perceived the land of the Imperturbable Buddha (Akṣobhya)[3] in the eastern region where I was admitted as a son of the Dharma king, serving all the Buddhas in the ten directions. My body and mind gave out rays of light that illumined everything without obstruction.

' "As the Buddha now asks about the best means of perfection, in my opinion the best consists in looking into the power of the element wind which has nothing (real) on which to rely, thereby awakening to the Bodhi mind so as to enter samādhi and (then) to unite with the Profound One Mind expounded by the Buddhas in the ten directions." '

22. Meditation on the element space

'Ākāśagarbha Bodhisattva then rose from his seat, prostrated himself with his head at the feet of the Buddha and declared: "When the Tathāgata and I were with Dīpaṁkara Buddha and realized our boundless bodies, I held in my hands four large precious gems[4] which illumined all Buddha lands

1. To wipe out space first and then time.

2. Tri-sahasra-mahā-sahasra-loka-dhātu. Mount Sumeru and its seven surrounding continents, eight seas and ring of iron mountains form one small world; 1,000 of these form a small chiliocosm; 1,000 of these small chiliocosms form a medium chiliocosm; 1,000 of these form a great chiliocosm, which consists of 1,000,000,000 small worlds.

3. One of the five Dhyāni Buddhas, viz. Vairocana, in the centre, Akṣobhya in the east, Ratnasaṁbhava in the south, Amitābha in the west and Amoghasiddhi in the north. He is the first of the sixteen sons of Mahābhijñā-jñānābhibhu, the great Buddha of supreme penetration and wisdom, who was also father of Amitābha and Śākyamuni in their former incarnations.

4. Ākāśagarbha had then succeeded in his meditation on the four elements: earth, water, fire and wind which he could perceive as identical with the underlying principle thus transmuting them into four precious gems.

in the ten directions, as uncountable as dust, and transmuted them into the (absolute) void. Then my own mind appeared like a great mirror emitting ten kinds of mysterious precious light[1] which penetrated the ten directions, reached the boundaries of space and caused all the pure lands of Buddhas to enter the mirror and then to intermingle freely with my own body which was like unobstructive space. (Then) my body could perfectly enter as many (saṁsāric) countries as there are grains of dust to carry out far and wide the Buddha works (of salvation) so that universality could prevail (everywhere). This great transcendental power derived from my close inquiry into the four elements which had nothing real to rely upon and into false thinking that rose and fell (alternately and ended in nothingness). I realized the non-duality of space and the sameness of the Buddhas' (pure lands) and saṁsāric worlds, thereby achieving the patient endurance of the uncreate.

' "As the Buddha now asks about the best means of perfection, according to my own experience, the best consists in close examination into boundless space, leading to entry into samādhi and perfecting thereby the mysterious spiritual power." '

23. Meditation on the element consciousness

'Maitreya Bodhisattva then rose from his seat, prostrated himself with his head at the feet of the Buddha and declared: "I remember that in the remotest of aeons as uncountable as the dust, there was a Buddha called Candra-sūrya-pradīpa[2] who appeared in the world (to convert others). I followed him in order to leave home. However, I (still) cherished worldly fame and liked to mix with noble clans. Then the Tathāgata taught me how to practise abstruse meditation (dhyāna) on the mind's consciousness[3] in order to realize the state of samādhi. Ever since in the following aeons, I have used this samādhi to serve Buddhas as many as the sands in the Ganges, thereby eliminating completely my (previous) mind set on worldly fame. When Dīpaṁkara Buddha appeared in the world, (under his instruction) I realized the consciousness-perfecting supreme samādhi of the mind which enabled me to perceive that all Tathāgata (stores) and saṁsāric worlds, purity and impurity and existence and non-existence were but appearances caused by my own mind's transformations. World Honoured One, because of my clear understanding that only the mind's consciousness was the cause (of all externals, I perceived) an unlimited number of Tathāgatas

1. To perceive the fundamental sameness in the ten dharmadhātus, i.e. the six saṁsāric worlds and the four saintly realms.

2. Or Candrākadīpa Buddha.

3. Mind only, the doctrine that nothing exists apart from mind, that the three worlds of existence (of desire, of form and beyond form) come from the *mind only* and that all things (dharma) are created by *consciousness only*.

coming out of the nature of consciousness, hence (the Buddha's) prophecy that I shall be His successor.

'"As the Buddha now asks about the best means of perfection, my opinion is that the best consists of close examination into all appearances in the ten directions, which are created by consciousness only, in order to perfect the conscious mind, thereby realizing complete reality and ensuring non-reliance on externals and the breaking of all attachments caused by discrimination, thus achieving the patient endurance of the uncreate."'

24. Meditation on the element perception

Mahāsthāma,[1] a son of the Dharma King, who was the head of a group of fifty two Bodhisattvas, rose from his seat, prostrated himself with his head at the feet of the Buddha and declared: "I remember that in the remotest of aeons countless as the sands in the Ganges, there was a Buddha called Amitābha[2] who was succeeded by eleven other Tathāgatas in that kalpa. The last one was called the 'Buddha whose light surpassed that of the sun and moon'; he taught me how to realize the state of samādhi by thinking exclusively of (Amitābha) Buddha. By way of illustration, if a man concentrates his mind on someone else while the latter is always forgetful of him, both may meet and see, but without recognizing, each other. However, if both are keen on thinking of each other, their keenness will grow from one incarnation to another until they become inseparable like a body and its shadow. The Tathāgatas in the ten directions have compassion for all living beings and always think of them, like a mother who never ceases thinking of her son. If the son runs away, her thoughts of him will not help. But if he also thinks of her with the same keenness, they will not be separated in spite of the passing of transmigrations. If a living being remembers and thinks of the Buddha, he is bound to behold Him in his present or future incarnation. He will not be far from the Buddha and thus without the aid of any other expedient, his mind will be opened. He is like a man whose body, perfumed by incense, gives out fragrance; hence his name 'One glorified by (Buddha's) fragrance and light.'[3] From my fundamental cause-ground and with all my thoughts concentrated on the Buddha, I achieved the patient endurance of the uncreate. (This is why) I help all living beings of this world to control their thoughts by repeating the Buddha's name so that they can reach the Pure Land.

'"As the Buddha now asks about the best means of perfection, I hold that

1. Or Mahāsthāmaprāpta, a Bodhisattva symbolizing the Buddha wisdom of Amitābha and standing on his right with Avalokiteśvara on the left. They are called the Trinity of the Western Paradise of Bliss.

2. Buddha of Infinite Light.

3. A term meaning that one whose mind meditates on Buddha becomes impregnated with Buddha-fragrance and glorified by Buddha-light.

nothing can surpass the perfect control of the six senses with continuous pure thoughts in order to realize samādhi." '

E. AVALOKITEŚVARA'S METHOD OF REALIZING COMPLETE ENLIGHTENMENT

25. Meditation on the organ of hearing

'Thereupon, Avalokiteśvara Bodhisattva rose from his seat, prostrated himself with his head at the feet of the Buddha and declared: "I remember that long before as uncountable a number of aeons as there are sandgrains in the Ganges, a Buddha by the name of Avalokiteśvara appeared in the world. When I was with Him, I developed the bodhi mind and for my entry into samādhi, I was instructed by Him to practise self-cultivation by means of the organ of hearing.

' "At first by directing the hearing (ear) into the stream
(Of meditation) this organ from its object was detached.
By wiping out (the concept of) both sound and stream entry,
Both disturbance and stillness
Were clearly non-existent.
Thus advancing step by step,
Both hearing and its object ceased;
But I did not stay where they ended.
When the awareness (of this state) and the state itself (were realized)
As non-existent, subject and object merged into the void
And awareness of that void became all embracing.
Then, when both creation and annihilation
Vanished, the state of nirvāṇa manifested.

' "Suddenly I leaped over both the mundane and supramundane, I realized an all-embracing brightness pervading the ten directions and acquired two unsurpassed (merits). The first was in accord with the fundamental Profound Enlightened Mind of all Buddhas high up in the ten directions and possessed the same merciful power as the Tathāgata. The second was in sympathy with all living beings in the six realms of existence here below in the ten directions and shared with them the same plea for compassion.

' "World Honoured One, as I (followed and) made offerings to the Tathāgata Avalokiteśvara He taught me how to use illusory hearing to develop (absolute) hearing in order to realize the Diamond (vajra) samādhi which was the same as that of all Buddhas and which enabled me to transform myself into thirty-two bodily forms for the purpose of visiting all countries in saṁsāra (to save living beings)." '

(The Bodhisattva then detailed the thirty-two different forms which he could take and stated that with the profound uncreative power of the same samādhi he could bestow fourteen kinds of fearlessness upon all living beings, and that in addition, he had acquired the four inconceivable and wonderful uncreative merits. He continued:)

' "As the Buddha now asks about the best means of perfection, according to my own experience, the best consists in employing the organ of hearing for an all-embracing concentration to ease the conditioned mind for its entry into the stream (of meditation), thereby achieving the state of samādhi that led to my personal experience of bodhi.

' "World Honoured One, that Buddha praised my skilful realization of Complete Enlightenment and, in the presence of the assembly, gave me the name of Avalokiteśvara, because of my ability to hear perfectly from the ten directions. For this reason, my name is known everywhere in the ten directions."

'Thereupon, the Tathāgata said to Mañjuśrī: "Son of the Dharma King, these twenty-five Bodhisattvas and arhats who no longer need to study and learn, have related the expedient methods used by them at the start of their self-cultivation for their realization of bodhi. In reality, each of these methods does not differ from, and is neither superior nor inferior to, the others. Tell me which one of them is suitable to Ānanda so that he can awaken to it and which one is easy of achievement, for the benefit of living beings who, after my nirvāṇa, wish to practise with the Bodhisattva vehicle in their quest of Supreme Bodhi."

'As commanded, Mañjuśrī rose from his seat, prostrated himself with his head at the feet of the Buddha and reverently chanted the following gāthā:

' "Perfect and clear by nature is the Bodhi ocean,
Pure and faultless Bodhi is in essence wonderful.[1]
Its fundamental brightness shone, so by chance creating
An object which then obscured its radiant nature.
Thus in delusion there appeared one-sided emptiness
In which an imaginary world arbitrarily was built.
Steadying itself, the thinking process made the continents
While the (illusory) knower became a living being.[2]
The voidness so created within Bodhi
Is but a bubble in the ocean. Worldly

1. These two lines describe the reality of the One Mind.
2. These six lines show how illusion sprang from reality.

Countries, countless as the dust, arose
In this (relative) emptiness.
When the bubble bursts, the void's unreality
Is exposed; how much more so is that of the three realms?[1]
Though all return to One Nature at the source,
There are many expedient methods for the purpose.[2]
Though holy nature pervades all, direct
Or inverse methods are expedients;
Hence newly initiated minds of different
Aptitudes are quick or slow to enter samādhi.[3]
Form which from thought crystallizes
Is too difficult to look through.
How can perfection be achieved
Through this impenetrable form?[4]
Sound, voice, word and speech are each confined
To specific definition
Which by itself is not all embracing.
How can they help to achieve perfection?[5]
Smell, perceived when in contact with the nose,
Without that contact is non-existent.
How can that which is not always present
Be a means to achieve perfection?[6]
Taste exists not of itself, but is
Perceived when flavour's present.
Since sense of taste is ever varied
How can it to perfection lead?[7]
Touch exists when there's an object touched;
Without an object touch is naught.
Since contact and its absence are not constant,
How can touch help to achieve perfection?[8]
Dharma is inner defilement called;
Reliance thereon implies an object.
Since subject and object are not all embracing,
How can dharma lead one to perfection?[9]

1. The three realms of desire, of form and beyond form are created in the unreal voidness.
2. Return to the non-dual nature.
3. Stress on the choice of a suitable method of self-cultivation.
4. Comment on Upaniṣad's choice of form as means of perfection.
5. Comment on Kauṇḍinya's meditation on sound.
6. Comment on Fragrance Adornment's meditation on smell.
7. Comment on meditation on taste by Bhaiṣajya-rāja and Bhaiṣajya-samudgata.
8. Comment on Bhadrapāla's meditation on touch.
9. Comment on Mahākāśyapa's meditation on things (dharma).

The organ of sight, although perceiving clearly,
Sees things in front but cannot see behind.
How can partial (sight of) the four quarters
Help one to achieve perfection?[1]
The inward and the outward breath
Have no link uniting them.
How can they, thus unconnected,
Be used to achieve perfection?[2]
The tongue is useless touching nothing;
When flavour is present, there is taste
Which vanishes when flavour's absent.
How can this help to achieve perfection?[3]
Body must be conditioned to the object touched;
Both cannot be used for all-embracing meditation
Which is beyond both subject and object with their limits.
How can this serve to achieve perfection?[4]
The tumult of thinking with the mind disturbs
The serenity of right perception.
Since stirring thoughts are most hard to eradicate
How can intellect serve to achieve perfection?[5]
Union of consciousness with eye and sight
Has three components that are not settled.
How can that which is devoid of substance
Be used as a means to win perfection?[6]
The hearing mind which reaches into space
Needs a great cause for its development;
But untrained men cannot realize it.[7]
How can this help to achieve perfection?[8]
Meditation on the nose is only an expedient
Means to control the mind by fixing it for the moment,
But wrong dwelling can create an illusory abode.
How can this be used to achieve perfection?[9]

1. Comment on Aniruddha's meditation on the organ of sight. We can see everything in front of us, but only partially on the right and left; how can incomplete sight be used to achieve perfection?

2. Comment on Kṣudrapanthaka's meditation on the organ of smell.

3. Comment on Gavāṁpati's meditation on the organ of taste.

4. Comment on Pilindavatsa's meditation on the body.

5. Comment on Subhūti's meditation on the intellect.

6. Comment on Śāriputra's meditation on sight-perception.

7. Lit. Newly initiated men cannot realize it.

8. Comment on Samantabhadra's meditation on ear-perception. The hearing mind can be perceived only because of a great cause, i.e. after a very long training.

9. Comment on Sundarananda's meditation on the perception of smell.

Preaching the Dharma plays upon voice and words
But awakening occurred during practice long ago,
Words and speeches never going beyond the worldly stream.
How can this be a means to achieve perfection?[1]
Observance of rules of discipline controls
The body but never that which is beyond it.
Since control of body is not all embracing
How can this serve to achieve perfection?[2]
Transcendental powers come from a former cause;
How can they derive from discriminating consciousness?[3]
Since thinking from externals cannot stray,
How can it serve to achieve perfection?[4]
If the element of earth be used for contemplation,
It is solid and cannot be penetrated;
Belonging to the worldly it lacks spirituality.
How can it be used to achieve perfection?[5]
If meditation be on the element of water,
The thoughts that then arise have no reality.
Beyond feeling and seeing is the absolute;
How then can water help to achieve perfection?[6]
If for meditation the element of fire be used,
Dislike of desire is not complete renunciation;
'Tis no expedient for newly initiated minds.
How then can fire become a means to achieve perfection?[7]
If meditation is on the element of wind,
Motion and stillness are a false duality
From which Supreme Bodhi cannot develop.
How can wind serve to achieve perfection?[8]
If the element of space be used for meditation,
Its dimness and dullness cannot be enlightenment.
Since whate'er is unenlightened differs much from Bodhi,
How can the element of space help to achieve perfection?[9]
If on the element of consciousness you meditate,

1. Comment on Pūrṇamaitrāyaṇīputra's meditation on the tongue consciousness.
2. Comment on Upāli's meditation on the body-perception.
3. 'Discriminating mind' in the gāthā is mano-vijñāna, the sixth consciousness, mental sense or intellect.
4. Comment on Mahā-Maudgalyāyana's meditation on the sixth consciousness.
5. Comment on Dharaṇiṁdhara's meditation on the element earth.
6. Comment on Candraprabha's meditation on the element water.
7. Comment on Ucchuṣma's meditation on the element fire.
8. Comment on Crystal-Light's meditation on the element wind.
9. Comment on Ākāśagarbha's meditation on the element space.

It changes and is not permanent.
The mind fixed on it being false
How then can that element help to achieve perfection?[1]
Phenomena are impermanent;
Thinking originally comes and goes.
Since cause ever differs from effect,
How can sense achieve perfection?[2]
I now submit to the World Honoured One
That all Buddhas from this world escaped
By following the teaching, here most suitable,
Which consists in sublimating sound.
The state of samādhi can be
Realized by means of hearing.[3]
Thus did Avalokiteśvara Bodhisattva win
Deliverance from suffering for self-liberation.
During aeons countless as the Ganges'
Sand, he entered as many Buddha lands,
Winning the power and comfort of his independence
And bestowing fearlessness upon all living beings.
O you of pure and wondrous voice like the ocean-tide,
You who look down on men of worldly speech,
Save us (poor) worldlings, give us security, ensure
Our liberation and attainment of eternity.[4]
Reverently I declare to the Tathāgata
What Avalokiteśvara said:
When one dwells in quietude,
Rolls of drums from ten directions
Simultaneously are heard,
So hearing is complete and perfect.[5]
The eyes cannot pierce a screen,
But neither can mouth nor nose.
Body only feels when it is touched.
Mind's thoughts are confused and unconnected,

1. Comment on Maitreya's meditation on the element consciousness.

2. Comment on Mahāsthāma's meditation on the element of sense.

3. These six lines show the Dharma most suitable for this world.

4. These ten lines praise the great achievements by Avalokiteśvara Bodhisattva. Wonderful voice is the voice by means of which he realized Supreme Bodhi for himself. Regarder of voice is his saving characteristic for the welfare of others. Pure voice stands for freedom from all attachments. Ocean-tide voice is unfailing response to the needs of men, like the ocean-tide which never fails to occur.

5. These six lines show the completeness of the faculty of hearing which nothing can hinder.

(But) voice whether near or far
At all times can be heard.
The five other organs are not perfect,
But hearing really is pervasive.[1]
The presence or absence of sound and voice
Is registered by ear as 'is' or 'is not'.
Absence of sound means nothing heard,
Not hearing devoid of nature.
Absence of sound is not the end of hearing,
And sound when present is not its beginning.
The faculty of hearing, beyond creation
And annihilation, truly is permanent.[2]
Even when isolated thoughts in a dream arise,
Though the thinking process stops, hearing does not end,[3]
For the faculty of hearing is beyond
All thought, beyond both mind and body.[4]
In this Sahā world
Teaching is by voice.[5]
Living beings who cognize not hearing's nature,
Follow sound to continue transmigrating.
Though Ānanda memorized all that he had
Heard, he could not avoid perverted thoughts.[6]
This is a fall into saṁsāra by clinging to sound;
Whilst reality is won against the worldly stream.[7]
Listen, Ānanda, listen closely.
In the name of Buddha I proclaim
The Vajra King of Enlightenment,
The inconceivable understanding that illusions
Are unreal, the true samādhi that begets all Buddhas.[8]
You may hear of esoteric methods

1. These eight lines point out the pervasiveness of the faculty of hearing.

2. These eight lines point out the permanence of the faculty of hearing.

3. Even in sleep, one still hears the sound of a pestle pounding rice, which one mistakes for the beating of a drum.

4. The faculty of hearing really surpasses all other organs.

5. While other means are employed to preach the Dharma in other worlds of existence, voice alone is used to teach human beings.

6. Ānanda succumbed to temptation when he knocked at the door of a Mātaṅgī girl to beg for food and was about to break the rule of chastity. The Buddha, who knew this, sent Mañjuśrī to rescue Ānanda and availed of this happening to preach the Śūraṅgama Sūtra, laying stress upon the eradication of sexual desire, the main obstruction to the realization of bodhi.

7. These eight lines show the main causes of delusion and enlightenment.

8. These five lines point out the true samādhi.

From Buddhas countless as the dust,
But if you cannot eradicate
Desire, to hear much causes errors.[1]
To hear your very Self, why not turn backward
That faculty employed to hear Buddha's words?[2]
Hearing is not of itself,
But owes its name to sound.[3]
Freed from sound by turning hearing backwards,
What do you call that which is disengaged?[4]
When one sense organ has to its source returned,
All the six senses thereby are liberated.[5]
Seeing and hearing are like optical illusions,
Just as all three worlds resemble flowers in the sky.
With hearing disengaged, the illusory organ vanishes;
With objects eradicated, perfectly pure is Bodhi.[6]
In utter purity, the bright light pervades all,
With its shining stillness enfolding the great void.
All worldly things, when closely looked at,
Are but illusions seen in dreams.
Dream-like was the Mātaṅgī maiden:
How could she keep your body with her?[7]
Like a clever showman
Presenting a puppet play,
Though movements are many,
There is but one controller.
When that control is stopped,
Figures show no nature.[8]
Likewise are the six organs
Derived from one ālaya
Which divides into six unions.
If one of these returns to source,
All six functions are ended.
With all infection ended,

1. These four lines show the futility of hearing and learning without following the correct method of practice.

2. These two lines point out the correct method of practice.

3. These two lines show the inter-dependence of hearing and sound. Therefore hearing does not lead to profound awakening.

4. Profound awakening is beyond names and terms.

5. Instantaneous enlightenment is past words and phrases.

6. This is meditation on the seeming, leading to entry into the void.

7. Mātaṅgī is the name of the low-caste girl who seduced Ānanda. These six lines show meditation on the void, leading to entry into the seeming.

8. Meditation on the void and the seeming shifted to that on the mean.

Bodhi is then realized.[1]
Any defiling remnant requires further study
Whereas full enlightenment is the Tathāgata.[2]
Ānanda and all you who listen here
Should inward turn your faculty
Of hearing to hear your own nature
Which alone achieves Supreme Bodhi.
That is how enlightenment is won.[3]
Buddhas as many as the Ganges' sand
Entered this one gateway to Nirvāṇa.
All past Tathāgatas
Have achieved this method.
All Bodhisattvas now
Enter this perfection.
All who practise in the future
On this Dharma should rely.
Avalokiteśvara did not practise
It alone, because through it I also passed.
The Enlightened and World Honoured One
Has asked about the best expedients
For those in the Dharma ending age
Who wish from saṁsāra to escape
In their search for nirvāṇa's heart.
It is best to contemplate on worldly sound;
All other methods are expedients
Used by Buddha in particular cases
To keep disciples from occasional trouble.
They are not good for indiscriminate practice
By men of different types (or natures).
I salute the Tathāgata Store
Which is beyond the worldly stream.
Blessed be coming generations
So that they have (abiding) faith
In this easy expedient.
'Tis good for teaching Ānanda
And those of the Dharma ending age
Who should use their hearing organ
Which surpasses all others
And with the True Mind accords." '

1. Result of meditation on the mean.
2. This shows partial or complete achievement.
3. This is the way to realize Bodhi.

The terms *wonderful form*, *wonderful fragrance*, *wonderful touch* and *wonderful dharma*, mentioned in the above passages from the Śūraṅgama Sūtra, refer to sense data which have been successfully looked into during meditation and have been found to be illusory and non-existent, thereby becoming identified with the mind which created them and which now reverts to its absolute condition of purity and cleanness, free from the duality of subject and object. The transmutation of the six sense data into a state of purity and cleanness is explained in the Sūtra of Complete Enlightenment, presented in the third series of *Ch'an and Zen Teaching*.

The method employed by Avalokiteśvara Bodhisattva which consists in turning inwards the organ of hearing to hear the self-nature, agrees perfectly with the Buddha's Teaching in the Sūtra of Complete Enlightenment which says that practice should begin from the self-moving cause-ground, that is from the self-nature which inadvertently moved and stirred and thereby split into the subjective knower and the objective relative voidness. This primal cause of separateness led to the creation of all sorts of illusion which are likened to the flowers in the sky produced by an optical illusion. In order to recover our inherent wisdom, it is necessary to realize the non-existence of illusions by stripping the mind first of all coarse conceptions of subject and object and then by disengaging it from the remaining subtle view of ego and things (dharma), as taught in the Diamond Sūtra.[1] After all externals have been eradicated, that which cannot be wiped out is the self-mind in its absolute condition, free from all relativities and contraries; this is Enlightenment.

Although all the above twenty-five methods of self-cultivation are excellent according to the Buddha, the one most suitable to us in this period of the decline of Dharma is that practised by Avalokiteśvara. If we examine it closely, we will find that it does not differ from the Ch'an technique which also consists in disentangling the self-mind from seeing, hearing,

1. See *Ch'an and Zen Teaching*, First Series, The Diamond Cutter of Doubts.

feeling and knowing to realize its absolute condition which alone can lead to the perception of self-nature and attainment of bodhi. Therefore, the only difference between the Mahāyāna Teaching and the Transmission lies in the latter's device which is a short cut to Enlightenment. The Teaching is complementary to the Transmission and serves to adjust the various stages achieved during Ch'an training and to seal, or to testify its final attainment.

Since it is now almost impossible to find enlightened masters to teach and guide us, it is imperative that we follow the Teaching left behind by the Buddha in anticipation of this Dharma ending age. Many masters followed this Teaching in their practice of the Dharma and we can cite Master Han Shan who practised it and realized enlightenment (bodhi) by himself. Even if enlightened teachers were available, we would still have to follow their instruction and undergo the training ourselves in our self-cultivation for self-realization and self-enlightenment.

Due to lack of space we are unable to present other passages of the Śūraṅgama Sūtra which deal with the rules of morality and discipline but we should know that discipline begets an unperturbed mind which in turn begets wisdom, and that we should begin by keeping the first five precepts, or prohibitions, against killing, stealing, carnality, lying and intoxicating liquor. We should also develop an unshakeable faith in the Dharma taught by the Buddha and great masters, and take the great vow to enlighten ourselves for the sole purpose of enlightening others. If we fail to observe these preliminary rules, we will never succeed in self-cultivation and will continue to drift about in the sea of suffering.

In the third series of *Ch'an and Zen Teaching* we have presented the Sūtra of Complete Englightenment and the Altar Sūtra of the Sixth Patriarch which all ancient masters in China read before their own enlightenment and which are the best guides for all students of the Supreme Vehicle in this period of the decline of Dharma.

2

SELF-CULTIVATION ACCORDING TO THE CH'AN (ZEN) SCHOOL

THE Buddha attained Enlightenment after gazing at the stars at night, that is after He had succeeded in stripping His mind of all feelings and passions and after it had returned to its normal, or absolute, condition and had resumed its unhindered function of perceiving externals. He then transmitted to Mahākāśyapa the Mind Dharma which was handed down to following generations until it reaches us today. The Buddha was not enlightened at birth and had to undergo rigorous training before He won bodhi. He did it alone without teachers and, out of compassion for us in this Dharma ending age, He left behind the Dharma so that we can follow His example to escape from the realm of miseries and sufferings. Therefore, we would be ungrateful to Him and would do Him a very great injustice if we now pretend that His Dharma is impracticable or that we are unable to practise it because learned teachers are not at hand.

THE MIND DHARMA OR DOCTRINE OF THE MIND

According to the Ch'an method, self-cultivation begins with the control of mind as the starting point. By mind is meant the wandering mind, always in search of something in the realm of unreality. It is said that he who realizes his self-mind can perceive his self-nature and attain enlightenment. By self-mind is meant the pure mind which is not stirred by a single thought. As man has been so inextricably enmeshed by his false thoughts since time without beginning, he finds it very difficult to free his mind from false views in order to uncover his inherent wisdom which they screen. He is, however, endowed with a latent potentiality which no amount of teaching can reach because of his obstinate clinging to the empty names and terms implicit in human language. Even Ānanda, who was one of the most intelligent disciples of the Buddha, was reprimanded by the World Honoured One for clinging to names and terms which caused him to neglect self-cultivation; how much more so are men in this period of the decline of the Dharma?

THE INNER POTENTIALITY

This inner potentiality can, however, be aroused and vitalized by the Ch'an technique and developed to the full so that it can absorb and unite with the Truth. This is the Transmission of the Mind Dharma, outside of the Teaching, which the Buddha handed down to Mahākāśyapa when He held up a flower to probe His disciples' abilities to perceive the substance of His essential body (Dharmakāya) through its function of raising the flower, and when His chief disciple understood His revealing gesture and acknowledged it with a broad smile.

THE ANCIENT TECHNIQUE

This Transmission was successively passed down through the Indian and Chinese Patriarchs and the techniques used since the beginning of the long Ch'an lineage until today have been discussed in detail in the three volumes of my Ch'an and Zen Teaching.[1] In ancient times, it was sufficient for an enlightened

1. Published by Rider.

teacher to give some hint of the presence of the self-nature inherent in his pupil who was immediately awakened to it, thereby attained enlightenment and succeeded to the Mind Dharma. Such a student was likened to a good horse which started galloping at the mere shadow of a whip. For life was so simple in olden times that a disciple had only a few desires which could be easily eliminated for the purpose of quieting his mind so that he could perceive his self-nature and attain enlightenment (bodhi).

THE KUNG AN DEVICE

Later with the advance of material civilization, when life became complicated with the result that spiritual awakening was very difficult to achieve, the masters were compelled to change their tactics by employing words, sentences, shouts, roars of laughter, gestures and blows of the staff to awaken their students so that the latter could perceive the essential bodies of their teachers through their revealing functions of speaking, shouting, laughing and gesticulating. All these acts were later called kung ans (Japanese, kōans), which were concurrent causes that provoked the awakening of deluded disciples whose minds were already disentangled from illusions and whose potentialities were vitalized to the full, ready to unite with the Truth. In fact, the kung an device had been used long ago by the Buddha when He held up a flower to cause Mahākāśyapa's enlightenment and later by Bodhidharma when he said: 'So have I quieted your mind' to awake Hui K'o, the first Chinese Patriarch.

Kung ans are, therefore, not riddles and riddle-like problems which students should solve before their enlightenment, for kung ans are full of meaning which is clear only to those who have rid themselves of discrimination and discernment. Obviously, they are incomprehensible to unenlightened people who grasp at externals and cling to the names and terms of conditioned human language. However, as soon as they keep from illusions, that is when their minds are not stirred by thoughts, or when they have taken the 'host' position, they will understand all kung ans without making the least effort.

Consequently it is misleading to pretend that Ch'an training begins with the so-called *solution* of these so-called *riddles* and that all the *seventeen hundred* kung ans, a number frequently mentioned in Ch'an texts, should be properly solved before awakening (Chinese, wu and Japanese, satori) can take place. This is tantamount to putting the cart before the horse and will never lead to awakening, for a student should first discipline his wandering mind so as to disengage himself from seeing, hearing, feeling and knowing for the purpose of realizing singleness of mind, in order to be able to see clearly and to take up the 'host' position before a kung an can be interpreted correctly. He will never understand it so long as his mind is screened by externals and if he takes up the 'guest' position, from which he cannot comprehend the esoteric meanings of kung ans. After he has succeeded in disciplining his mind, with no further thoughts arising therein, he is able to understand not only the seventeen hundred ancient kung ans, but also all the others beginning with the seventeen hundred and first, without exception, and will see that there is nothing strange, absurd or eccentric in this Ch'an technique.

If, instead of disciplining his mind, a student is urged to stir it in search of the so-called solution of kung ans, he will be turned round by the unending flow of his thoughts and will never be able to pause for a moment to see clearly; he will mistake a robber for his own son, as the masters put it. Consequently, the prerequisite of Ch'an training is to apply a brake to the wandering mind so that it can be quieted and that, after all illusions have vanished, the self-possessed wisdom can return to its normal state and function as it should. Therefore, even before starting Ch'an practice, it is imperative that we know how to stop the ever-flowing thoughts that have been stirring our minds since time without beginning. We 'live' because we 'think', and if we want to escape from this realm of suffering, the first thing is to realize a mind free from all thoughts. We know that the human body and the ego which is supposed to be its owner are but phenomenal creations of our deluded minds and are, therefore, false because they have no permanent nature and no existence of their own. The sūtra says: 'Just by mind control, all things become possible to us.'

Since Mind is an aspect of the self-nature, the Sixth Patriarch said to his disciples: *Our self-natured bodhi is fundamentally pure and clean. Use only this mind (of yours) for your direct understanding and attainment of Buddhahood.* He also said: *This business should begin with the self-nature. At all times, instant after instant, you should purify your own minds, practise self-cultivation, realize your own Dharma-kāyas, perceive the Buddha of your own minds, effect your self-liberation and observe self-discipline so that you will not have come (to this meeting) in vain.*[1]

THE HUA T'OU TECHNIQUE

We now know that we should control the wandering mind and strip it of all thoughts before we can speak of Ch'an practice. Therefore, the first step is to put an end to the flow of thoughts, but we also know that this is the most difficult thing to achieve. If we fail to stop our stirring thoughts, we will not be able to practise self-cultivation. For this reason, the ancients devised a technique which can help us to prevent thoughts from arising in our minds. This is the hua t'ou device. Hua t'ou means the mind before it is stirred by a thought or a mental word, and its English equivalent is ante-word or ante-thought. It consists in looking into, or in concentrating on, the self-mind and is also an impure thought used as a device to put an end to the thinking process. It is a

1. See *Ch'an and Zen Teaching*, Series Three, Part One.

pointed concentration to cut down all thoughts and eventual visions which assail the meditator during his training. Since the student cannot stop all his thoughts at one stroke, he is taught to use this poison-against-poison device to realize singleness of thought which is fundamentally wrong but will disappear when it falls into disuse and gives way to singleness of mind which is a pre-condition of the realization of the self-mind for perception of self-nature and attainment of bodhi. The late Ch'an Master Hsu Yun[1] said:

All hua t'ous have only one meaning which is very ordinary and has nothing peculiar about it. If you look into him 'Who is reciting a sūtra?', 'Who is holding a mantra?', 'Who is worshipping Buddha?', 'Who is taking a meal?' . . . or 'Who is sleeping?', the reply to 'WHO?' will invariably be the same: 'It is Mind.' Word arises from Mind and Mind is the head of (i.e. ante-) Word. Thought arises from Mind and Mind is the head of Thought. Myriad things come from Mind and Mind is the head of myriad things. In reality, a hua t'ou is the head of a thought. The head of a thought is nothing but Mind. To make it plain, before a thought arises, it is hua t'ou. From the above, we know that to look into a hua t'ou is to look into the Mind. The fundamental face before one's birth is Mind. To look into one's fundamental face before one's birth is to look into one's mind. Self-nature is Mind and to 'turn inwards the hearing to hear the self-nature' is to 'turn inwards one's contemplation to contemplate the self-mind'.

Thus we come exactly to the same method practised by Avalokiteśvara Bodhisattva (Kuan Yin) who turned inward the ear to hear the all-embracing awareness, or the self-natured bodhi, as described in Chapter 1. Therefore, the pretension that the Ch'an Transmission is different from the Teaching in the sūtras is totally groundless, for the principle is the same in both.

1. See *Ch'an and Zen Teaching*, First Series, p. 23.

The late Ch'an Master Hsu Yun in 1959

I CH'ING OR THE FEELING OF DOUBT

Even if we know how to look into a hua t'ou, or into the self-mind, it is very difficult to maintain this mental state all the time, that is while walking, standing, sitting or reclining. Ch'an practice has nothing to do with whether one sits or not, but sitting with crossed legs is the most convenient way for beginners to control their bodies and minds which can be easily disciplined in that position. However, when they know how to exercise this control while sitting in meditation, they should continue to do so while walking, standing, reclining or performing all the common acts of daily life. For this reason, the ancients taught their students to give rise to a gentle feeling of doubt (i ch'ing) about the above-mentioned 'WHO?' at all times, so as to strip the mind of seeing, hearing, feeling and knowing and to ensure its constant rest, or undisturbed condition.

It is necessary to remember the warning given by Master Hsu Yun when he said that we should not push up the hua t'ou for this would cause its dimness, that we should not hold it in the chest where it would cause pain and that we should not push it down, for it would expand the belly and cause us to fall into the realm of the five aggregates, resulting in all kinds of defect. The reason is that the prāṇa, or vital principle, will follow our mental concentration and will affect the head, chest or belly. Years ago I was very impatient during my Ch'an practice and wrongly concentrated with force on my hua t'ou, thus inadvertently pushing up the prāṇa which caused my lower teeth to loosen, with the result that I had to have three of them pulled out. However, this small sacrifice was worth while for it enabled me to make some little progress in my practice. Therefore, when looking into a hua t'ou, we should not fix our minds anywhere, but should concentrate without using force solely on the I Ch'ing after giving rise to it.

In order to acquaint readers with the proper methods of practice at the start of training, we translate below some of the instructions given by enlightened masters to their disciples.

1. Instruction given by the late Master Hsu Yun (1840–1959)[1]

'When one looks into a hua t'ou, the most important thing is to give rise to a doubt. Doubt is the crutch of hua t'ou. For instance, when one is asked: "Who is repeating Buddha's name?" everybody knows that he himself repeats it, but is it repeated by the mouth or by the mind? If the mouth repeats it, why does it not do so when one sleeps? If the mind repeats it, what does the mind look like? As mind is intangible, one is not clear about it. Consequently some slight feeling of doubt arises about "WHO?" This doubt should not be coarse; the finer it is, the better. At all times and in all places, this doubt should be looked into unremittingly, like an ever-flowing stream, without giving rise to a second thought. If this doubt persists, do not try to shake it; if it ceases to exist, one should gently give rise to it again. Beginners will find the hua t'ou more effective in some still place than amidst disturbance. However, one should never give rise to a discriminating mind; one should remain indifferent to either the effectiveness or ineffectiveness (of the hua t'ou) and one should take no notice of either stillness or disturbance. Thus, one should work at the training with singleness of mind. . . .

'Usually beginners give rise to a doubt which is very coarse; it is apt to stop abruptly and to continue again, and seems suddenly familiar and suddenly unfamiliar. This is (certainly) not doubt and can only be their thinking (process). When the mad (wandering) mind has gradually been brought under control, one will be able to apply the brake on the thinking process, and only thus can this be called "looking into" (a hua t'ou). Furthermore, little by little, one will gain experience in the training and then there will be no need to give rise to the doubt which will rise of itself automatically. In reality, at the beginning, there is no effective training at all as there is only (an effort) to put an end to false thinking. When real doubt rises of itself, this can be called true training. This is the moment when one reaches a "strategic gateway" where it is easy to go out of one's way (as follows).

'Firstly, there is the moment when one will experience utter purity and boundless ease and if one fails to be aware of and look into this, one will slip into a state of dullness. If a learned teacher is present, he will immediately see clearly that the student is in such a state and will strike the meditator with the (usual) flat stick, thus clearing away the confusing dullness; a great many are thereby awakened to the Truth.

'Secondly, when the state of purity and emptiness appears, if the doubt

1. See *Ch'an and Zen Teaching*, First Series, pp. 38–40.

ceases to exist, this is the unrecordable state in which the meditator is likened to a withered tree which is lifeless and to a stone which cannot be soaked with water. When one reaches this state, one should arouse the doubt to be immediately followed by one's awareness and contemplation (of this state). Awareness (of this state) is freedom from illusion; this is wisdom. Contemplation (of this state) wipes out confusion; this is imperturbability. This singleness of mind will be thoroughly still and shining, in its imperturbable absoluteness, spiritual clearness and thorough understanding, like the continuous smoke of a solitary fire. When this state is attained, one should be provided with a diamond eye (i.e. the indestructible eye of wisdom) and should refrain from giving rise to anything else, as if one does, one will (simply) add another head (i.e. an illusory external) upon one's head (i.e. one's own mind).

'Formerly, when a monk asked (Master) Chao Chou: "What should one do when there is not a thing to bring with the Self?" Chao Chou replied: "Lay it down." The monk said: "What shall I lay down when I do not bring a thing with me?" Chao Chou replied: "If you cannot lay it down, carry it away." This is exactly the state (above mentioned) which is like that of a drinker of water who alone knows whether it is cold or warm. This cannot be expressed in words and speeches, and one who reaches this state will clearly know it.'

2. Instruction given by Master Han Shan (1546–1623)

(From *Han Shan's Journey in Dreamland*—Han Shan Meng Yu Chi)

(a) The Ch'an sect transmits the Buddha's sealing of mind and is no small matter. When Bodhidharma came from the West (India), he set up only the doctrine of the Transmission of Mind and used the four books of the Laṅkāvatāra Sūtra to seal the Mind. Although Ch'an is a Transmission outside of the Teaching, it uses sūtras to testify spiritual awakening. Therefore, the Buddha's Teaching and the Patriarchs' Transmission are one (and the same).[1] As to Ch'an practice, it also derives from the Teaching. The Laṅkāvatāra Sūtra says: 'When one sits in meditation in a mountain grove and practises all-embracing self-cultivation, one perceives the endless flow of false thoughts arising in the self-mind.' This is the World Honoured One's revelation of the secret of self-cultivation.

The sūtra continues: 'As mind, thought and perception are realized as false states of the self-nature appearing in the self-mind, one is liberated from all causes (producing) the saṁsāric sea of existence and ignorant karmic desire.' This is the Tathāgata's profound teaching of the method of awakening to the self-mind.

1. Śākyamuni Buddha was also a Patriarch of the Transmission school. (See *Ch'an and Zen Teaching*, Second Series, Part I.

It says: 'From olden times, the saints handed down, from one to another, the teaching according to which all false thinking is devoid of independent nature.' This is the esoteric sealing of mind.

The above are the essentials of self-cultivation taught by the yellow-faced Grand Old Man.[1]

When Bodhidharma said to the (Chinese) Second Patriarch: 'Put an end to the formation of all causes without and have no panting heart (mind) within; then with a mind like an (impenetrable) wall, you will be able to enter the Tao (Truth),' this was the essence of self-cultivation as taught by Bodhidharma.

When Huang Mei sought for a successor to his Dharma, the Sixth Patriarch inherited the robe and bowl after merely saying: 'Fundamentally there is not a thing.' This was the Transmission of the Sealing of Mind.

When the Sixth Patriarch returned to the South, he met Tao Ming and said to him: 'Do not think of either good or evil, at this very moment, what is the Venerable Sir's fundamental face?' This was the Sixth Patriarch's first revelation of the secret of self-realization.

Therefore, we know that formerly the Buddha and Patriarchs taught only how to awaken to the self-mind and how to cognize one's Self. There were then neither kung ans nor hua t'ous. Later at the time of Nan Yo and Ch'ing Yuan,[2] and after them, when a master trained his disciples, he took advantage of their giving rise to doubts to hit them in their weaker spots in order to turn them away from their thoughts so that they could set their minds at rest. In the case of those who could not be awakened at once, the master, although continuing to press them hard, had to wait for opportune times and concurrent circumstances. It was Huang Nieh who taught people to look into hua t'ous and then Ta Hui[3] definitely decided on the use of this device. He taught his students to use an ancient kung an as something to lay hold of, called a hua t'ou on which they were urged to concentrate their attention. The reason was that in the store (ālaya) of the eighth consciousness the seeds of evil habits, contracted since time without beginning, continued to exercise their contaminating influence, thus sustaining the flow of false thoughts. Since there was no other alternative, a meaningless sentence was given to students to grasp firmly. As they had to lay down all false thoughts of inner mind and outer objects, but since they could not do so, they were taught to use this hua t'ou to cut all these 'ravelled threads' at one stroke, so that the flow of thoughts could not

1. i.e. Śākyamuni Buddha.

2. The two great Dharma successors of the Sixth Patriarch, whose Dharma descendants founded the Five Ch'an Sects of China. See Genealogical Chart of the Five Ch'an Sects in *Ch'an and Zen Teaching*, Second Series, p. 56.

3. Ta Hui: an eminent Ch'an master in the Sung dynasty; died in 1163 in his seventy-fifth year.

continue. This is exactly what Bodhidharma meant by: 'Put an end to the formation of all causes without and have no panting mind within until your mind becomes like an impenetrable wall.' If one does not proceed in this manner from the start, one will never be able to perceive one's fundamental face. This does not mean that you are taught to think of a kung an and to regard this thinking as a feeling of doubt that will give a result. This is also what Ta Hui meant when he used a poison-against-poison method by urging his students to look into a hua t'ou so that they could cut off their remiss minds. For instance, he once said to them: 'Ch'an practice consists solely in emptying the mind; you should fix on your foreheads the two words "birth" and "death" and remember them as if you owe a debt of ten thousand strings of (threaded) coins (which you must repay). Day and night, while drinking or eating; when walking, standing, sitting or reclining; when receiving friends and chatting with them; as well as in a still or moving state, you should give rise to the hua t'ou: "Does a dog have the Buddha nature? Chao Chou replied: 'Wu.' (No.)" Look into it again and again, until you are completely disgusted with it and this is the moment when you seem to come into collision with an (impenetrable) wall, like a mouse trying to enter the horn of a cow, resulting in all your attempts recoiling upon themselves. You are required to develop a long-enduring body and mind to keep on looking into the hua t'ou, and all of a sudden, the mind-flower will blossom and radiate, illuminating all the ten directions. Thus once awakened, you will be so thoroughly for ever.' This was the usual method employed by the old master Ta Hui to press hard those coming for his instruction. He meant this: 'You should use a hua t'ou to cut down all false thoughts arising in your minds so that they cannot continue to flow and should then perceive your fundamental face by looking into where they cease.' This does not mean that you should think about a kung an and regard this (thinking) as a feeling of doubt that can give you an expected result. When he said that the mind-flower blossomed and radiated, did this imply something gained from without? When the Buddha and Patriarchs gave instruction, they wanted you only to look into your own Self but not to grasp at beautiful and wonderful words and phrases.

Nowadays, everyone practising Ch'an says that he looks into a hua t'ou and gives rise to a doubt, but instead of concentrating on the fundamental, he only seeks (something) from the hua t'ou and continues seeking it again and again. If suddenly he succeeds in visualizing some (mental) state, he will immediately speak of his awakening, will write gāthās and hymns, will regard this as a remarkable achievement and will pretend that he has attained bodhi, without knowing that he has already been caught in the net of false thoughts and perverted views. Will not such a Ch'an practice be harmful to the coming generation all over the country? Nowadays, even before they are properly seated on their mats, the young practisers boast of their awakening to the Tao and talk nonsense which they claim to be the product of their (so-called) spiritual dialectics. They write empty sentences which they read loudly and call them their hymns in praise of the ancients. All this comes from their wrong thinking; have they ever dreamt of (understanding) the past masters? If people can be so easily awakened now, and if we compare them with those ancient disciplinarians such as Ch'ang Ch'ing[1] who sat in meditation until he had worn out and torn seven mats and Chao Chou[2] who spent thirty years without allowing his mind to be stirred by a single thought, the latter would be really stupid and would not even be qualified to carry straw sandals for the former. These people are only arrogant for they claim that they have won bodhi although they are still ignorant. Is it not a dreadful thing?

It is true that during the training when a hua t'ou is looked into, it is imperative to give rise to a feeling of doubt. It is also known that a little doubt leads to a minor awakening, that a great doubt leads to a major awakening and that absence of doubt leads to no awakening, but the essential lies in the skilful use of this feeling of doubt and when this doubt bursts, all the noses of the Buddha and Patriarchs can be pierced and tied together with a string.

For instance, when employing the kung an: 'Who is the repeater of Buddha's name?' it is essential to look into HIM who repeats it but not to doubt about who Buddha is. If you give rise to a doubt about who the Buddha is, you can go and listen to any commentator who will explain that Amitābha Buddha is the Buddha of Infinite Light. If you then write a few gāthās on the Infinite Light and claim that this is your awakening to the Tao, those who were to be so awakened would be as countless as hemp (seeds) and (grains of) maize What a pity, what a pity!

The ancients likened the hua t'ou to a (broken) tile which one picks up to knock at the door so that when the door is opened one can see the man inside the house, instead of remaining outside and playing with external things. Thus we know that the feeling of doubt (in connection with) a hua t'ou is not a doubt about its meaning, but about the fundamental (face). For instance when Chia Shan[3] called on the Boat Monk,[4] the latter asked him: 'When a thousand feet of fishing line is let down, the quarry is

1. Ch'ang Ch'ing: an eminent Ch'an master, Dharma successor to Shueh Feng. Died in 932 in his seventy-ninth year.

2. Chao Chou: an eminent Ch'an master, Dharma successor to Nan Chuan. Died in 894 in his 120th year.

3. Chia Shan: eminent Ch'an master, disciple of the Boat Monk. Died in 881.

4. The Boat Monk: Ch'an master Teh Ch'eng of Hua Ting, nicknamed the Boat Monk, was Dharma successor of Yo Shan and teacher of Chia Shan—ninth century. See *Ch'an and Zen Teaching*, First Series, pp. 123–8.

deep in the pond. Three inches beyond the hook, why don't you speak?' Chia Shan (guessed and) was on the point of opening his mouth, when the Boat Monk gave him, with the paddle, a blow that knocked him into the water. As soon as Chia Shan scrambled back into the boat, his master said again: 'Speak! Speak!' Before the pupil could open his mouth, the master hit him again. Thereupon, Chia Shan won a major awakening and nodded thrice (in approval and gratitude). His master said: 'You can play with the silken line at the end of the rod, but so long as you do not disturb the clear water (i.e. the mind), the meaning will be different.' If Chia Shan only played with the line and hook, how would the Boat Monk agree to sacrifice the pupil's life solely for the latter's enlightenment?

This shows how the ancients were skilful and quick in finding their own ways. Formerly, when the Ch'an sect flourished, enlightened teachers could be found everywhere, and all over the country there were many cases of real awakening. Hence the saying: 'There is no lack of Ch'an but only of teachers.'[1] Nowadays, true practisers of Ch'an are very rare, and although there are many who wish to practise it, their teachers merely make a rough estimate of the capabilities of the pupils, give way to worldly feelings and seal their achievements; the latter, because of superficiality, (wrongly) think that they have achieved real success. Moreover, because of their contempt of the Tathāgata's holy Teaching,[2] these instructors do not seek the right Way but act carelessly, thus using a pumpkin-seal to testify others' achievements.[3] Thus not only do they mislead themselves but they also misguide their students. Is this not a dreadful thing? The ancient scholars and upāsakas whose names are recorded in the Transmission of the Lamp were very few, but nowadays worldlings, who do not even care to observe the elementary precepts but who indulge in stirring their minds aimlessly and only rely on their intellect, just read a few ancient kung ans, boast of their own superior roots, delight in all sorts of argument when meeting a member of the Saṅgha and claim that they have realized the Tao. This is not only a sign of the times, but is also the result of a blind man leading a group of blind people.

In conformity with the right method of training as taught by the Buddha and Patriarchs I now point out what is essential for your study and those of high spirituality will certainly not disagree with me.

(b) In your Ch'an practice, when for a time thoughts cease to rise, this

1. A quotation from Huang Po's *Essentials of the Transmission of Mind.*

2. This is also the case of people who now pretend that śīla and sūtra can be dispensed with in Ch'an practice.

3. This is wrong testifying for a pumpkin-seal is an external and leaves traces behind whereas the correct sealing of mind by mind leaves no traces due to the immateriality of both minds. A pumpkin-seal is a Ch'an term frequently used by enlightened masters when rebuking impostors.

does not mean that they have really stopped, but that the hua t'ou has begun to take effect. This effectiveness is not permanent for it can be swept away if you find yourselves in an (adverse) causal state or it can be weakened by externals. In such cases, there will be produced the two states of stillness and disturbance which will appear and disappear alternately without interruption. If you can make effective use of your mind, by concentrating on (that which is self-existent) before a thought arises, you will gradually become accustomed to it, and with the passing of time, will realize your personal experience of it. When thoughts no longer arise, your (spiritual) substance will appear bright and clear, without being affected by either light or darkness, and will remain in its thusness amidst stillness or disturbance. Only then can you realize the oneness (of mind and its objects). This is the culmination of concurrent causes and is beyond all control; it automatically unites with the Tao.

The Ch'an training consists solely of concentration on that which is (self-existent) before your mind is disturbed by a thought, and if you exert yourself unremittingly, self-realization is bound to follow very quickly. However, if you regard a transient stillness in a flash of lightning as real attainment, you will slip into the realm of feelings and passions.

(c) A student determined to escape from the wheel of birth and death, should know that, because of the unceasing flow of his thoughts, he is unable to put an end to saṁsāra. If he now wishes to stop it, he should lay down all his feelings and passions, and lay them down again and again until he is rid of them all. However, there still remain the seeds of his old habits which he cannot destroy at one stroke. He is, therefore, required to look into a hua t'ou. He can find hua t'ous in the books but he does not know the secret of their practice. Consequently, he should call on learned masters who already know the method of practice.

For instance, when the Sixth Patriarch heard the sentence: 'One should develop a mind that does not abide anywhere', he was instantaneously enlightened. Deluded people mistake this for an abstruse doctrine. In reality, there is nothing abstruse in it, because formerly the Sixth Patriarch had thought of an abiding (place) but since he now heard that there was none, he merely laid down everything and was thereby enlightened. So where is all this abstruseness?

Ordinary people mistake Ch'an for a doctrine, without knowing that Ch'an is but the self-mind which is beyond birth and death according to the sūtra. If you want to be clear about the important question of birth and death, you should respect and observe the precepts and prohibitions and should never break them. You should develop a firm faith, have a dogged determination and lay down all abstruse words and profound doctrines as well as all worldly feelings and passions. The Ch'an practice has nothing abstruse, wonderful and extraordinary in it for it is very simple, but will you believe me? If you really do, just lay down all your old thoughts without allowing new ones to arise. Then, slowly, call: 'Amitābha!' and without loosening your grip on this word, look into where this thought arises, with the same keenness as when you let down a fishing line into a deep pond. If a new thought arises, this is because of your habits contracted since the time without beginning. You should lay it down at once but on no account use your mind to cut it off. Just sit up straight without thinking of anything and look into where this thought arises. Then lay down everything again and again. Call the Buddha's name once more and strive to see where this call comes from. Repeat this five or seven times and your thoughts will cease to arise. Now give rise to this doubt: 'Who is repeating the Buddha's name?' People mistake this for a sentence of the hua t'ou and do not know that the effectiveness of training comes solely from this feeling of doubt. If another thought arises, shout at it and ask: 'Who are you?' and it will vanish at once.

The Buddha said: 'Except when you sleep, you should control your mind unceasingly.' You cannot control your mind in your sleep, but when you wake up, you should again look into the hua t'ou not only when you are sitting, standing, drinking or eating but also when you are in the midst of stillness or disturbance. Thus you will not notice a single man while passing through a crowd and will not perceive any motion in the midst of disturbance. If you can achieve this, you will gradually advance further until you come to where your seventh consciousness becomes impotent. Then, day and night, you will continue your training without loosening your grip (of the hua t'ou), and one day, your eighth consciousness (ālaya-vijñāna) will suddenly burst, exposing your fundamental face. You will then be clear about birth and death and will realize the goal for which you left home.

During your training, do not wait for your awakening. If you behold the Buddha, Patriarchs or demons appearing in your meditation, just remain unperturbed and do not loosen your grip of the hua t'ou. Thus without straying from the hua t'ou and with unbroken singleness of mind, your efforts will be successful.

(d) When the ancients disciplined their minds, they employed a sentence of the hua t'ou which they regarded as an iron wall or a silver hill, against which they could lean as a prop in support of their efforts. When you succeed in realizing the non-arising of thoughts, this shows only the effectiveness of your training but should not be mistaken for the ultimate result. Even when you can practise without involving the thinking process, thereby disengaging yourselves from body and mind, this shows further advanced progress but not the ultimate state. When you come to this, you will automatically experience weightlessness, bliss and a comfortable independence. You will be filled with joy but this is the characteristic of your Self, which has nothing extraordinary in itself. If you regard it as extraordinary, you will slip into the realm of joyful demons and will be involved in all sorts of wrong views. This is the most dangerous pass which I have myself experienced. An ancient said:

Before the grotto with withered logs[1] *false paths are many*
On which all who arrive are liable to slip and fall.

'If you have enough vigour to pass through all sorts of states, exert yourselves in your training to preserve the good results you have so far achieved, but you have not yet reached home. If you think that your realization is complete, you will give rise to all kinds of wrong thinking which are precisely the causes of the five desires.[2] This pass is the most difficult one to get through and only one or two per cent of practisers succeed in negotiating it. If you have not obtained the same result achieved by the ancients, do not pretend that some small progress of yours is complete attainment.'

3. Instructions given by Master Kao Feng (1238–1295)
(From *The Sayings of Ch'an Master Yuan Miao of Kao Feng peak—* Kao Feng Miao Ch'an Shih Yu Lu)

(a) The practice of self-cultivation is like throwing into a deep pond a stone that goes straight to the bottom. If self-cultivation, practised in this manner, with unbroken continuity, is not successful, I shall consent to fall into the avīci hell[3] for my deceitful sin.

(b) If we train in self-cultivation, we should strive like a prisoner condemned to death and awaiting execution in a jail. It happens that one evening the jailer has a few drinks, gets drunk and falls into a heavy sleep. Taking advantage of this unique chance, the prisoner rids himself of the cangue and fetters and escapes under cover of darkness. The place is infested with tigers and poisonous snakes but he runs away without paying attention to them. Why is it possible? Because his keenness is to escape at all costs. If we develop the same keen mind in our self-cultivation, we are bound to succeed.

(c) Usually students are taught to look into the kung an: 'All things are

1. i.e. when the mind is stripped of all feelings and passions, it is as dead as a withered log, before the resurrection of the self-nature.

2. Arising from the objects of the five senses, things seen, heard, smelt, tasted or touched.

3. Avīci hell: the last and deepest of the eight hot hells, where sinners suffer, die and are instantly reborn to suffering, without interruption.

returnable to the One, to where does the One return?' When you look into this kung an, you should give rise to a great doubt (by asking yourselves): 'All worldly things are returnable to One thing, to where does this One thing return?'[1] So, while you are walking, standing, sitting or reclining, when you are wearing your robes and taking your meals, and whether you are stooling or urinating, you should raise your spirits and continue to harbour your doubt about 'To where does that One return?' as if you are determined to be clear about this at all costs. You should give way neither to indifference nor to confused and aimless thoughts. Your doubt should be fine and continuous, like a homogeneous block, causing you to look like a man gravely ill, devoid of the sense of taste when eating or drinking, and with a stupid and idiotic mien. While in this state, you will be unable to distinguish between east and west or between north and south. If you can achieve this, your mind-flower will (open and) radiate and you will be thoroughly awakened to your fundamental face. Lay down all thoughts and feelings about the worldly and your inclination for the Tao will automatically grow stronger. An ancient said: 'One should be intimate with the unfamiliar and distant towards the familiar.' In your leisure moments, do not read sūtras to kill the time, because if you do, you will never achieve the state of homogeneity (i.e. oneness). Just get up to tread the Path, raise your spirits and look into: 'To where does that One return?' There is no need to read sūtras (at this juncture) for the kung an is also a sūtra which has no beginning and which turns round day and night;[2] why should you add another head to your own? If you practise self-cultivation in this manner, all devas and nāgas will automatically be your guardians and there will be no need to offer prayers. The only thing is to cut off all worldly causes and you can thus save many words and speeches. An ancient said: 'For twenty years, I have not opened my mouth to speak; if you can do this, even the Buddha will be unable to contradict you.' The question of birth and death is important and impermanence is fast closing in. Like those climbing a hill, you should strive and exert yourselves. Listen to my gāthā:

In this bustling world strive as on a hill to dwell;
Still mind and body, your Tao will lack naught.
Just empty your mind of all you like and hate,
This is training too, though Ch'an is not practised.

1. All phenomena are created by, and can be returned to, the One Mind, but where is this One Mind?

2. A sūtra is a sermon on the Dharma and since the Dharma is inherent in ourselves, when we realize our mind and perceive our self-nature, our self-natured Dharma will manifest itself as an eternal Dharma which has neither beginning nor end and which turns round day and night, i.e. functions in unbroken continuity.

4. Instruction given by Master Chung Feng (1263–1323)
(From *The Sayings of Chung Feng*—Chung Feng Kuang Lu)

(a) To upāsaka Hai Yin

'My late Master Kao Feng stayed thirty years in his monastery without descending from the mountain. He taught his disciples to look into the kung an: "All things are returnable to the One, to where does the One return?" He urged them to look into it with all their energy and to forget all about the length of time required for the purpose, until they were awakened to it. (Thus) they should, in their daily activities, hold on to this kung an which should be fixed in their minds and held firmly in silence without interruption. He compared this to one losing control of both hands while hanging from the top of a cliff, to one ready to step forward from the top of a high pole, to one defending a pass alone against assault by ten thousand enemies and to one trying to make fire by rubbing two pieces of wood together. This is how the ancients exerted themselves to the utmost so that what they said accorded well with the truth and their words were certainly not deceitful. Hence, an ancient said:

If intense cold strikes not to the bone,
How can plum blossoms fragrant be?[1]

He also said:

Though the pavilion's old and the surroundings quiet,
One should continuously strive until they are won back.[2]

Are these deceitful words?

'Another ancient said: "There is no secret in Ch'an training which requires but keenness in (solving the question of) birth and death." Why so? Because the Buddhas of the past, present and future and the Patriarchs and great masters in succeeding generations set up so many rules and spoke in so many ways to wipe out all worldly feelings and passions (which cause) the birth and death of all living beings. If not so, why should they establish all sorts of Dharma? If students of this generation are not really keen about their own business, what can they expect from their morning and evening practices?

1. A quotation from Huang Po's sayings. See *Ch'an and Zen Teaching*, First Series, Part I, p. 63.

2. Although the self-nature is self-possessed and its condition is eternally still, one should practise self-cultivation in order to recover both (i.e. self-nature and its still condition).

(b) To the Japanese ascetic Ting I (Tei-ichi)

'Saṅgha is not Saṅgha and laity is not laity (for) six times six is thirty-six.[1] Laity is laity and Saṅgha is Saṅgha (for) the third night watch is struck at noon according to the Teaching.[2] Either Saṅgha or laity is acceptable for fundamentally there is no separateness.[3] If one is suddenly awakened to this absence of separateness, one will laugh at the sight of an (old) tiger with two wings.[4] Do you understand? If not, you should not be careless.

'Why have you left behind all your filial duties to follow a master and stay in a monastery? Is it because you search for food and clothing or for fame and wealth? If not, then why? You have come thousands of miles by sea solely because there was close on your heels something pertaining to the impermanence of birth and death (i.e. life). For aeons till this day, the more you have tried to be awakened to the Great Cause,[5] the more you have been confused and have sunk deeper in your fall.[6] From now on, cast away (all your ideas of) body and life, exhaust all your energy to look silently and closely into a meaningless ancient kung an and to continue so doing in unbroken continuity with a mind expecting nothing, an intellect (manas) free from wandering outside, a consciousness no longer seeking externals and all thoughts that have stopped flowing. Be indifferent to your surroundings, whether in a silent mountain grove or a noisy town, whether in the midst of stillness or disturbance and whether you are working or at leisure. Look into this kung an today, do the same thing tomorrow and continue without interruption. Suddenly, your eyelids will be pierced and your skull broken.[7] You will then behold the Tao which will be obvious and will prevail everywhere.[8] When the Tao is evident, all sorts of things will be auspicious.[9] From the Eastern Sea, a black Persian will emerge with eyebrows and

1. Saṅgha and laity are two empty names and are just a duality that does not exist in the absolute noumenon. Noumenon cannot be named but can be perceived through its function of saying that six by six equals thirty-six. This is the real which is inconceivable and inexpressible.

2. It is through the phenomenal that the noumenal can be revealed according to the expedient Teaching, for the still self-nature, symbolized by night, can be revealed in the midst of activities, symbolized by noon. This is the seeming which springs from the real.

3. Both noumenon and phenomenon come from the undivided whole which is beyond both. This is the mean which is inclusive of the absolute and the relative.

4. 'An old toothless tiger' is a Ch'an term for self-nature powerless in the midst of illusions caused by attachment to dualities, symbolized by the two wings.

5. i.e. the discovery of the self-natured wisdom inherent in every being.

6. i.e. into the sea of suffering. This is the phenomenal realm with differentiation.

7. This is how to destroy all obstructions, i.e. discriminations and prejudices.

8. This is the noumenal realm with unity.

9. The noumenon and phenomenon are interdependent.

nostrils three feet long,[1] speaking of birth, death, transmigration, empty falsity and real truth. The two eyelets of your straw sandals will suddenly hear his voice but both Saṅgha and laity are completely unknown.[2] But who is aware that they are unknown?[3]

> *'When the spring breeze scatters the flowers in Ling Nan*
> *The plugging of all leaks brings tidings that are true.'*[4]

5. Instruction given by Master Ta Kuan, alias Tsu Pai (1543–1604)
(From *The Sayings of Master Tsu Pai*—Tsu Pai Lao Jen Chi)

(a) Instruction given to one of his disciples.

'If you take Master Chao Chou's "Wu" (No) as a hua t'ou for your continued training, with the passing of time your thoughts will become identical with the hua t'ou and the hua t'ou with your thoughts, amidst all states such as birth or death, and in adverse or favourable circumstances. Then, everywhere you will find yourself in the condition of oneness.

'The secret of Ch'an training lies in your mind's ability to realize the oneness of all contraries such as adversity and prosperity, etc., and if you can achieve this, your awakening will be imminent.'

(b) The Story of Master Ta Kuan's awakening.

One day, the master heard a monk reading Chang Chue's Gāthā of Awakening. When the reader came to the lines:

> *To stop wrong thinking aggravates the illness*
> *But to seek the absolute is also wrong.*[5]

Ta Kuan observed:

'These are wrong and should read:

1. The Persian gulf was called the Western sea by the ancients. After enlightenment, all phenomena are turned upside down with elimination of location and direction, because all springs from the noumenal.

2. All phenomena are also interdependent. Thus the teaching reveals the four Dharma realms: (a) the phenomenal realm, with differentiation; (b) the noumenal realm, with unity; (c) both the noumenal and phenomenal are interdependent; and (d) all phenomena are also interdependent.

3. This is the 'mean' which is inclusive of both phenomenon and noumenon.

4. Spring stands for Enlightenment, and breeze, for its function that disperses the flowers, symbol of illusions, according to the Southern school of the Sixth Patriarch Hui Neng in Ling Nan, i.e. south of the range of mountains, or Kuang Tung province. When the stream of transmigration stops flowing, the One Reality is bound to appear.

5. To stop thinking and to seek the absolute imply subjects and objects and do not ensure the realization of absolute bodhi.

To stop wrong thinking avoids illness
But to seek the absolute is right.'

The monk retorted: 'You are wrong but Chang Chue was not.' This retort caused a great doubt to rise in Ta Kuan's mind and after that, wherever he went, he wrote these two lines on the wall. His doubt was so intense that his head became swollen. One day, while eating, he was instantaneously enlightened and the swelling disappeared. He said: 'Had I been with (enlightened masters like) Lin Chi or Te Shan, a slap would have awakened me immediately and saved me a great deal of trouble.'[1]

From the above instructions given by enlightened masters, we know that a kung an is a sentence or any concurrent cause that leads to enlightenment, and that the hua t'ou is a technique devised to strip the mind of hearing, seeing, feeling and discerning so that it can return to its absolute state, the pre-condition of awakening. In olden times, life was not so complicated as it is today and a student had so few desires that he could forsake them without much difficulty to achieve singleness of mind; hence his ability to win bodhi without having recourse to the hua t'ou technique which was later devised to deal with recalcitrant pupils who were unable to look directly into their self-minds. With the successful use of this technique, the mind, relieved from all hindrances, resumes its function of seeing and hearing without further handicap; thus the sight of one's reflection in the water or the sound of a stone hitting a bamboo will suffice to cause instantaneous enlightenment. These sights and sounds are also kung ans, or concurrent causes leading to the perception of self-nature and attainment of bodhi. The blow given by an enlightened master to clear away the confusing dullness of his student and to provoke his awakening, mentioned earlier in our translation of Master Hsu Yun's instruction, is also a kung an which contributes to the enlightenment of a pupil who has reached the 'strategic gateway' where he is about to go astray. It is, therefore, wrong to think that kung ans can be dispensed with when the hua t'ou technique is employed.

1. Quotations from Han Shan's Foreword to *The Sayings of Master Tsu Pai.*

According to astronauts, beautiful colours are seen and weightlessness is experienced when flying in space. It is impossible for all of us to be spacemen and although many are eager, only a very few are chosen for this type of travel. There is, however, no need to go to this expense since if we practise the Ch'an Dharma seriously, we too, without leaving our homes, can see colours more beautiful than any we have seen before. If we close our eyes and concentrate on the 'third eye' between the eyebrows, we too will see very attractive colours and those perceived by the mind are much more beautiful than those seen by the eyes. These colours, however attractive they may be, are only illusions and we should on no account cling to them, but remain indifferent to all visions seen during our meditation in order to disengage ourselves from externals.

As to weightlessness, any serious Ch'an practiser can experience it as soon as he succeeds in realizing singleness of mind and in entering the dhyāna stream. By relinquishing all his attachments to the world and laying down both body and mind which suddenly vanish to be replaced by the brightness of his inner wisdom, he will experience a weightlessness and boundless bliss which no scientists can provide and which no earthly wealth can buy. He will be an 'unconcerned man' as the ancients call it, and this is the key to our escape from saṁsāra. Moreover, with this partial appearance of his self-natured wisdom, he is able to interpret correctly sūtras and kung ans, as well as Dharma words, that is the language of the uncreate, as upāsaka P'ang Yun called it, used by enlightened masters when giving instruction to their disciples or when probing their spiritual achievements. This experience will not cost him a penny and can be realized while sitting before his home shrine or in his bedroom. However, he should be indifferent to all such attractive states which unfold during his meditation, for they are but illusions which can hinder him in his quest of the ultimate goal.

FREEZING THE WANDERING MIND FOR THE RESURRECTION OF SELF-NATURE

After the mind has been disengaged from seeing, hearing, feeling and discerning, that is after it has been frozen in the training, the student reaches a state where he perceives only his eighth consciousness (ālaya-vijñāna), a storehouse holding the germs of all things, on which he depends for existence in the realm of illusions. It is here that the subtle and imperceptible dualism of ego and things (dharma) still remains. Although he has, when entering upon the stream of meditation, been able to distinguish between the coarse aspects of 'host' and 'guest', as taught in the Śūraṅgama Sūtra,[1] he is now confronted with their fine aspects, and if he is unable to distinguish between them, he will remain stationary and so be unable to advance. This is the state reached by Avalokiteśvara Bodhisattva who said:

Thus advancing step by step
Both hearing and its object ceased:
But I stopped not where they ended.

This is what the ancients called 'stagnant water', 'a withered log', 'the top of a hundred-foot pole', 'a stone girl', 'a wooden horse', 'an incense burner in an ancient temple', 'an iron tree', etc., and is but the wandering mind reduced to impotence, for it still retains a subtle view of ego and things (dharma) which is imperceptible to the practiser. It is the last of the four aspects of an ego, which are the I, a man, a being and a life, mentioned in the Diamond Sūtra.[2] If the practiser fails to get out of this state which still belongs to saṁsāra, and since he who does not advance will backslide, he will fall into one of

1. See *Ch'an and Zen Teaching*, First Series, Part I, Master Hsu Yun's Discourses (p. 94).
2. See *Ch'an and Zen Teaching*, First Series, Part III, The Diamond Cutter of Doubts.

the six heretical ways mentioned in the sūtras. He is confronted with a dull emptiness, or the relative voidness which implies a subjective awareness of this state. If he does not loosen his grip of the hua t'ou, he will be aware of this pitfall and will strive to leap over it; then he will reach the stage which Avalokiteśvara Bodhisattva described in the following lines:

When the awareness (of this state) and this state itself were realized
As non-existent, subject and object merged into the void
And awareness of the void became all embracing.
Then when creation and annihilation
Vanished, the state of nirvāṇa manifested

RELATIVE NIRVĀṆA

This state is called Relative, or Partial Nirvāṇa, and although it is already beyond the realm of birth and death, it is not the aim of enlightened Ch'an masters who seek nothing short of the Dharmakāya. After this stage has been attained, a student should advance further and here a very great and long endurance is required so that he can reach the state of the uncreate; this is called anutpattika-dharma-kṣānti, or patient endurance of the uncreate, a pre-condition of the realization of absolute nirvāṇa.

THE YUN MEN DHARMA (UMMON ZEN)

Here, Yun Men gave the following warning:

When light does not penetrate, there are two kinds of illness. The first is when there is absence of clearness everywhere with the presence of something ahead. The other is when although the light penetrates the void, there is still the semblance of something through which the light does not entirely penetrate.

The Dharmakāya has also two kinds of illness. The first is that when reaching the Dharmakāya, one cannot forsake the reality of things (dharma), thereby preserving the conception of an ego; one thus stops on the borderline. The other illness is that even after one has penetrated through the Dharmakāya, one still grasps it and pants for the hereafter.

The Yun Men Dharma is not easily understood by beginners as it is rather for men of high spirituality. It is noted for its cakes, its one-word answers, its Three Gates and its seemingly offensive words which have only one aim, to wipe out the disciples' prejudices and hesitations when distinguishing between the immutable Self and changing illusions; in other words, to remove all remaining traces of the subtle view of ego and things (dharma), so that the disciples can realize the absolute Dharmakāya. This is what Han Shan called the self-preservation and self-awareness of the ego.[1]

THE LIN CHI DHARMA (RINZAI ZEN)

If an advanced disciple still clung to the remaining traces of ego and things (dharma), Lin Chi, in order to wake him up, would give a shout which the master called 'a shout not used as a shout'[2] in performance of the teacher's 'great function' of awakening the fully vitalized potentiality of a student so that it could unite with the absolute. Lin Chi taught his pupils not to cling to anything in order to get out of the realm of illusions. He said:

Sometimes the subject is snatched away but the object is not; sometimes the object is snatched away but the subject is not; sometimes both subject and object are snatched away; and sometimes both subject and object are not snatched away.

1. See *Ch'an and Zen Teaching*, First Series, Part III, The Diamond Cutter of Doubts, p. 189.

2. See *Ch'an and Zen Teaching*, Second Series, The Lin Chi Sect.

His Dharma consists, therefore, in eradicating the subject when there is no attachment to an object; in eliminating the object when there is no attachment to a subject; in wiping out both subject and object when there is attachment to both; and in forsaking nothing when both subject and object are not grasped.

He urged his disciples to interpret the Dharma correctly, that is from the 'host' position, and to disregard all illusions which are but aspects of the non-existent 'guest'. He taught them to hit the first rate meaning in order to realize the absolute, for the second rate meaning leads only to the realization of the non-existence of phenomena and the third rate meaning only to the comprehension of the teaching without experiential realization of it. He then explained that in order to realize the first rate meaning, they should pass through Three Profound Gateways, each with three Vital Stages, that is nine vital phases of training, in order to realize the Dharmakāya. These nine Vital Stages include both the Hīnayāna and Mahāyāna Teachings. Readers will find an account of all the five Ch'an sects with detailed explanations in Series Two of my *Ch'an and Zen Teaching*.

Lin Chi is noted for his use of four kinds of shout in his teaching. He also urged his disciples to distinguish clearly between 'host' and 'guest' in order to avoid confusion in their meditation. According to his Dharma, relations between 'Host' and 'Guest' are classified into four positions: that of guest looking at host; that of host looking at guest; that of guest looking at guest and that of host looking at host, so that students can be clear about the absolute Self and relative illusions.

THE KUEI YANG DHARMA (IKYŌ ZEN)

A student should overcome the last obstructions—ego and things (dharma)—to realize his Dharmakāya, or essential body, which is called 'Substance' in Buddhist terminology. A substance which is incapable of performing its saving function is useless, and a master should train his disciples in the right performance of 'Function'. The story of the Kuei Yang sect relates how Kuei Shan trained his disciple Yang Shan in the realization of Substance and Function. For instance, he would say to his pupil that the latter only realized function but did not realize its body or vice versa so that the student became well versed in the doctrine of Substance and Function. As substance should be all-embracing in order to realize Universal Enlightenment, that is the fifty-first stage of Bodhisattva development for welfare of Self, its function should also be universal for realizing Wonderful Enlightenment, that is the fifty-second or last stage of Bodhisattva development into Buddhahood for the welfare of all living beings. When Yang Shan asked about the abode of the real Buddha, his master Kuei Shan replied:

Turn inwards the subtleness of your thoughtless thinking to think of spiritual brightness until your thinking is exhausted, then return it to its source where the fundamental nature and its formal expressions eternally abide, where activity and principle are not a dualism and where is the suchness of the real Buddha.

This is the region where the fundamental nature, or Substance, and its beneficial activity, or Function, are but the One Reality of the absolute Dharmakāya.

THE TS'AO TUNG DHARMA (SŌTŌ ZEN)

In order to make the Dharma more clear, Tung Shan and his disciple Ts'ao Shan classified the progressive stages of self-cultivation into five positions of (1) Host, or Prince, or the real containing the seeming; (2) Guest, or Minister, or the seeming containing the real; (3) Host coming to light, or Prince looking at Minister, or Resurgence of the real; (4) Guest returning to Host, or Minister returning to Prince, or the seeming uniting with the real; and (5) Host in Host, or Prince and Minister in harmony, or Integration of the real and the seeming. In practice, these five progressive positions are: Shift, Submission, Achievement, Collective Achievement and Absolute Achievement. These five positions serve to enable a student to distinguish between the Host, or Self, and the Guest, or illusory externals, and if he can do so in practice, he will not be misled by his old habits contracted since time without beginning.

Followers of the Ts'ao Tung sect should know its Dharma which is summarized in Tung Shan's Gāthā of the Seal of the Precious Mirror Samādhi.[1]

THE FA YEN DHARMA (HOGEN ZEN)

This Dharma is based on the Buddha's teaching according to which the triple world of desire, form and beyond form are but creations of the One Mind and all phenomena are but the product of its consciousness. It urges all students to realize the identity of this One Mind with its surroundings for realizing the absolute state and he who succeeds in personally experiencing this Dharma will remain immutable in the midst of changing phenomena. This is the state where the fundamental nature and its formal expressions eternally abide, where activity and principle are not a dualism and where is the suchness of the real Buddha as taught by the Kuei Yang sect.

ABSOLUTE NIRVĀṆA

Absolute, or final, nirvāna is attained when there are no further traces of the real and the seeming, that is when a disciple reaches the source of all, where the fundamental nature and its

1. *Ch'an and Zen Teaching*, Series Two, p. 149 ff.

formal expression eternally abide, where activity and principle are not a dualism and where is the suchness of the real Buddha, according to the Kuei Yang sect; when he hits the first rate meaning or has reached the final stage of the Third Profound Door to Enlightenment according to the Lin Chi sect; when he reaches the position of Host in Host according to the Ts'ao Tung sect; when he realizes the identity of Mind with cakes or when he succeeds in following an arrow shot through the Three Gates according to the Yun Men sect; and when he has personal experience of the doctrine of only One Mind according to the Fa Yen sect.

This Final Nirvāṇa was realized by Avalokiteśvara Bodhisattva and described by him in the following lines:

Suddenly I leaped over both the mundane and supramundane and realized an all-embracing brightness pervading the ten directions, acquiring two unsurpassed (merits). The first was in accord with the fundamental Profound Enlightened Mind of all Buddhas high up in the ten directions, possessing the same merciful power as the Tathāgata. The second was in sympathy with all living beings in the six realms of existence here below in the ten directions, sharing with them the same plea of compassion.

According to the Ch'an sect, this absolute nirvāṇa is attained when a disciple is thoroughly awakened to his enlightened master's 'Final Sentence' or 'Real Aim', or, in plain English, the object of his doctrine, that is 'the object of the coming from the West', and if he does not understand it, he is not qualified to be his master's Dharma successor.

THE FINAL SENTENCE

In order to give an idea of the term 'Final Sentence', we present the story of Master Tao Ch'ien of Chiu Feng peak.[1]

1. From *The Imperial Selection of Ch'an Sayings*—Yu Hsuan Yu Lu. Tao Ch'ien was an eminent master who died about 921.

Master Tao Ch'ien was Shih Shuang's attendant and when the latter died, the community invited its leader to succeed him as abbot. The master said to the monks: 'The leader should realize the aim of our late master before he is qualified to be his Dharma successor.' The leader retorted: 'What was the aim of our late master?' The master replied: 'Our late master said: "Halt and rest;[1] be cold and indifferent;[2] equate the moment of a thought (kṣaṇa) with a myriad years (kalpa);[3] go your way like cold ashes and a withered log;[4] be like an incense burner in an ancient temple;[5] and like a thread of white silk."[6] I do not ask you about all this, but tell me what did he mean by "Be like a thread of white silk?" ' The leader replied: 'This is only understanding uniformity.' The master said: 'So you do not really understand the aim of our late master!' The leader said: 'If you do not agree with me, let me light an incense stick and if I fail to depart before it burns out, this will mean that I do not understand the aim of our late master.' Then he lit an incense stick and before it burnt out, he passed away. The master patted him on the back, saying: 'There are cases of those who pass away while sitting or standing, but you have not even dreamt of our late master's aim!'

This shows that the leader did not understand the silk thread that was really white and stood for the all-embracing purity and cleanness of the Dharmakāya, which he mistook for one-sided uniformity, hence his realization only of dhyāna which enabled him to pass away at will, without achieving wisdom (prajñā) in the same proportion, for he was not completely awakened to Shih Shuang's aim. We know that dhyāna should be on an equality with wisdom, as the Sixth Patriarch taught us, in order to realize absolute nirvāṇa.

When the absolute state is achieved, one will be sovereign, that is one will be free to go and to come. Enlightened masters

1. Lay down body and mind and cease discriminating.
2. To perceive the emptiness of phenomena to realize transcendental wu wei.
3. To wipe out the element of time in order to realize eternity.
4. To realize the impotence of the mind.
5. To cut off all feelings and passions.
6. To realize the condition of purity and cleanness of the Dharmakāya which is likened to a silk thread which is white throughout.

used to probe their disciples who had just passed away by saying, for instance: 'You know only how to go but you do not know how to come.' We cite below cases of those who enjoyed complete freedom to go and to come.

1. When Chih I passed away while standing in front of Master Ts'ao Shan, the latter said: 'You know only how to go but you do not know how to come.' Thereupon, Chih I opened his eyes, saying: *Venerable Master, please take good care of yourself* and departed.[1]

2. Although Master Tung Shan had been dead for some time, his disciples continued to weep bitterly without interruption. Suddenly he opened his eyes and said: *Those who leave home should be mindless of illusory externals; this is true practice. What is the use of being anxious for life and death?*[1] He then postponed his death for seven days.

3. When Master Ta Kuan was falsely accused and jailed, he heard that a government official wanted to put him to death. He took a bath, sat erect and chanted the following gāthā before passing away:

A smile comes not without a special cause.
Who knows that Nothingness contains no dust?
Henceforth I tuck up the feet my mother gave me:
The iron tree waits not for the spring to blossom.[2]

When a friend heard of his death, he hurried to the prison, patted the body and said: 'Your leave is well taken.' Thereupon the master opened his eyes, smiled and departed.

The above show that when a man is completely enlightened,

1. See *Ch'an and Zen Teaching*, Second Series, The Ts'ao Tung sect.

2. The first line means: 'I have appeared in the world to teach deluded beings to realize their self-natured bodhi'; this is a special cause. The second line means: 'The absolute immateriality of the self-nature does not admit any foreign matter', i.e. all illusory externals, including the killing of my illusory body, are non-existent in the Nothingness. The third line means: 'I am returning Function to Substance'. To let down the feet is a Ch'an term meaning the performance of Function, and to draw them up is to return its activity to the still self-nature. Iron tree is a Ch'an idiom meaning the mind stripped of all feelings and passions, ready for enlightenment, without depending on the spring, or changing phenomena.

he is free to die or to return to life without hindrance. This is true realization of a teacher's last sentence or the true aim of his Dharma, without which a pupil is not qualified to be his successor.

BODHI OR ENLIGHTENMENT

We now know the pre-condition of Complete Enlightenment and present below a few cases of Ch'an masters attaining bodhi.

1. The Late Master Hsu Yun

After fleeing his home at the age of nineteen, Master Hsu Yun went to Ku Shan monastery where he joined the Saṅgha and received full ordination. He hid himself in a grotto for three years and lived as a hermit. Then he returned to the monastery where he stayed for about four years, after which he started on his long journey to Hua Ting mountain at Wenchow. There he met Master Yang Ching, of the T'ien T'ai (Tendai) school, who taught him to look into the kung an: 'Who is dragging this corpse of yours?' He also practised the T'ien T'ai system of meditation. He then went to other places to study the Ch'an and Lotus doctrines and began his pilgrimage to P'u T'o, the holy place of Avalokiteśvara Bodhisattva; to the monastery of king Aśoka at Ningpo where the relics of the Buddha were kept for worship; to Wu T'ai mountain, the holy place of Mañjuśrī; and to mount O Mei, the bodhimaṇḍala of Samantabhadra Bodhisattva. Thence, he went to Tibet, Bhutan, India, Ceylon and Burma and returned to China where he passed through the provinces of Yunnan, Kweichow, Hunan, Anhwei and Kiangsi and stayed for two years on Ts'ui Feng peak to read the Tripiṭaka. During his travels, the master succeeded in realizing singleness of mind, and in his fifty-sixth year, one evening, in Kao Ming monastery at Yangchow, after a long meditation, he opened his eyes and saw everything inside and outside the monastery. Through the wall, he saw a monk urinating outside, a guest monk in the latrine and far away, boats plying on the river and trees on both its banks. On the third night, at the end of a long meditation, an attendant came to pour tea into his cup. As the boiling water splashed over his hand, he dropped the cup which fell to the ground and broke. Instantly, he cut off his last doubt about his Self and rejoiced at the realization of his cherished aim. He said he was like someone awakening from a dream, and chanted the following gāthā:

A cup fell to the ground
With a sound clearly heard.
As space was pulverized,
The mad mind came to a stop.

He chanted a second gāthā which reads:

When the hand released its hold, the cup fell and was shattered;
'Tis hard to talk when family breaks up or someone dies.[1]
Spring comes with fragrant flowers exuberating everywhere;[2]
Mountains, rivers and the great earth are only the Tathāgata.[3]

2. Master Han Shan[4]

When Master Han Shan was nine years old, his mother sent him to a monastery where he was taught sūtras and literature. At nineteen, he was urged by a learned monk to read *The Sayings of Chung Feng* and to practise Ch'an meditation. Since he did not know its essentials, he concentrated his mind on the repetition of Amitābha Buddha's name continuously for days

1. It is impossible to describe the state attained after one has cut off all earthly feelings and passions.

2. This is the condition of nirvāṇa, full of bliss.

3. All phenomena are identical with the suchness of the self-nature from which they spring.

4. See also Han Shan's autobiography—contracted for publication by Charles E. Tuttle, Tokyo, Japan.

and nights on end. One night in a dream he beheld Amitābha Buddha with his two attendant Bodhisattvas. After that the three saints of the Western Paradise appeared constantly before his eyes and he was confident that he would succeed in his self-cultivation.

One day, as he was listening to a commentary on the samādhi of the Ocean Symbol as taught in the Avataṁsaka Sūtra, he awakened to the profound meaning of the unhindered interdependence of all phenomena in the Dharma realm. The enlightened lecturer, Master Wu Chi, urged him to attend a meditation meeting and to look into the kung an: 'Who is the repeater of the Buddha's name?' Han Shan succeeded in achieving singleness of thought and for three months he did not notice the presence of the community and was mindless of their activities. After this long meditation, when he left his seat, his mind was in the same state as when he sat. He went out and did not see a single person in the crowded market place. At twenty-eight, he went to Wu T'ai mountain with the intention of staying there to meditate but he could not stand the bitter cold and proceeded to the capital. One day, he climbed the peak of P'an Shan mountain where he met a hermit who refused to talk with him. However, he stayed with his speechless host in a grotto, and one evening, he went out for his usual walk. All of a sudden, his forehead seemed to burst with a loud noise like thunder, and his surroundings disappeared completely. This state of voidness lasted about half an hour, and gradually he felt again the presence of his body and mind and became aware of his surroundings once more. He experienced weightlessness and bliss which were beyond description. The hermit began to talk and warned him that the state he had just experienced was only the manifestation of the aggregate of 'form' which should not be clung to.[1] From the capital, he returned to Wu T'ai mountain, passing through

1. Master Hsu Yun also advised his disciples not to push down the hua t'ou into the belly in order to avoid the bad influence of the five aggregates. (See *Ch'an and Zen Teaching*, First Series, Part I.)

Shao Lin monastery where Bodhidharma once stayed and Ho Tung where he stopped to supervise the carving of printing blocks for an edition of Chao Lun[1] with a commentary. He was still not very clear about the doctrine of the immutability of all phenomena, but after reading the treatise again he was instantaneously awakened to the profound teaching. He got up from his meditation bed and went to the Buddha shrine but perceived motionlessness everywhere. He raised the blind and leaves whirling in the wind seemed to stand still. From that moment all his doubts about birth and death disappeared. Then he went on to Wu T'ai mountain in his thirtieth year, and first felt disturbed by the loud roar of water rushing down the mountain. He remembered the story of Avalokiteśvara's Complete Enlightenment by means of the hearing faculty and went to a wooden bridge where he sat in meditation. The noise was very disturbing but with his pointed concentration, after a long while, he only heard it when his mind was stirred by thoughts. All of a sudden, his body seemed to vanish and the noise was no longer heard. One day, after a meal, while he was standing, suddenly he entered the state of samādhi and his body and mind disappeared completely and were replaced by a vast brightness, like a round mirror wherein his surroundings appeared. He then felt at ease in this serenity without meeting any hindrance from externals. He was alone and did not know how long he was in this samādhi state, and when he came out of it, his hearth was covered with a layer of dust. He opened the Śūraṅgama Sūtra to check his awakening. Soon afterwards, he contracted the Ch'an illness[2] and rid himself of it after sitting in meditation for five consecutive days and nights, after which he experienced an indescribable bliss. He had many experiences

1. A treatise written by the eminent master Seng Chao who was Kumārajīva's chief disciple and helped him to translate Indian sūtras into Chinese.

2. The Ch'an illness is sometimes contracted after a major awakening, when the vital principle does not circulate freely through the psychic centres in the body. The meditator is then seized with an irresistable desire to dance, jump, gesticulate, hum, talk and act strangely without apparent reason. Words that he has read before come to him in an endless succession and cannot be stopped. See also Chapter 6 and the preface to *Ch'an and Zen Teaching*, Series Two.

but two of them were of special significance. In each he sat cross-legged, face to face with another enlightened friend, for forty successive days and nights, without sleeping.

3. Master San Feng (1573–1635)

(From *Master San Feng's Autobiography*—San Feng Ho Shang Nien P'u) At the age of thirty, Master San Feng isolated himself in seclusion to look into the kung an: 'All things are returnable to One, to what does the One return?' and he trained for days and nights without interruption.

When he was forty he decided to live in silent seclusion with another monk. As soon as he sat on his cushion, he felt dizzy, vomited and fell asleep, feeling as if he was falling into a very deep pit without anything on which to hold for support. On the fifth day, as he was sleeping soundly, two monks outside the window broke a large bamboo with a loud crack which struck him like a clap of thunder. Instantaneously, he perceived the pulverization of space, the disappearance of the great earth, the vanishing of ego and things (dharma), the invalidity of the One Reality and the non-existence of even traces of imperfection—all this being beyond description and comparison. To him, all the scriptures he had read before were but printed paper, for the profound meaning was beyond thought. He sat in this state the whole night which passed like a finger-snap. In this condition of thoughtlessness, he remembered ancient kung ans, such as Chao Chou's 'At Ch'ing Chou I bought a robe weighing seven (Chinese) pounds', 'An old cypress', 'A toilet stick', 'A bride riding on a donkey led by her mother-in-law', 'An octagonal millstone turning in the air', including Yun Men's 'A fan that jumps up to the thirty-third heaven', so that he experienced all kinds of samādhi.[1]

As a result, he understood that arguing back and forth, blows and shouts, etc., did not reach the transcendental; that even Yun Men's saying: 'The great earth is completely free from all imperfection' was just a way of turning words; that the non-seeing of uniformity was only partial achievement and that there was the transcendental whole which could be experienced only at a propitious moment.[2] If Lin Chi did not understand that 'Huang Po's Buddha Dharma was mainly so little',[3] and if Te Shan still harboured 'doubts about the tips of the tongues of old monks all over the country',[4] how could a shout or a stroke of the staff provoke the realization

1. If these six meaningless kung ans are skilfully looked into, they can be traced back to that which speaks of them; this is direct pointing at the self-mind.

2. This state is indescribable and he who attains it is like a drinker of water who alone knows whether it is cold or warm.

3. See *Ch'an and Zen Teaching*, Second Series, The Lin Chi sect, p. 85.

4. See *Ch'an and Zen Teaching*, First Series, Part I, p. 60.

of Universal Enlightenment? When asked about which sentence he found the most effective, the master replied: 'When I got out of bed, I trod on and flattened my rush sandals.'[1]

4. The Japanese Zen Master Yin Yuan (In-gen)
(From the Supplementary Edition of *A Finger Pointing at the Moon—Hsu Chih Yueh Lu*)

The master was a native of Hsiang Chou (Sō-shū now Kamakura) in Japan. His lay surname was T'eng (Fujiwara) and the T'engs (Fujiwara clan) were noblemen. There were auspicious signs when the master was born. At thirteen, he left his parents, had his head shaved and received full ordination. Then he crossed the sea to China where he called on abbot Wu Chien at T'ien T'ai. Wu Chien urged him to see Chung Feng at T'ien Mu. The latter received him and allowed him to be his attendant.

The master had several times submitted his understanding (of the Dharma) to Chung Feng and one day the Chinese teacher scolded him, saying: 'How can you be free from bondage if you are not disengaged from sense organs and sense data?' The master withdrew sadly and wept bitterly. After that, he had no mind to eat and sleep. Chung Feng was compassionately impressed by his earnestness and said to him: 'The Mind contains a myriad phenomena; when it is deluded, it is subject to birth and death and when it is enlightened, it is nirvāṇa. Although the saṁsāric delusion cannot be easily cast away, yet the nirvāṇic enlightenment is likened to gold dust thrown in the eyes. You should know that wisdom (prajñā) is like a mass of fire that burns everything touching it. If you give rise to a thought that does not turn back and can preserve it in your transmigration through birth and death, you will naturally be in accord with the Tao. But before your awakening, even if a thousand Śākyamunis and ten thousand Maitreyas poured all the water of the four great oceans into your organ of hearing, it would still be falsity and infection which are far away from the ultimate.' These words frightened the master so much that he perspired profusely. One day, he awakened to the profound meaning and came to see Chung Feng, saying: 'I have collided with and penetrated the silver hill and the iron wall.'[2] Chung Feng said: 'If you have penetrated the silver hill

1. The most effective thing is that which speaks these words, or performs its function. If function can be traced back to its source, that is substance, realization of the self-mind will be possible; this is Bodhidharma's direct pointing at the Mind.

2. Presumably the master was so attached to the idea of enlightenment that Chung Feng's words about the absolute, which could not be described even by the Buddha and Maitreya, made such a strong impression on him that he perspired profusely. A profuse perspiration always precedes awakening and this explains why the master was awakened after leaping over all obstructions, symbolized by the silver hill and iron wall.

and the iron wall, why do you come and see me?'[1] The master immediately understood what his teacher meant and the latter said: 'Take good care of your awakening and do your best to preserve it.'[2]

One day, the master felt unwell and said to his attendant: 'The time has come; bring me pen and ink.' He added: 'My stūpa is ready but lacks an inscription.' Then he wrote the two characters 'hsin yin' (mental impression), sat erect and passed away.

Before his death, as his disciples intended to paint a portrait of him and asked him to write an inscription in his own calligraphy, the master drew a circle[3] on the paper and wrote the following gāthā:

Mysterious form is crystal clear,[4]
Absolute is it and unchanging.[5]
It is found everywhere;[6]
What then is its face?[7]

1. Chung Feng urged the master to cast away even the idea of overcoming all obstructions in order to wipe out his last clinging.

2. After awakening, one still has to cut off gradually old habits contracted since the time without beginning. Therefore, one should be very careful in order to preserve the 'holy foetus' and to nourish it, as the masters put it.

3. A circle stands for the all-embracing Dharmakāya which has neither beginning nor end.

4. Mysterious, or wonderful, form is that which is inclusive of both noumenon and phenomenon. See also p. 41 for explanation.

5. It is the immutable thatness.

6. It is omnipresent.

7. It is inconceivable and indescribable but is expediently called 'the fundamental face'. According to the text, the master did not return to Japan and passed away in China.

The three Holy Ones of the Western Paradise

3

SELF-CULTIVATION ACCORDING TO THE PURE LAND SCHOOL

THE chief tenet of the Pure Land school (Chin T'u Tsung) is salvation by faith in Amitābha Buddha, noted for his forty-eight great vows taken in a previous incarnation when he was Bhikṣu Dharmākara (Fa Tsang or Dharma Store). His eighteenth vow was:

After my attainment of Buddhahood, if living beings in the ten directions—except those committing the five rebellious acts[1] *and vilifying the right Dharma—who have developed their unshakeable faith in me, who desire to be reborn in my realm and who have repeated my name ten times, fail to reach their goal, I shall give up saṁbodhi.*[2]

In anticipation of the Dharma ending age when all sūtras and śāstras, beginning with the Śūraṅgama Sūtra, will gradually disappear, Śākyamuni Buddha expounded:

1. the Sūtra of Amitābha (O Mi T'o Ching) which describes the Pure Land of the Buddha of Infinite Light:
2. the Sūtra of Amitāyus (The Buddha of Boundless Age—Wu Liang Shou Ching) which tells the story of Bhikṣu Dharmākara and his forty-eight great vows; and
3. the Sūtra of the Contemplation of Amitāyus (Kuan Wu

1. The five rebellious acts are: parricide, matricide, killing an arhat, shedding the blood of a Buddha and destroying the harmony of the Saṅgha.

2. Saṁbodhi: perfect universal awareness; perfect enlightenment.

Liang Shou Ching) which teaches the method of meditation on this Buddha, so that all living beings can have something to hold on to when the right Dharma is about to be buried in oblivion. It is said that in this period of darkness, when hatred and harm prevail everywhere, only very few fortunate beings will remember even the name of Amitābha and will still have the chance of calling it.

THE LINEAGE OF THE PURE LAND SCHOOL

According to records, Samantabhadra Bodhisattva founded the Pure Land school. In his treatise 'The Awakening of Faith', Aśvaghoṣa, the twelfth Patriarch of the Ch'an sect, urged Buddhists to strive for rebirth in the Pure Land. In their writings, Nāgārjuna and Vasubandhu, respectively the fourteenth and twenty-first Patriarchs of the Ch'an sect, also gave the same advice to those who are unable to awaken to the mind Dharma.

In China, the Pure Land school began to flourish with Master Hui Yuan[1] who was regarded as its second Patriarch, after Samantabhadra Bodhisattva. Hui Yuan was followed by T'an Luan[2] and Tao Ch'o[3] who were regarded at the time as the third and fourth Patriarchs.

This school is also called the Lotus sect (Lien Tsung) in China and its nine Patriarchs, now recognized, are: Hui Yuan,[1] Shan Tao,[4] Ch'eng Yuan,[5] Fa Chao,[6] Shao K'ang,[7] Yen Shou,[8] Hsing Ch'ang,[9] Lien Ch'ih,[10] and Hsing An.[11]

1. Died in 416 at the age of eighty-three.
2. Died in 542 at the age of sixty-seven.
3. Died in 645.
4. Died in 681.
5. Died in 802 at the age of ninety-one.
6. Died in 772.
7. Died in 805.
8. Died in 975 at the age of seventy-two.
9. Died in 1020 at the age of sixty-two.
10. Died in 1615 at the age of eighty-one.
11. In the Ch'ing dynasty (1662–1911).

Among them, Yen Shou and Lien Ch'ih were two enlightened Ch'an masters, and they spread the Pure Land Teaching because the Ch'an Transmission was not suitable for men having affinity with and faith in Amitābha Buddha.

METHODS OF PRACTICE

The three well-known methods of practice are:

1. Repetition of Amitābha's Name.

It consists in calling, either mentally or in a loud or low voice, the name of Amitābha Buddha, the repetition of which, with or without the aid of a rosary of 108 beads, will enable a practiser to concentrate all his attention on that Buddha, thereby realizing singleness of thought. It is an excellent way of controlling the mind and many a devotee thereby succeeds in beholding Amitābha and the two assistant Bodhisattvas, Avalokiteśvara and Mahāsthāmaprāpta.[1]

Followers of this school usually set a fixed number of repetitions a day, from 50,000 to 500,000 or more, and wherever they may happen to be, they mentally call the Buddha's name without interruption. This enables them to put an end to all other thoughts and to purify their minds without difficulty. This practice is supported by unshakeable faith in Amitābha's forty-eight vows and by strict observance of the five precepts. Devotees usually vow to save all living beings after their own self-enlightenment and when their vows unite with those of Amitābha, the combined power of their devotion will enable them to experience an all-embracing state of purity and cleanness. The Chinese founder of this school, Master Hui Yuen, beheld Amitābha thrice and when he was about to die, he saw the three Saints of the Western Realm of Bliss who came to receive him. The Second Patriarch,

1. Before his Ch'an practice, Han Shan beheld the Three Holy Ones of the Realm of Bliss when he concentrated his mind on them. See p. 75.

Shan Tao, repeated the Buddha's name for days and nights without interruption, and each time he called it, a ray of light came out of his mouth. For this reason, emperor Kao Tsung of the T'ang dynasty gave him the name of Great Master 'Kuang Ming' (Bright Light). There are many adherents of this school who succeed in purifying their minds with the aid of this practice and who know in advance the exact time of their death. There are numerous cases of old people who bathed, put on their best clothes, sat cross-legged and passed away peacefully. To preserve stillness of mind they did not tell their families that they were about to die, lest their last moments be disturbed by weeping.

The method of silently calling the Buddha's name is the most convenient for people in all walks of life who wish to control their minds and can be practised even in times of persecution.

2. Repetition of the Mantra of Amitābha
(Chinese, Wang Sheng Chou—mantra for rebirth in the Pure Land)

This mantra is very popular in China and when I was only seven years old my mother taught me to recite it and I could repeat it by heart. Its Chinese transliteration is as corrupt as that of any other, but in spite of this, mantras are said to be very effective when the repeater has realized singleness of mind for they work exactly like the hua t'ou or any kung an. Consequently, a corruptly transliterated mantra can become full of wonder in the same way that the sense data can be sublimated and made wonderful as explained on p. 41. When a devotee is about to die, either the Buddha's name or this mantra is repeated by himself, his family or his Buddhist friends.

We are indebted to the Venerable Bhikkhu Āryadeva who sent us from India a few years ago a correct transliteration of this mantra which we reproduce below for the benefit of those who follow the Pure Land school:

Namo Amitābhaya Tathāgatāya Tadyathā Amṛtabhave Amṛtasambhave Amṛtavikrante Amṛtavikrantagamini Gagana Kīrtīchare Swāhā!

The Indian masters who came to China to translate Siddham texts into Chinese never translated mantras because they said it was impossible to find Chinese equivalents. Nevertheless Bhikkhu Āryadeva rendered it thus:

We take refuge in the Tathāgata Amitābha. Be it thus: that Immortality has become, that Immortality has perfectly become, that Immortality has progressed, that Immortality is progressing, going forward in the glorious Transcendental Way—Swāhā!

According to the Venerable Bhikkhu, the above translation is only approximate because it is impossible to put into words the esoteric meaning of mantras. It is said that when a devotee succeeds in realizing singleness of mind by repeating a mantra, its profound meaning will be clearly revealed to him.

3. The Contemplation of Amitāyus Buddha

We now translate the Sūtra of the Contemplation of Amitāyus, which teaches sixteen methods of meditation leading to the realization of either one of the following nine stages of rebirth in the Pure Land of Amitābha:

1–3. The high, medium and low stages of the superior class of birth;
4–6. the high, medium and low stages of the middle class of birth;
7–9. the high, medium and low stages of the inferior class of birth.

THE SŪTRA OF THE CONTEMPLATION OF AMITĀYUS
(Kuan Wu Liang Shou Ching)

Thus have I heard. Once upon a time, the Buddha sojourned on Gṛdhrakūṭa (Vulture) mountain, near Rājagṛha (city), with an assembly of twelve hundred and fifty bhiksus and a company of thirty-two thousand Bodhisattvas under the leadership of Mañjuśrī, a son of the Dharmarāja (King of the Law).

At the time, in Rājagṛha (city) prince Ajātaśatru,[1] encouraged by his evil friend Devadatta,[2] arrested his own father, king Bimbisāra, and held him in a room inside a sevenfold enclosure, where all the ministers and officials were forbidden to go. The queen, Vaidehī, served the king with great respect and, after bathing him, anointed his body with an ointment made of cream and roast rice powder and offered him grape-juice in a jade vessel. After taking the grape-juice, the king rinsed his mouth, turned towards Gṛdhrakūṭa mountain, brought his two palms together and knelt down to pay in the distance his reverence to the World Honoured One, saying: 'May my relative and friend Maudgalaputra[3] be compassionate enough to teach me the eight prohibitions.'[4]

Thereupon, Maudgalaputra went to the palace with the speed of a flying eagle; and thus every day, he came to teach the eight prohibitions to the king. The World Honoured One also ordered Pūrṇamaitrāyaṇīputra[5] to expound the Dharma to the king. Thus three weeks passed, during which, thanks to the ointment, grape-juice and Dharma, the prisoner continued to look cheerful. (One day), prince Ajātaśatru asked the door-keeper: 'Is the king still alive?' The door-keeper replied: '(Each day) the queen anoints him with an ointment of roast rice powder and gives him grape-juice in a jade vessel. The two monks, Maudgalaputra and Pūrṇamaitrāyaṇīputra, fly every day to expound the Dharma to him. I regret nothing can be done to prevent them.' When Ajātaśatru heard this, he was enraged and said: 'My mother is just a bandit, keeping company with another bandit, and the monks are wicked men using unorthodox mantras to help this wicked king escape from death for so long.' After saying this, he drew his sharp sword with the intention of killing his mother.

Moon-light, an intelligent and wise minister, and Jīva[6] made obeisance to the prince and said: 'Your Majesty, we have read in the Vedas that from

1. Ajātaśatru: king of Magadha who killed his father to ascend to the throne. At first hostile to the Buddha, later he was converted and became noted for liberality.

2. A cousin of the Buddha, of whom he was an enemy and rival.

3. Or Mahā-maudgalyāyana, one of the ten chief disciples of the Buddha, especially noted for his miraculous power.

4. Prohibitions against (1) killing, (2) stealing, (3) sexual intercourse, (4) lying, (5) intoxicating liquors, (6) using garlands or perfumes for personal adornment, singing and dancing, (7) sitting and sleeping on luxurious beds, and (8) eating after midday.

5. Or Maitrāyaṇīputra, son of Bhava by a slave girl; he was the chief preacher among the ten great disciples of the Buddha.

6. Or Jīvaka, son of Bimbisāra by the concubine Āmrapālī, noted for his medical skill.

the beginning of this aeon, there have been 108,000 cases of princes usurping the throne by killing their royal fathers but no prince has murdered his mother the queen. If you now commit this rebellious act which will bring disgrace upon the kṣatriya (royal) caste, we cannot bear to witness this lowest and most despicable of acts. We must leave.' The two ministers then grasped their swords and began to withdraw. Ajātaśatru was astounded and scared, and said to Jīva: 'Are you going to desert me?' Jīva replied: 'Your Majesty should be very careful not to kill your mother.' At this, Ajātaśatru, now in deep remorse, put away his sword and gave up the idea of murdering his mother. He then ordered a court official to confine her in an inner courtyard and to forbid her to leave it.

As Queen Vaidehī was now a prisoner, her heart was full of sadness and anxiety, and turning towards Gṛdhrakūta mountain, she knelt down and from the distance, said to the Buddha: 'O Tathāgata, the World Honoured One used to send Ānanda to comfort me. I am now very sad and will have no chance of seeing the World Honoured One again. Please send Maudgalaputra and Ānanda to come and console me.' Then she wept bitterly and the tears ran down her cheeks; she bowed upon her knees, but even before she raised her head, the World Honoured One who was on Gṛdhrakūta mountain and knew the queen's thoughts as they rose in her mind, ordered Maudgalaputra and Ānanda to fly to comfort her. The Buddha also left the mountain and appeared in the palace. When the queen looked up, she saw the golden body of the World Honoured One, seated on a hundred gemmed lotus, with Maudgalaputra on His left and Ānanda on His right, while the guardians of the Dharma, including Indra and Brahmā, offered celestial flowers which rained from the heavens. She threw away her necklace of precious stones, cast herself at His feet, wept and cried out, saying: 'O World Honoured One, what sin have I committed to be given this wicked son? World Honoured One, what causes led to my becoming a relative of Devadatta? Please tell me of a place free from troubles and afflictions, where I can be reborn, because I do not like this impure earth (Jambudvīpa) where there are so many hells, hungry ghosts and animals which are all evil. May I not hear wicked voices and see evil people in future! I now throw myself at the feet of the World Honoured One and beg for a chance to repent and reform. May the Buddha teach me every day how to look where there is only pure and clean karma!'

Thereupon, the World Honoured One sent out from between His eyebrows a radiant ray of golden light which lit up an incalculable number of worlds in the ten directions and then returned to the top of His head where it turned into a golden tower like mount Sumeru, wherein the mysterious Pure Lands of Buddhas in the ten directions appeared. Some of these Buddha lands were made either of the seven precious gems or of lotus flowers; some were like the heavens of Īśvaradeva while others resembled crystal mirrors reflecting all the worlds in the ten directions. When queen Vaidehī saw these countless Buddha lands, she said: 'World Honoured One, although these Buddha lands are pure and bright, I hope to be born in Amitābha Buddha's Realm of Bliss. Will the World Honoured One teach me how to control my thoughts so as to realize the right samādhi (for this rebirth)?'

Thereupon, the World Honoured One sent out from His mouth rays of a five coloured light which lit up the top of king Bimbisāra's head. Although the king was shut up, his mind's eye was not obstructed and, in the distance, he beheld the World Honoured One. He then bowed his head to pay reverence to Him, and thus making spiritual progress, he realized the anāgāmin stage.[1]

The World Honoured One then said to Vaidehī: 'Know you not that Amitābha Buddha is not distant?[2] Fix your mind on and contemplate his realm which is the produce of pure deeds. I will now use expedients to give you full instruction, and also for the benefit of those in the coming generations who wish to act purely so that they can be born in the Western Realm of Bliss. Those seeking rebirth in that Buddha's land should practise three kinds of blessed virtues. Firstly, they should fulfil their filial duties by taking good care of their parents, obey their teachers, be kind (to others), refrain from killing and perform the ten good deeds.[3] Secondly, they should practise the three formulas of refuge (in Buddha, Dharma and Saṅgha), keep all precepts and refrain from breaking the rules of discipline. Thirdly, they should develop the bodhi mind, believe in the law of causality, read and recite the Mahāyāna sūtras and encourage practisers (of Dharma). These are pure deeds.'[4]

The Buddha continued: 'You should know that these three virtues are the direct causes of the pure deeds of all Buddhas of the past, present and future.'

The Buddha then said to Ānanda and Vaidehī: 'Listen carefully and give serious thought to what the Tathāgata is telling you about these pure deeds for the benefit of all living beings who will suffer from troubles (kleśa) in the coming generations. It is good that you, Vaidehī, have asked about this. And you, Ānanda, should keep these words of the Buddha and spread them

1. Anāgāmin: the stage of a 'non-returning' arhat who will not be reborn in this world, but in heaven where he will attain to nirvāṇa.

2. See also *Ch'an and Zen Teaching*, Third Series, the Altar Sūtra of the Sixth Patriarch, chapter III, Queries.

3. The ten good deeds are strict observance of the ten prohibitions against killing stealing, carnality, lying, double-tongue, coarse language, filthy language, covetousness, anger and perverted views.

4. These words of the Buddha refute the groundless contention that sūtras and śīla can be dispensed with in the practice of the Supreme Vehicle.

widely. I will now teach Vaidehī and also all living beings in coming generations how to contemplate the Western Realm of Bliss so that, with the aid of the Buddha's (transcendental) powers, they will behold that Pure Land as easily as they can see their own faces in a mirror. After they have experienced the wonderful bliss of that land, they will be filled with joy and will realize the patient endurance of the uncreate.'[1]

1. CONTEMPLATION OF THE SETTING SUN

The Buddha then said to Vaidehī: 'Your worldly (faculty of) thinking is inferior and since you have not realized divine sight,[1] you are unable to see (things) from a distance. (But) all Buddhas have wonderful expedients which can cause you to see clearly.' Vaidehī said: 'World Honoured One, by means of the Buddha's transcendental powers, I have been able to see that Land, but after the Buddha's nirvāṇa, how can impure and perverted living beings who are subject to the five forms of suffering[2] perceive Amitābha Buddha's Realm of Bliss?' The Buddha replied: 'You and all living beings should concentrate your minds pointedly on the sole thought of the West. What does "thought" mean? It means that all living beings are not born blind and all those who have eyes can see the setting sun. You should give rise to a thought of it, sit erect with your face towards the west, and direct your mind pointedly to where the sun usually sets like a hanging (red) drum. After you have succeeded in visualizing it, it should be clearly visible whether you open or close your eyes. This is visualization of the sun and is called the First Contemplation.'[3]

2. CONTEMPLATION OF WATER

'Next visualize pure and limpid water which should be clearly seen and absolutely still. After beholding water, visualize ice which should be clear and transparent. After seeing ice, visualize crystal. Then visualize the

1. Deva eye: divine sight, unlimited vision.
2. The five forms of suffering in each of three categories:
   a. (1) Birth, age, sickness and death; (2) parting with those loved; (3) meeting the hated and disliked; (4) inability to satisfy one's desires; and (5) mental and physical suffering from the five aggregates.
   b. Birth, age, sickness, death and fetters.
   c. Suffering in the five realms of hells, hungry ghosts, animals, asuras and human beings
3. This first contemplation is easy to achieve and he who practises it seriously will have no difficulty in beholding the setting red sun which is a very pleasing sight, but is usually followed by profuse perspiration.

ground as crystal which should be really transparent and below it, supporting flagstaffs made of diamonds and seven other gems. Each flagstaff is octagonal, with a hundred gems on each side. Each gem emits a thousand rays of light. Each ray has 84,000 colours and lights up the crystal ground, thus revealing myriads of suns which are too numerous to be all seen. The crystal ground is bounded by a golden rope adorned with seven gems each of which emits five hundred coloured lights which look like a flower, a star or a moon hanging in the air. They form a radiant tower with tens of thousands of upper chambers each made of a hundred gems. The sides of the tower are ornamented with a hundred lacs[1] of flagstaffs and countless musical instruments, played by eight clear breezes produced by these bright lights, and proclaiming (the doctrine of) "suffering, unreality, impermanence and absence of ego". This is visualization of water and is the Second Contemplation.'

3. CONTEMPLATION OF THE GROUND

'When the (above) contemplation has been achieved, the visualization should be clearly seen whether you open or close your eyes, and should be constantly kept in your mind except when you sleep. This is a coarse view of the Realm of Bliss.[2] If you succeed in realizing the state of samādhi, you will perceive very clearly that Realm which it is impossible to describe fully.[3] This is visualization of the Ground and is the Third Contemplation.'

The Buddha said to Ānanda: 'Keep these words of the Buddha; for the benefit of those of coming generations who wish to escape from sufferings, teach them this method of visualizing the ground. He who achieves it will be rid of saṁsāric sins committed in eighty lacs of aeons and when he dies, he will be reborn in the Pure Land about which he will no longer have doubt. This contemplation is right and any other is wrong.'

4. CONTEMPLATION OF PRECIOUS TREES

The Buddha then said to Ānanda and Vaidehī: 'After achieving this contemplation of the Ground, you should visualize its jewelled trees. They should be seen clearly in seven lines (or avenues), each tree reaching the height of eight thousand yojanas.[4] These trees have their seven gemmed

1. Lac or lakh: a hundred thousand.
2. This is still the realm of relativities.
3. This is the realm of the absolute.
4. Described as a distance covered by a royal day's march for the army.

leaves and flowers, each leaf and flower being of different colours. If (each leaf or flower) is made of lapis lazuli, it emits a ray of golden light, if of crystal, a ray of red light. If it is made of cornelian, it emits a ray of agate light, if of agate, a ray of pearl-green light. Above these trees are pearl nets adorned with coral, amber and all other gems. Above each tree, there are seven layers of nets. Each net contains five hundred lacs of beautifully decorated palaces like those of Brahmā and each has its complement of youths. Each youth wears necklaces of five hundred lacs of maṇi pearls, which light up the land for a hundred yojanas, and the whole thing resembles an indescribable mass of myriads of bright suns and moons. These gems are mixed together and their colours are incomparably beautiful. The lines of jewelled trees are in perfect order and so are their leaves. Amidst these leaves are beautiful flowers above which are seven gemmed fruits. Each leaf is twenty yojanas long and wide and has a thousand colours and a hundred ribs, similar to the necklaces of the gods (devas). These beautiful flowers are of the colour of the Jambū river's gold and look like turning torches shining amidst the leaves and producing fruits which resemble the vase of Śakra.[1] There is (also) a great light which produces banners and countless canopies. Inside each canopy can be seen all the Buddha works (of salvation) in all the worlds of the great chiliocosm and all the Buddha lands in the ten directions. When these trees appear, they should be distinctly contemplated, one by one, with their trunks, branches, leaves, flowers and fruits which should be clearly visible. This is visualization of trees and is the Fourth Contemplation.'

5. CONTEMPLATION OF MERIT-GIVING WATER

'Next visualize merit-giving water. In the Realm of Bliss, there are eight pools, and the water of each consists of seven gems in liquid form, begotten by the royal maṇi pearl.[2] The water of each pool flows into fourteen channels, each of which has the beautiful colours of the seven gems, with a golden gutter and a bed of diamond sands. In each pool, there are sixty lacs of seven gemmed lotus, each being perfectly round and twelve yojanas (across). Its pearly water flows amidst the lotus, rising and falling between their stalks and producing mysterious voices which proclaim the (doctrine of) suffering, unreality, impermanence and absence of ego, tell of the various perfections (pāramitā) and praise the physical marks and excellent characteristics of Buddhas. The royal maṇi pearl emits wonderful rays of golden light which turn into multi-coloured jewelled birds which melodiously

1. The vase of Śakra, from which come all things required by him.
2. Cintāmaṇi: a fabulous gem, responding to every wish.

sing praise to the Buddha, Dharma and Saṅgha. This is visualization of the eight pools of merit-giving water and is the Fifth Contemplation.'

6. CONTEMPLATION OF THE REALM OF BLISS WITH PRECIOUS TREES, GROUND AND WATER

'In this Realm of precious gems, there are overhead five hundred lacs of precious palaces, with upper chambers wherein countless devas play heavenly music. Musical instruments hang in the air, like heavenly flag-staffs, producing voices that proclaim the Buddha, Dharma and Saṅgha. The realization of this vision is called the coarse view of the Realm of Bliss (with its) precious trees, ground and pools. This complete visualization is called the Sixth Contemplation. He who achieves it, rids himself of the most evil karmas formed in countless lacs of aeons and will, at his death, be reborn in that Land. Such a contemplation is right and any different one is wrong.'

7. CONTEMPLATION OF THE LOTUS SEAT

The Buddha then said to Ānanda and Vaidehī: 'Listen carefully and give serious thought to what I now tell you about how to escape from troubles and afflictions so that you can remember and expound it widely to others.' As the Buddha was speaking, Amitāyus appeared in the air, flanked by the two attendant Bodhisattvas, in a mass of brightness which was so vast that it could not be seen completely and outshone the hundreds and thousands of brilliant gold pieces in the Jambū river.

Upon seeing Amitāyus, Vaidehī prostrated herself with her head at the feet of the Buddha, saying: 'World Honoured One, thanks to the Buddha's transcendental powers, I can now behold Amitāyus with the two attendant Bodhisattvas. What should living beings of future generations do in order to see them?' The Buddha replied: 'He who wishes to behold that Buddha, should visualize a lotus on the seven gemmed ground. Each of its petals is of the colour of a hundred gems and has 84,000 veins which seem to have been drawn by the devas and send out 84,000 rays of light which make them clearly visible. Each small petal is two hundred and fifty yojanas long and wide and each lotus has 84,000 such petals. Each petal is adorned with a hundred lacs of mani pearls and each pearl emits a thousand rays of light. These lights form an umbrella which seems to be made of seven precious gems and which covers the whole ground. The seed case (of the lotus) is surrounded by and adorned with a net of 80,000 gems, such as diamonds, rubies (kiṁśuka), cintāmaṇi and beautiful pearls. From the seed case rise four precious flagstaffs, each of which looks like a hundred, a thousand, ten thousand and a hundred thousand mount Sumerus, with at the top of each, a precious tent similar to (that of) Yama's heaven,[1] and adorned with five hundred lacs of precious pearls. Each pearl emits 84,000 rays of light, each ray having the same number of golden colours. These golden lights penetrate everywhere and turn into various forms and shapes, such as diamond seats, nets of pearls and clouds of mixed flowers appearing in the ten directions and performing the Buddha works. This is visualization of the lotus seat and is called the Seventh Contemplation.'

The Buddha then said to Ānanda: 'This lotus is the crystallization of Bhikṣu Dharmākara's former vows, and those thinking of that Buddha should first visualize his lotus seat. When so doing they should refrain from contemplating anything else. In this visualization, every leaf, every gem, every ray of light, the lotus seat and each flagstaff should be clearly visible as when one sees one's own face in a mirror. Realization of this vision will eradicate all karmic sins committed in fifty thousand lacs of aeons and will ensure rebirth in the Realm of Bliss. Such a contemplation is right whereas any other is wrong.'

8. CONTEMPLATION OF THE IMAGES OF THE THREE HOLY ONES

The Buddha then said to Ānanda and Vaidehī: 'After seeing all this, one should think of that Buddha (Amitāyus). Why? Because the Buddha-kāyas of all Tathāgatas are but the Dharmadhātu which contains and pervades the thinking minds of all living beings. Therefore, when the mind is set on thinking of (that) Buddha, it is identical with the thirty-two physical marks and eighty excellent characteristics (of a Nirmāṇakāya-Buddha), because Mind realizes Buddhahood; Mind is Buddha; and the Buddha's ocean of universal knowledge comes from Mind's thought. Therefore, one should concentrate one's mind exclusively on contemplating that Buddha (as) Tathāgata, Arhat and Samyak-sambuddha.[2]

'When contemplating that Buddha, the first step is to visualize his precious golden image seated on a lotus (until) one beholds it with either open or closed eyes. When this image is seen, the mind's eye will open and will see clearly the Realm of Bliss with its seven gemmed ground, precious

1. Yama heaven, or Yamaloka, the third devaloka, the place where the seasons are always good.

2. The first three of the ten titles of a Buddha: (1) Tathāgata is he who came as did all Buddhas, who took the absolute way of cause and effect and attained to perfect wisdom; one of the highest titles of a Buddha; (2) Arhat is he who overcomes mortality; the second title of a Buddha and (3) Samyak-sambuddha is he who has perfect universal knowledge; the third title of a Buddha.

pools and avenues of precious trees, covered by heavenly jewelled tents, with nets of gems filling the whole of space. This visualization should be as clearly visible as one's own hand.

'After achieving this contemplation, visualize another great lotus, identical with the first one, on the left of the Buddha and then another identical one on his right, then the image of Avalokiteśvara of the same golden hue (as the Buddha), seated on the left lotus and then the image of Mahāsthāma on the right lotus. After this has been visualized that Buddha and the two attendant Bodhisattvas send out rays of golden light which illuminates all the precious trees. At the foot of each tree appear three lotus with that Buddha and the two attendant Bodhisattvas seated on them. Thus the Realm of Bliss is filled with an uncountable number of lotus with the three holy ones seated on them.

'When this visualization is achieved, the practiser will hear the Profound Dharma intoned by the flowing waters, rays of light, precious trees, wild geese and mandarin ducks. Thus he will constantly hear the wonderful Dharma whether or not he sits in meditation.[1] At the end of his contemplation, he should remember what he has heard during it and should not stray from the Dharma which should accord with the sūtras.[2] If it disagrees with the sūtras, this (comes from) his wrong thinking and if it agrees, this is a coarse form of meditation.[3] This seeing of the Realm of Bliss entails the visualization of images and is called the Eighth Contemplation. It eliminates karmic sins committed in countless former aeons and ensures the practiser's realization in his present bodily form of the samādhi (due to) pointed concentration on the Buddha.'[4]

9. CONTEMPLATION OF THE BODILY FORM OF AMITĀYUS BUDDHA

The Buddha then said to Ānanda and Vaidehī: 'After achieving this contemplation, you should visualize the radiant body of Amitāyus Buddha. Ānanda, you should know that his body is coloured like the pure gold in a hundred, a thousand, ten thousand and a hundred thousand Yamalokas (making a pile reaching the height of) as many yojanas as there are sand

1. Lit. whether he enters into meditation or comes out of it.

2. Here the contemplation taught by the Buddha is the correct one, and if the Dharma heard by the practiser does not accord with the sūtras, this shows that the practiser gives rise to discrimination and so strays from right concentration; hence the heterodox doctrine arising in his mind in contrast with the profound Dharma.

3. Meditation in its coarse aspect.

4. This samādhi results either from the above visualization or from constant repetition of the Buddha's name until singleness of mind is achieved.

grains in six hundred thousand lacs of nayutas[1] of Ganges rivers. The white hair between his eyebrows[2] curls five times to the right like five mount Sumerus. His eyes are like the water of four oceans with the blue and white clearly distinguishable. The pores of his body send out rays of light as great as mount Sumeru. The halo (round his head) contains a hundred lacs of great chiliocosms, wherein appear Nirmāṇakāya Buddhas as many as there are sandgrains in a million lacs of nayutas of Ganges rivers. Each Nirmāṇakāya Buddha has a following of countless Transformation Bodhisattvas serving him. Amitāyus Buddha has 84,000 (physical) marks; each mark has 84,000 excellent characteristics; each characteristic sends out 84,000 rays of light; and each ray of light illumines and attracts to it all living beings in all the worlds in the ten directions who (earnestly) think of him. The radiant marks and characteristics of these Nirmāṇakāya Buddhas cannot be detailed, but the meditator should just keep (the visualization) in mind and remember it so that his mind's eye will (ultimately) see them. When this is achieved, he will behold all the Buddhas in the ten directions. When all the Buddhas are seen, it is called the samādhi of pointed concentration on the Buddha. This visualization is called contemplation of all Buddhakāyas. As the Buddhakāya is seen, so is the Buddha's mind, by which is meant the great kindness (maitrī) and compassion (karuṇā) which consist in the uncaused merciful reception of living beings. This contemplation ensures, at the end of one's present life, rebirth in front of all the Buddhas, with realization of the patient endurance of the uncreate. Wise men therefore should concentrate their minds on the contemplation of Amitāyus Buddha, which consists in first visualizing a single mark, that is the white curl between his eyebrows until it is clearly seen. When this is achieved, all the 84,000 marks appear. When Amitāyus Buddha is beheld, countless Buddhas in the ten directions will be perceptible. Because countless Buddhas are beheld, they will come to predict the future attainment (of the practiser). This is the all-embracing visualization of the bodily forms (of all Buddhas) and is called the Ninth Contemplation. Such a contemplation is right whereas any other is wrong.'

10. CONTEMPLATION OF AVALOKITEŚVARA BODHISATTVA

The Buddha then said to Ānanda and Vaidehī: 'After clearly beholding Amitāyus Buddha, one should visualize Avalokiteśvara Bodhisattva whose golden body reaches the height of 800,000 lacs of nayutas of yojanas, with a fleshy lump on the top of his head[3] and a halo round his neck. His face,

1. Nayuta: a number, 100,000 or one million or ten million.
2. White curl or ūrṇā, one of the thirty-two signs of a Buddha.
3. Uṣṇīṣa, one of the thirty-two physical marks of a Buddha.

fleshy lump and halo are each a hundred and a thousand yojanas high. Within the halo, there are five hundred Nirmāṇakāya Buddhas who look like Śākyamuni Buddha. Each Nirmāṇakāya Buddha has a following of five hundred transformation Bodhisattvas together with an incalculable number of devas who serve him.

'The body of Avalokiteśvara Bodhisattva sends out rays of light in which all living beings in the five worlds of existence appear. His deva crown is made of maṇi pearls, in each of which stands a Nirmāṇakāya Buddha whose body is twenty-five yojanas high.

'The Bodhisattva's face is of golden hue and between his eyebrows a curl of seven colours emits rays of 84,000 kinds of light. Inside each ray there is a countless number of Nirmāṇakāya Buddhas. Each Buddha is surrounded by an incalculable number of Transformation Bodhisattvas who serve him and reproduce at will all the transformations that fill all the worlds in the ten directions.

'The (two) arms of the Bodhisattva are red like a lotus and adorned with bracelets whose majesty is revealed by eighty lacs of beautiful rays of light.

'The Bodhisattva's palms are coloured like five hundred lacs of many hued lotus. Each finger tip has 84,000 lines as (clear as) if they had been printed thereon. Each line has 84,000 hues each of which sends out 84,000 rays of soft light which illumine everything. With these precious hands he receives and delivers living beings.

'When the Bodhisattva raises his foot, its sole is seen to be marked with a wheel of a thousand spokes which turn into five hundred lacs of shining towers. When he lowers it, lotus made of maṇi pearls are scattered everywhere and fill the whole realm. The other marks and characteristics of his body are identical with those of the Buddha, except that the fleshy lump on the top of his head and the smallness of his brow cannot be compared to those of the World Honoured One. This is the visualization of the bodily form of Avalokiteśvara Bodhisattva and is called the Tenth Contemplation.

The Buddha then said to Ānanda: 'He who wishes to visualize Avalokiteśvara Bodhisattva should make this contemplation. He who does so, will escape from all calamities, rid himself of karmic obstructions and wipe out all mortal sins committed in countless aeons. Just to hear this Bodhisattva's name wins boundless blessings; how much more so does contemplating upon him. This contemplation begins with visualizing the fleshy lump on his head, then his heavenly crown and then gradually his other physical marks until he is seen as clearly as the palm of one's own hand. Such a contemplation is right whereas any other is wrong.

11. CONTEMPLATION OF MAHĀSTHĀMA BODHISATTVA

'Next visualize Mahāsthāma (or Mahāsthāmaprāpta) Bodhisattva whose body is the same size as that of Avalokiteśvara. His face and halo are each twenty five yojanas high and send out rays of light for two hundred and fifty yojanas. His radiant body illumines all continents in the ten directions and those living beings having causal affinities with him can behold his golden body. He who sees only a ray of light coming from one of his pores, will behold the pure light of boundless Buddhas in the ten directions; hence, this Bodhisattva's name of "Boundless Light". As he uses the light of wisdom to illumine all living beings and to lead them out of the three lower realms (of hungry ghosts, animals and hells) so that they can acquire unsurpassed powers,[1] he is called the Bodhisattva whose power of wisdom reaches everywhere (Mahāsthāmaprāpta). His heavenly crown consists of five hundred precious lotus, everyone of which has five hundred precious towers. Inside each tower appear all the wondrous Pure Lands in the ten directions, with Buddhas revealing their broad and long red tongues.[2] The fleshy lump on the top of his head is like a red lotus with, above it, a precious vase of all kinds of light revealing all the Buddha works.[3] His other physical marks are identical with those of Avalokiteśvara. When he walks, all the worlds in the ten directions shake, and wherever the tremor is felt, five hundred lacs of precious lotus appear, each as majestic as the Realm of Bliss. When he sits, the seven gemmed ground shakes and from the lower land of the Golden Light Buddha to the upper land of the Buddha of Glory, a countless dust-like number of Transformation Amitāyus Buddhas, each with Avalokiteśvara and Mahāsthāma, gather in the Realm of Bliss and fill the whole space, seated on their lotus seats and proclaiming the Profound Dharma to deliver suffering people. This is the visualization of Mahāsthāma Bodhisattva or the contemplation of his bodily form and is called the Eleventh Contemplation which roots out mortal sins committed in countless endless aeons (asaṅkhya). He who so contemplates will never abide again in the womb and will always enjoy his walks in the Pure Lands of all the Buddhas.'

12. CONTEMPLATION OF AMITĀYUS' REALM OF BLISS

'By the above successful visualization, the practiser will have achieved (what is) called the complete contemplation of the two attendant Bodhisattvas,

1. e.g. to eradicate miseries.
2. One of the thirty-two marks of a Buddha; this tongue is big enough to cover his face to prove that his words are true and not deceitful.
3. Of delivering living beings.

Avalokiteśvara and Mahāsthāma. Then one should give rise to a wish for rebirth in the Western Realm of Bliss where one will find oneself seated with crossed legs within a lotus, the flower of which then opens and closes. When it opens rays of five hundred coloured lights illumine one's body. Then one visualizes one's own eyes that open and the (countless) Buddhas and Bodhisattvas filling the whole space with waters, birds, trees, groves and the voices (of these Buddhas) proclaiming the Profound Dharma which accords with the teaching in the twelve divisions of the Tripiṭaka. If, after this meditation,[1] one can preserve it, this is the vision of Amitāyus' Realm of Bliss. This is its complete visualization and is called the Twelfth Contemplation. Amitāyus Buddha (will then turn into) a boundless number of Nirmāṇakāya Buddhas and will, with Avalokiteśvara and Mahāsthāma, always come to the meditator's dwelling place.'

13. CONTEMPLATION OF THE THREE HOLY ONES OF THE REALM OF BLISS[2]

The Buddha then said to Ānanda and Vaidehī: 'He who is determined to be reborn in the Western Realm should first visualize a sixteen-foot image (of Amitābha Buddha) above a pool as described earlier, for it is impossible for the worldling's mind to reach the boundless body of Amitāyus Buddha. However, because of the powerful vows taken in a former life by that Tathāgata, those who think of and concentrate on him will have their wishes answered. Even mere visualization of his image can result in boundless blessings; how much more so contemplation of his complete Buddhakāya? Amitābha Buddha, by means of his transcendental powers, can reproduce at will his Nirmāṇakāyas in the ten directions, either appearing in a boundless body filling the whole of space or in a small one, eight or sixteen feet high. The golden body, halo and lotus seat of his transformation body have been described earlier. As to Avolakiteśvara and Mahāsthāma, their bodies are alike but can be distinguished by looking at their heads. These two Bodhisattvas assist Amitābha Buddha to convert and deliver all living beings. This is a multiple visualization and is called the Thirteenth Contemplation.'

1. Lit. 'If after coming out of this still condition'.

2. Before his Ch'an practice, Master Han Shan succeeded in visualizing the three Saints of the Western Realm of Bliss when he began his mental concentration on them. See p. 76.

14. THE SUPERIOR CLASS OF BIRTH IN THE REALM OF BLISS

(a) The high stage of the Superior Class of Birth

The Buddha then said to Ānanda and Vaidehī: 'The high stage of the superior class of birth (in the Realm of Bliss) is attainable by those who, in their quest for rebirth there, develop three kinds of mind: the truthful mind, the profound mind and the mind fixed on the vow to devote all one's merits to being reborn there. He who develops these three kinds of mind is bound to be born in that Pure Land.

'There are also three classes of living beings who will be reborn there, namely: he who refrains from killing because of his compassionate heart and who observes all the other prohibitions; he who reads and recites (i.e. practises) Vaipulya and Mahāyāna sūtras; and he who does not stray from the six kinds of thought[1] and devotes all the merits derived therefrom to his rebirth in that Realm of Bliss. The accumulation of all these merits ensures his rebirth there within one to seven days, and because of his intense zeal and devotion, the Tathāgata Amitābha will, together with his two attendant Bodhisattvas, Avalokiteśvara and Mahāsthāma, an incalculable number of Nirmāṇakāya Buddhas, hundreds and thousands of devotees including bhikṣus and śrāvakas and countless heavenly palaces made of the seven gems will (appear to) welcome him. Avalokiteśvara Bodhisattva, holding a diamond seat, will come with Mahāsthāma Bodhisattva in front of him. Amitābha Buddha will send out rays of great light to illumine his body while he and the Bodhisattvas (present) will extend their hands to receive him. Then Avalokiteśvara and Mahāsthāma and countless Bodhisattvas will praise and comfort the practiser who, on seeing them, feels great joy and (suddenly) finds himself riding in the diamond seat which then follows that Buddha; in a finger-snap, he will be reborn in the Realm of Bliss.

'At his birth there, he will behold that Buddha and all Bodhisattvas in their completely perfect bodily forms, while the radiant precious groves proclaim the Profound Dharma. After hearing it, he will realize the patient endurance of the uncreate and, in an instant, he will be able to serve all the Buddhas in the ten directions. After receiving their predictions of his future attainment, he will return to his Realm (of Bliss) where he will immediately understand an incalculable number of dhāraṇi doors (to enlightenment). This is the high stage of the Superior Class of Birth.'

(b) The medium stage of the Superior Class of Birth

'The medium stage of the Superior Class of Birth is attainable by one who, without studying the Vaipulya sūtras, understands very well the path of

1. The six thoughts of Buddha, Dharma, Saṅgha, discipline (śīla), charity (dāna) and heavenly happiness.

truth, whose mind remains unshakeable in the Supreme Reality, who has deep faith in the law of causality, who does not criticize the Mahāyāna and who devotes all the merits thus accumulated to his rebirth in the Realm of Bliss. When he is about to die, Amitābha Buddha, flanked by the two attendant Bodhisattvas, Avalokiteśvara and Mahāsthāma, with their countless followers, will come with a golden seat to praise him, saying: "Son of Dharma,[1] because of your practice of the Mahāyāna and your understanding of Supreme Reality, I now come to receive you." (Thereupon), together with thousands of Nirmāṇakāya Buddhas, they extend their hands to welcome him, and he will find himself seated on the golden seat, and will bring his two palms together, with crossed fingers, praising all the Buddhas. In the time of a thought, he will be born in that Realm, seated on that seat, above a seven gemmed pool. This seat is like a great precious lotus which will open the following day. His body will be golden hued and under each of his feet there will be a seven jewelled lotus. Then the Buddha and Bodhisattvas will illumine him with rays of light which cause his eyes to open. Because of his former practice, he will hear voices proclaiming the very profound Supreme Reality. He will then descend from his golden seat, put his two palms together, pay reverence to the Buddha and praise the World Honoured One. Within seven days, he will develop an unflinching faith in the unexcelled Universal Enlightenment (anuttara-samyak-saṁbodhi) which will enable him to fly in the air and to go everywhere in the ten directions to (revere and) serve all Buddhas under whose teaching he will practise all kinds of samādhi. At the end of a small aeon (antara-kalpa), he will realize the patient endurance of the uncreate and will be told of his future attainments.

This is the medium stage of the Superior Class of Birth.'

(c) The low stage of the Superioı Class of Birth

'The low stage of the Superior Class of Birth is attainable by him who believes in the law of causality, refrains from criticizing the Mahāyāna, determines to seek Supreme Tao and devotes all the merits thus accumulated to his rebirth in the Realm of Bliss. When he is about to die, Amitābha Buddha, flanked by his two attendant Bodhisattvas, Avalokiteśvara and Mahāsthāma, and followed by other Bodhisattvas, appears with a golden lotus and causes, with his transformation powers, five hundred Nirmāṇakāya Buddhas to come and extend their hands to welcome and praise the practiser, saying: "Son of Dharma, as you live in purity and are determined to seek Supreme Tao, we now come to receive you." Upon beholding them, he will find himself seated on the golden lotus which will close and follow the World Honoured One. He will then be born on a seven

1. Son of Dharma: a practiser of the Buddha Dharma.

gemmed pool, and after a day and night, the lotus will open. Seven days later, he will behold the Buddha, and although he sees him, the latter's physical marks and excellent characteristics are still dim and will not become clearly visible for twenty-one days. Then he will hear voices proclaiming the subtle Dharma and will be able to roam in the ten directions to make offerings to all Buddhas, under whose guidance he will hear about the very Profound Dharma. Three small aeons later, he will be awakened to the door to Correct Understanding of the Hundred Divisions of Phenomena[1] and will realize the stage of joy (pramuditā).[2] This is the low stage of the Superior Class of Birth.'

'The above are (visualizations of) the Superior Class of Birth and are (jointly) called the Fourteenth Contemplation.'

15. THE MIDDLE CLASS OF BIRTH IN THE REALM OF BLISS

(a) The high stage of the Middle Class of Birth

The Buddha then said to Ānanda and Vaidehī: 'The high stage of the Middle Class of Birth is attainable by him who receives and observes the five precepts,[3] keeps the eight commandments,[4] practises the other rules of morality, does not commit the five rebellious acts, is free from other faults and devotes all the merits derived from these good roots to achieving his birth in the Western Realm of Bliss. When he is about to die, Amitābha Buddha, with his following of bhikṣus, will send out rays of golden light to illumine the devotee's place of abode, teaching him the doctrine about suffering,

1. The hundred divisions of all mental qualities and their agents, classified into five groups: (1) the eight consciousnesses; (2) the fifty-one mental ideas; (3) the five physical organs and their six modes of sense; e.g. eye and form, etc.; (4) the twenty-four indefinities; and (5) the six inactive concepts.

2. The first of the ten stages of a Mahāyāna Bodhisattva's development which are: (1) pramuditā, joy at having overcome all obstructions for present entry upon the path to bodhi; (2) vimala, a state of purity free from all defilement; (3) prabhākarī, appearance of the light of wisdom; (4) arciṣmatī, glowing wisdom; (5) sudurjayā, overcoming utmost difficulties; (6) abhimukhī, appearance of the absolute; (7) dūraṁgamā, condition of immateriality, beyond the worldly, śrāvaka and pratyeka buddha states; (8) acalā, state of immutability in the midst of changing phenomena; (9) sādhumatī, acquisition of the four unhindered powers of interpretation with ability to expound all Dharma doors everywhere. The four unhindered Bodhisattva powers of reasoning, or pratisaṁvid, are: (a) in the Dharma, the letter of the Law; (b) artha, its meaning; (c) nirukti, form of expression and (d) pratibhāna, in eloquence, or pleasure in preaching; (10) dharmamegha, the stage of Dharma clouds raining amṛta to save living beings.

3. Prohibitions against killing, stealing, adultery, lying and intoxicating liquors.

4. Against (1) killing, (2) stealing, (3) carnality, (4) lying, (5) drinking wine, (6) personal adornments, singing and dancing, (7) sleeping and sitting on luxurious beds, and (8) eating out of regulation hours.

unreality, impermanence and absence of ego, and praising those who leave their homes to escape from miseries. After seeing this, the practiser will be filled with joy and will find himself seated on a lotus seat. He will bring his two palms together and kneel to pay reverence to the Buddha and, even before he raises his head, he is already born in the Realm of Bliss where the lotus will open. As it opens, he will hear voices praising the Four Noble Truths,[1] and will realize arhatship, thus perfecting the three insights,[2] the six supernatural powers[3] and the eight forms of liberation.[4] This is the high stage of the Middle Class of Birth.'

(b) The medium stage of the Middle Class of Birth

'The medium stage of the Middle Class of Birth is attainable by him who, in a day and night, faultlessly observes the eight commandments, the ten prohibitions of the śrāmaṇera,[5] and the complete set of disciplinary rules,[6] does not fail to remain dignified (when walking, standing, sitting and lying) and devotes all the merits derived from his correct conduct to realizing his birth in the Realm of Bliss. Being thus purified by the fragrance of discipline, when he is about to die, he will behold Amitābha Buddha, surrounded by his retinue, who will send out a ray of golden light and will come with a seven jewelled lotus in front of the practiser. The

1. Catvāriārya-satyāni: suffering (duḥkha) its cause (samudaya), its ending (nirodha) and the way thereto (mārga). These four dogmas were first preached by the Buddha to his five former ascetic companions, and those who accepted them in the śrāvaka stage.

2. Insight into (1) the mortal condition of self and others in previous lives; (2) into future lives, and (3) into present mortal sufferings to put an end to all passions.

3. Ṣaḍabhijñā: (1) divine sight; (2) divine hearing; (3) knowledge of the minds of all other living beings; (4) knowledge of all forms of previous existences of self and others; (5) power to appear at will in any place and to have absolute freedom; and (6) insight into the ending of the stream of birth and death.

4. Aṣṭavimokṣa, the eight stages of meditation leading to (1) deliverance when there is attachment to form by examination of form and realization of its filthiness; (2) deliverance, when there is no attachment to form, by examination of form and realization of its filthiness—these two are deliverance by meditation on impurity, the next on purity; (3) deliverance by meditation on purity and realization of a state free from desire; (4) deliverance in realization of boundless immateriality; (5) deliverance in realization of boundless knowledge; (6) deliverance in realization of nothingness; (7) deliverance in the state wherein there is neither thought nor absence of thought; (8) deliverance in the state wherein the two aggregates, feeling (vedanā) and ideation (sañjñā) are entirely eliminated.

5. The ten commandments of the religious novice against (1) killing, (2) stealing, (3) carnality, (4) lying, (5) drinking wine, (6) taking food out of regulated hours, (7) using garlands or perfumes, (8) sitting and sleeping on luxurious beds, (9) taking part in singing, dancing, musical or theatrical performances, and (10) acquiring gold, silver and jewels.

6. 250 for a monk and 500 for a nun.

latter will hear a voice in the air praising him: "Virtuous man, as you have kept the Teaching of all the Buddhas of the three times, I now come to receive you," and will find himself seated on the lotus. Then the lotus will close and he will be reborn in the precious pool of the Realm of Bliss. Seven days later, the lotus will open and he will open his eyes, bring his two palms together and praise that Tathāgata. He will hear about the Dharma, will be filled with joy and will attain the śrota-āpanna stage,[1] and half an aeon later, he will realize arhatship.[2] This is the medium stage of the Middle Class of Birth.'

(c) The low stage of the Middle Class of Birth

'The low stage of the Middle Class of Birth is attainable by a virtuous man or woman who fulfils all filial duties and practises worldly compassion.[3] When about to die, he or she will meet an enlightened teacher who will tell him or her about the blissful conditions in the Realm of Amitābha Buddha and also about Bhikṣu Dharmākara's forty-eight vows. After hearing this, that person will die and, in the short time that a strong man (vīra) takes to bend and stretch his arm, will be born in the Western Realm of Bliss where, seven days later, he or she will meet the two Bodhisattvas, Avalokiteśvara and Mahāsthāma, who will expound the Dharma to the practiser. The latter will be filled with joy and will attain the śrota-āpanna stage. After the passing of a small aeon, the devotee will realize arhatship. This is the low stage of the Middle Class of Birth.

'The above are the visualizations of the Middle Class of Birth and are (jointly) called the Fifteenth Contemplation.'

16. THE INFERIOR CLASS OF BIRTH IN THE REALM OF BLISS

(a) The high stage of the Inferior Class of Birth

The Buddha then said to Ānanda and Vaidehī: 'The high stage of the Inferior Class of Birth is attainable by him who does not criticize the Vaipulya sūtras although he has created (other) evil karmas. In spite of his stupidity and of his many evil actions, he is not ashamed of his conduct. (However) before he dies, he meets an enlightened teacher who tells him the titles of the sūtras of the twelve divisions of the Mahāyāna canon. Because

1. One who enters the stream of holy living, the first stage of Hīnayāna, that of a śrāvaka.

2. A saintly man, the highest type or ideal saint in Hīnayāna in contrast with a Bodhisattva as the saint in Mahāyāna.

3. The conditioned compassion on earth, in contrast with the uncaused compassion of the Bodhisattva.

he hears the names of the sūtras, the evil effects of his actions committed in a thousand aeons will be wiped out. The teacher will also instruct him to join together his two palms with crossed fingers, and to call: "Namo Amitābha Buddhāya!" By thus calling the Buddha's name, he will wipe out the evil effects of saṁsāric sins committed in fifty lacs of aeons. Thereupon, that Buddha will send a Nirmāṇakāya Buddha who will come with two transformation Bodhisattvas, Avalokiteśvara and Mahāsthāma, in front of that person to praise him: "Virtuous man, your calling the Buddha's name has wiped out all your sins and I now come to welcome you." After hearing this, the practiser will see his room filled with the light of the Nirmāṇakāya Buddha. He will be filled with joy and will pass away. He will find (himself) riding in a precious lotus and will follow that Buddha to be born in the precious pool. After forty-nine days, the lotus will open and he will behold the compassionate Avalokiteśvara and mighty Mahāsthāma who will send out rays of light to illumine him. The two Bodhisattvas will expound the very profound Teaching of the twelve divisions of the Mahāyāna canon. Upon hearing it, he will believe and understand it, and will set his mind on the quest of Supreme Tao. After ten small aeons have passed, he will be awakened to the Door to the correct interpretation of the hundred divisions of phenomena and will enter upon the first stage of Bodhisattva development. This is the high stage of the Inferior Class of Birth.'

(b) The medium stage of the Inferior Class of Birth

The Buddha then said to Ānanda and Vaidehī: 'The medium stage of the Inferior Class of Birth is attainable to him who, in spite of having broken both the five and eight commandments and the complete set of rules of discipline; of his stupid usurpation of monastic property and theft of the monks' personal possessions; and of his "unclean" preaching,[1] without being ashamed of the evil conduct that stains him, will, when he is about to die and ready to fall into hell as retribution for his bad karma and when the fires of hell are already apparent, meet a learned teacher who takes pity on him, teaches him the awe-inspiring ten powers (daśabala) of Amitābha Buddha and the transcendental power of that Buddha's light, and praises the teaching of discipline, meditation, wisdom, liberation and knowledge of liberation.[2] The effect of what he thus hears wipes out his karmic sins in eighty lacs of aeons, and the fierce fire of hell will be transmuted into a cool breeze that fans the heavenly lotus (causing) the appearance thereon of a

1. Preaching of the Dharma, whether rightly or wrongly, from selfish and impure motives, e.g. for money or reputation.

2. Pañca-dharmakāya, the five attributes of the essential body of the Buddha. See *Ch'an and Zen Teaching*, Third Series, The Altar Sūtra of the Sixth Patriarch.

Nirmāṇakāya Buddha with transformation Bodhisattvas coming to receive him. In the flash of a thought, he will be born in a lotus in the seven gemmed pool. After the passing of six aeons, the lotus will open and Avalokiteśvara and Mahāsthāma Bodhisattvas will come to comfort him with their deep and resonant voice[1] and to teach him the very profound Mahāyāna sūtras. After hearing the Dharma, he will be able to set his mind on the quest of Supreme Tao. This is the medium stage of the Inferior Class of Birth.'

(c) The low stage of the Inferior Class of Birth

The Buddha then said to Ānanda and Vaidehī: 'The low stage of the Inferior Class of Birth is attainable by him who, in spite of his evil karma, and of his having committed the five rebellious acts and broken the ten commandments, the retributive effect of which should cause his fall into the realms of miseries where he would endure endless suffering in many aeons, will, when he is about to die, meet a learned teacher who will comfort him, will explain the Profound Dharma to him and will teach him how to think of the Buddha. As the man is suffering so much that he is incapable of thinking of Buddha, that teacher will say: "If you cannot think of Amitābha Buddha, you should call his name." Then by concentrating on repeating aloud ten times: "Namo Amitābha Buddhāya!" he will each time cancel the effect of karmic sins committed in eighty lacs of aeons, and will, when he is about to die, see a golden lotus similar to the (setting) sun appear before him. In the flash of a thought, he will be born in the Realm of Bliss and will stay (asleep) in the lotus for twelve great aeons. At the end of this long period, the lotus will open and he will see Avalokiteśvara and Mahāsthāma who will, with their merciful voices, expound to him the fundamental reality of all phenomena and teach him how to eradicate his sins. After hearing this, he will be filled with joy and will be able to develop the bodhi mind. This is the low stage of the Inferior Class of Birth.

'The above are the visualizations of the Inferior Class of Birth and are (jointly) called the Sixteenth Contemplation.'

After the Buddha had spoken these words, Vaidehī and five hundred maids of honour beheld the immense Realm of Bliss with (Amitābha) and the two Bodhisattvas. They were filled with joy and praised the remarkable occurrence which they had never witnessed before. Thereupon, they experienced a great awakening and realized the patient endurance of the uncreate. The five hundred maids developed the highest universal bodhi mind and vowed to be born in the Realm of Bliss. The World Honoured One then foretold their future realization, after their birth in that Realm,

1. Lit. Brahman voice, pure, clear, melodious, deep and far-reaching; one of the thirty-two marks of a Buddha.

of the samādhi for attaining the absolute (bhūtatathatā).[1] A countless number of devas developed minds (set on) the quest of Supreme Tao.

Ānanda then rose from his seat and said: 'World Honoured One, what is the name of this sūtra; how should we receive and observe the essentials of its Dharma?' The Buddha replied: 'It is the Sūtra of the Contemplation of Amitāyus Buddha and Avalokiteśvara and Mahāsthāma Bodhisattvas in the Realm of Bliss—also called the Sūtra of the Eradication of karmic hindrance for birth in the presence of all Buddhas—under which names you should receive and observe it, without allowing it to be forgotten. He who realizes the (above) samādhi will, in his present life, behold Amitāyus and his two attendant Bodhisattvas. A virtuous man or woman who only hears of their names is able to eradicate karmic sins in countless aeons; how much more so is one who remembers and calls their names? You should know that he who calls that Buddha's name, is a real white lotus flower (puṇḍarīka)[2] amongst men and the two Bodhisattvas will be his best friends. He will sit in a Bodhimaṇḍala and will be born in the Family of Buddhas.'

The Buddha then said to Ānanda: 'You should keep my words and to keep them is to hold (in mind) the name of Amitāyus Buddha.'

After hearing this sermon, Maudgalaputra, Ānanda and Vaidehī were filled with joy. Then the World Honoured One walked in the air to return to Gṛdhrakūṭa mountain.

Ānanda then spread this sūtra widely and a countless number of heavenly dragons (nāga) and demons (yakṣa)[3] who heard of it, were filled with joy, paid reverence to the Buddha and withdrew.[4]

When I was young, I first read the Diamond Sūtra and then the Sūtra of Amitābha Buddha. Although I did not understand the Diamond Sūtra very well, I knew that its meaning was very profound and that if one put it into practice, one would be bound to attain enlightenment. Then I read the Sūtra of Amitābha Buddha but after only a few pages I was so shocked that I put it aside for several years because I could not reconcile the Enlightened One's Teaching of the absolute Buddha nature inherent in every being with His description of the Western Realm of Bliss which pertains to the region of

1. The sixth of the ten stages of Bodhisattva development.

2. An unexcelled man.

3. Yakṣa: a demon in the earth, air or lower heavens: they are cruel and violent and eat human flesh.

4. Cf. C. G. Jung, *Collected Works XI: Psychology and Religion: West and East*, p. 558, for his interesting commentary on the Sūtra of Contemplation of Amitāyus.

relativities. I called on a Dharma master who, however, failed to give satisfaction and it was only after I had read other sūtras, such as the Altar Sūtra of the Sixth Patriarch, the Sūtra of Complete Enlightenment, the Mahāparinirvāṇa, Avataṁsaka and Śūraṅgama Sūtras, etc., that I realized that the Buddha was compelled to expound the Sūtra of the Buddha of Infinite Light to those who were unable to be awakened to the Absolute Reality but who, after developing an unshakeable faith in Amitābha, would also be able to relinquish their earthly attachments and to develop singleness of mind. Thus though the means are different, the ultimate result is the same in both Sūtras, that is attainment of the pure, still and imperturbable condition leading to enlightenment.

In the Sūtra of the Contemplation of Amitāyus Buddha numbers such as 6, 8, 25, 500, 600, 80,000, 84,000, etc., etc., are symbolic and stand for the six consciousnesses, the eight distresses, the eighteen realms of sense with the seven elements that make a universe, the five aggregates, the sixth consciousness, the ālaya-vijñāna or eighth consciousness, and the eighth consciousness abiding in the illusory body of four elements; that is space, whereas the zeros stand for time. These numbers suggest relativities which are sublimated by a trustful and profound mind, by a mind fixed on the vow for rebirth in the Realm of Bliss, by observance of the rules of discipline and by the accumulation of other concurrent merits. They are then transmuted into the six thoughts of Buddha, Dharma, Saṅgha, discipline, charity and blessings; the eight pools of merit-giving water or eight forms of liberation; a halo reaching a height of twenty-five yojanas; 500 transformation Bodhisattvas or Nirmāṇakāya Buddhas; 600 lacs of precious pearls; 80,000 gems and 84,000 kinds of light or excellent bodily marks.

Although the mind is now fixed on the Realm of Bliss which is beyond birth and death, it is still in the region of relativities. Hence, the Buddha said: 'This is only the coarse view of the Realm of Bliss. If you succeed in realizing the state of samādhi, you will perceive very clearly that Realm which it is impossible fully to describe.' Therefore, after a devotee's birth in that Realm, he will meet either Amitābha Buddha or the two attendant Bodhisattvas who will teach him the right Dharma and he will then realize Samādhi which will enable him to reach the region of the absolute which is inconceivable and inexpressible.

Ānanda and Vaidehī were also urged to refrain from visualizing differently from that taught by the Buddha, because He taught the correct meditation which put an end to discrimination and discerning and because if the mind strays from this right contemplation, it will wander outside in search of all mental states, will again abide in illusion and falsehood and will be bound to return to saṁsāra.

4

SELF-CULTIVATION ACCORDING TO THE T'IEN T'AI (TENDAI) SCHOOL

THE T'ien T'ai (Japanese, Tendai) school bases its tenets mainly on the Lotus Sūtra and also on the Mahāparinirvāṇa Sūtra, Nāgārjuna's commentary on the 'Long Chapter' of the Mahāprajñāpāramitā Sūtra[1] and his Mādhyamika Śāstra. For this reason, Nāgārjuna was regarded as the first Patriarch of the T'ien T'ai school.

When Hui Wen of the Pei Ch'i dynasty (550–78) read the above commentary, he awakened to the profound meaning of Nāgārjuna's words: 'The three wisdoms[2] are realizable in the One Mind.' He then read the Mādhyamika Śāstra and achieved perfect insight into the three aspects of the One Mind[3] when he came to the following gāthā:

All things causally produced
I say are void,

1. Ta Chih Tu Lun, a commentary by Nāgārjuna on the 'Long Chapter' of the Mahāprajñāpāramitā Sūtra.

2. The Three Wisdoms: śrāvaka and pratyeka-buddha wisdom, Bodhisattva wisdom and Buddha wisdom. The T'ien T'ai school associates them with worldly wisdom, supramundane wisdom and Supreme Wisdom.

3. Also called the combined triple insight, the inconceivable triple insight and the simultaneous triple insight which is the meditative study of the T'ien T'ai school, appropriate for those of high spirituality and derived from Nāgārjuna's commentary on the 'Long Chapter' of the Mahārprajñāpāramitā Sūtra. It is a simultaneous insight into the three aspects of the mind, i.e. insight into the void, the unreal and the Mean, without passing through stages and accords with the Buddha's Teaching in the Sūtra of Complete Enlightenment. (See *Ch'an and Zen Teaching*, Third Series).

Are but false names
And also indicate the Mean.

Hence, Hui Wen was regarded as the second Patriarch.

Hui Wen transmitted the Teaching to Hui Szu of Nan Yo who became the third Patriarch.[1] In one of his meditations, Hui Szu realized the Lotus Samādhi.[2] He was the author of the Ta Ch'eng Chih Kuan (the Mahāyāna's śamatha-vipaśyanā).

The successor to Hui Szu was Chih I, also called Chih Che, who became the fourth Patriarch.[3] He also practised the Lotus Samādhi and realized within two weeks his major awakening. He was the author of many treaties of which the Mo Ho Chih Kuan (Mahā-śamatha-vipaśyanā), the T'ung Meng Chih Kuan (Śamatha-vipaśyanā for Beginners) and the Lu Miao Fa Meng (the Six Profound Dharma Doors) are the most widely read in China. As he stayed and died on T'ien T'ai mountain,[4] the school was named after the mountain.

The T'ien T'ai lineage continued with Kuan Ting as its fifth Patriarch, Fa Hua, its sixth, T'ien Kung, its seventh, Tso Ch'i, its eighth,[5] Chan Jan, its ninth,[6] and Tao Sui, its tenth Patriarch[7] whose Japanese disciple, Dengyo Daishi, introduced the Teaching to Japan in the ninth century.

T'IEN T'AI MEDITATION

The T'ien T'ai teaching of meditation is the most comprehensive of all and in order to acquaint readers with its methods of practice, we present below versions of two of the treatises by its fourth Patriarch, master Chih I, also called Chih Che.

1. Died in 577.

2. A state of samādhi wherein the meditator looks into the void (noumenon), the unreal (phenomenon) and the Mean (the absolute) that unites them. It derives from the sixteen samādhis in the Lotus Sūtra, Chapter 24.

3. Died in 598 at the age of sixty.

4. T'ien T'ai or Heaven Terrace, is a district south-west of Ningpo in Chekiang province.

5. Died in 742 at the age of eighty-three.

6. Died in 782 at the age of seventy-two.

7. In the eighth century.

(I) ŚAMATHA-VIPAŚYANĀ FOR BEGINNERS (T'UNG MENG CHIH KUAN)

(by Master Chih I of Hsiu Ch'an monastery on T'ien T'ai mountain)

To avoid evil actions,
To do actions that are good
And to purify the mind
Is the essence of Buddha's Teaching.

The attainment of Nirvāṇa is realizable by many methods whose essentials do not go beyond the practice of chih (śamatha) and kuan (vipaśyanā).[1] Chih is the first step to untie all bonds and kuan is essential to root out delusion. Chih provides nourishment for the preservation of a knowing mind[2] and kuan is the skilful art of promoting spiritual understanding. Chih is the unsurpassed cause of dhyāna and kuan begets wisdom. He who achieves both chih and kuan is fully competent to work for the welfare of self and others. Hence the Lotus Sūtra says: 'The Buddha while dwelling in Mahāyāna used the transcendental power of the dhyāna and wisdom (prajñā) which he had realized to liberate living beings from birth and death.' Therefore, we know that this twin realization is like the two wheels of a cart and the two wings of a bird. Partial practice of them is wrong. Hence the sūtra says: 'The practice of dhyāna alone, while wisdom is disregarded, (causes) stupidity and the practice of wisdom alone, while dhyāna is disregarded, causes infatuation.' Although stupidity and infatuation are relatively minor faults which differ from each other, their contribution to recurrent wrong views is identical.

If dhyāna and wisdom are not in equal proportion, the practice is deficient; how can it lead to speedy realization of the Supreme Fruit? This is why the sūtra says: 'Śrāvakas cannot perceive the Buddha nature because of their excessive dhyāna; Bodhisattvas of the tenth stage do not perceive it clearly because of their excessive wisdom; (and) all Tathāgata Buddhas perceive it clearly because their dhyāna and wisdom are in equal proportion.' Therefore, chih-kuan is the main gate to the great nirvāṇa, the unsurpassed

1. Chih Kuan: śamatha-vipaśyanā. Chih is silencing the active mind and getting rid of discrimination, and kuan is observing, examining, introspecting. When the physical organism is at rest, it is called chih and when the mind is seeing clearly it is kuan. The chief object is the concentration of mind by special methods for the purpose of clear insight into the truth and to be rid of illusion.

2. Or discerning mind, as contrasted with the differentiating, or discriminating, mind.

path of self-cultivation, the index to perfection of all excellent virtues and the true substance of the Supreme Fruit. Consequently the chih-kuan Dharma door to enlightenment is not shallow. When receiving beginners to initiate them to the Path, it is easy to preach the Dharma which is, however, very difficult to practise. How, then, is it possible to expound in full what is deep and subtle? For the benefit of beginners, I now briefly present the following ten essentials for treading the right Path so that they can achieve the progressive stages leading to (their realization of) nirvāṇa. Instead of slighting the seeming shallowness of the text, Truth seekers should blush to find that these steps are difficult to practise. However, if their minds are ripe for the teaching, in the twinkling of an eye their sharp wisdom[1] will have no limit and their spiritual understanding will become unfathomable. If they aimlessly drag about words and terms and allow their feelings (and passions) to distort the teaching, they will fritter away their time and will fail to achieve realization; thus they are like a man who counts the treasures belonging to others. What advantage can they expect therefrom? (These ten essential steps are:)

1. Formation of concurrent causes,
2. rebuking all desires,
3. removal of screens,
4. regulating (food, sleep, body, breath and mind),
5. expedient lines of conduct,
6. the main practice,
7. manifestation of good roots (qualities),
8. discerning the harmful influence of māra,
9. healing of ailments, and
10. final realization.

These ten steps are given to elucidate the Teaching of chih and kuan and are essential for those who begin their practice of meditation. If they really understand and follow them in their self-cultivation, they will be able to quiet their minds and avoid all difficulties; will realize dhyāna and achieve understanding; and will attain the transcendental holy stage.

I. FORMATION OF CONCURRENT CAUSES[2]

Those who resolve to practise the chih-kuan method should provide themselves with five concurrent causes:

1. Lit. 'their wisdom that cuts off all miseries will become boundless'.

2. Concurrent causes: a Buddhist term equivalent to 'favourable condition' which causes the practice to succeed. According to Buddhist teaching, the law of causality is in force in the realm of illusions wherein nothing occurs by chance.

(a) Strict observance of discipline and morality (śīla),
(b) adequate supply of food and clothing,
(c) leisure in a tranquil place,
(d) lay down all causal activities, and
(e) search for helpful friends.

(a) Strict observance of śīla

The rules of discipline and morality (śīla) should be kept strictly. As the sūtra says, discipline causes the realization of dhyāna and the manifestation of wisdom that put an end to all suffering. Therefore, all bhikṣus should keep śīla strictly. There are three categories of people who observe the precepts in different ways:

The first category comprises those who, before being admitted as disciples, do not commit the five rebellious acts and later meet enlightened teachers who instruct them in the three formulas of refuge and the five commandments, thereby entitling them to be disciples of Buddha. If they leave their homes, they will receive first the ten precepts of a novice (śrāmaṇera) and then full ordination to become bhikṣus or bhikṣuṇīs. After their ordination, they will keep all the commandments and will refrain from breaking them; they are the best keepers of śīla. You should know that when these people practise chih-kuan, they are bound to realize the Buddha Dharma, like immaculate clothes that dye well.

The second category comprises those who, after receiving the precepts, break only the minor rules but not the important ones. Before their practice of meditation, if they carry out correctly the rites of repentance and reform, theirs is that strict observance which causes dhyāna and wisdom to manifest. They are like dirty and greasy clothes that have been washed clean and can be worn after being dyed again.

The third category comprises those who after receiving śīla are unable to observe it and break many minor and grave prohibitions. They cannot follow the Hīnayāna rules which do not provide for repentance and reform after committing the four grave prohibitions.[1] If they follow the Mahāyāna rules, they will be able to root out their sins. Hence the sūtra says: 'According to the Buddha Dharma, there are two kinds of virile men, those who never commit evil acts and those who repent after committing them.'

True repentance and reform are possible if the following ten conditions are fulfilled:

1. Belief in the law of causality;
2. great fear (of consequences);

1. Pārājikas: killing, stealing, carnality and deception under the mask of true preaching.

3. strong feeling of shame;
4. keen search for the methods of eradicating sins, such as those taught in the Mahāyāna sūtras which should be strictly followed;
5. exposure of all sins committed;
6. stopping all evil mental activities;
7. keenness to protect the Dharma;
8. taking the great vow to deliver all living beings;
9. constant remembrance of all Buddhas in the ten directions, and
10. introspection into the non-existent nature of sins.[1]

If these ten conditions can be fulfilled, the repentant disciple should, after taking a bath and putting on clean garments, offer incense and flowers to the Three Precious Ones (Buddha, Dharma and Saṅgha) and (pray for) true repentance and reform. For seven to twenty-one days, one to three months, or sometimes a year, he should concentrate his mind on repentance and reform because of the grave prohibitions he has broken until his sins are rooted out. How will he know that all his sins have been eradicated? If, while he concentrates on true repentance and reform, he feels that both his body and mind are light and at ease, has auspicious dreams, sees remarkable things, perceives some manifestation of his excellent mental state, feels as if his body is like clouds and shadows thereby gradually realizing the various stages of dhyāna, suddenly awakening to and understanding all things (dharma), or easily grasping the profound meaning of sūtras when he hears them—he will feel joy in the Dharma and will be free from anxiety and remorse; all this proves that he has really removed all sinful obstructions to the Tao, previously caused by his breaking of śīla. From then on he keeps firmly all the precepts; his śīla is also spotless and he can practise dhyāna. This is like a ragged and dirty robe which can be mended, washed, dyed and worn again.

If a man, after breaking the grave prohibitions, is afraid of the resulting obstruction to his (achievement of) dhyāna, and instead of following the methods of rooting out sins as taught in the sūtras, he repents bitterly for the wrong done of which he is now sincerely ashamed, exposes his weakness to the Three Precious Ones, vows to cut off his evil mind, sits erect to contemplate the non-existent nature of sins, thinks of the Buddhas in the ten directions and, at the end of each meditation, with the same eagerness for repentance and reform, he burns incense and pays reverence (to the Buddha), recites the rules of discipline and reads the Mahāyāna sūtras, all hindrances to his realization of the Tao will be gradually eliminated, so that his śīla also becomes spotless and he realizes the state of dhyāna. The sūtra says: 'If a man is seized with great fear after breaking the grave prohibitions and

1. This last condition is the basic repentance and reform of the Mahāyāna which differs greatly from those of Hīnayāna and other religions.

hopes to eliminate the evil effects, he has no other way than to practise dhyāna which alone can root out his sins.' This man should sit in a quiet place to control his mind at all times and recite the Mahāyāna sūtras; all his sins will then be wiped out and the state of dhyāna will manifest to him.

(b) Adequate supply of food and clothing

There are three kinds of garments (for a monk): firstly, the single robe worn by the greast masters in the Snow Mountains (i.e. the Himālayas), just enough to cover their bodies because they have cut off all contact with the world and because of their great endurance; secondly, the three garments of cast-off rags[1] worn by Mahākāśyapa who had no other clothes when keeping the rules of austerity; and thirdly, the three usual garments[2] with an extra supply of 101 other kinds of clothing permitted by the Tathāgata for disciples living in cold countries who are not yet able to achieve endurance. If a monk is greedy and keeps more clothes than he needs, this will upset his mind and hinder his practice of Tao.

As regards food, there are four proper ways of obtaining it:

1. The great masters who stay deep in the mountains to retire from the world, eat only herbs and fruits to preserve their bodies.

2. The ascetics who beg for food and whose way of life enables them to abstain from improper ways of making a living and to adhere to right livelihood[3] which contributes to their realization of holy Tao. There are four improper ways (for monks) to obtain a living: by working with their hands, by astrology, by magic and soothsaying, and by guile and flattery, all of which was taught by Śāriputra to the blue-eyed maiden.

3. Those living in places of retirement where they receive food offered by the patrons (dānapati) who support them.

4. Those living in a community where the way of life is prescribed by the monastery's regulations.

When devotees are provided with clothes and food, this is adequate for their needs (and a causal condition for their successful meditation). Why so? Because without this concurrent cause, their minds cannot be set at rest and their Path will be blocked.

(c) Leisure in a tranquil place

'Leisure' implies the absence of all (worldly) activities and 'tranquil' suggests freedom from disturbance. There are three places where dhyāna can be

1. Cast-off rags were picked up in cemeteries, washed and mended to make garments.

2. These are: (1) antarvāsas or antarvāsaka, an inner garment, the five-piece cassock, (2) uttarāsaṅga, an outer garment, the seven-piece cassock, and (3) saṅghāṭī, an assembly robe of from nine to twenty-five pieces.

3. The fifth of the Eightfold Noble Path.

practised: on a retired and uninhabitated mountain; in an ascetic's hermitage some three or four miles from an inhabitated area, too far away for herdsmen to visit and where stillness prevails; and in a quiet monastery far away from the dwellings of laymen.

(d) Lay down all causal activities

To lay down all causal occupations consists of: ending all causal means of livelihood by giving up work on the earthly plane; cutting all links with worldlings including relatives, friends and acquaintances; relinquishing all cause-producing arts and crafts, such as worldly skill, ingenuity, quackery, magic, divination, physiognomy, writing, counting and recording; and stopping the search for earthly knowledge by giving up all reading, reciting and listening.

All the above concern the laying down of causal activities which, if continued, will block the Path and make it difficult to control the stirred mind.

(e) Search for helpful friends

There are three kinds of helpful friends: outsiders who provide you with all the necessities of life and look after you; fellow-practisers who give you good advice and never disturb you; and enlightened teachers who are keen to employ all expedients to teach you how to practise dhyāna.

The above ((a) to (e)) are the five concurrent causes (in the practice of chih-kuan).

2. REBUKING ALL DESIRES

The desires that should be rebuked are the five kinds of craving which should not arise during chih-kuan practice. They are longings for form, sound, smell, taste, and touch which deceive all worldlings into clinging to them. If desires are known as wrong, they should be repulsed and this is called rebuking.

1. To repulse craving for form involves all pleasant appearances of the male and female, with attractive eyes and brows, red lips and white teeth as well as precious gems of beautiful colours, such as blue, yellow, red, white, purple, green, etc., which can deceive the ignorant into craving to possess them so that they commit evil karmic actions. For instance, king Bimbisāra who, to satisfy his sexual desire, went to a hostile country to have intercourse with a prostitute, and king Udayana who was defiled by form and cut off the hands and feet of five hundred seers (ṛṣi). This shows the mistakes and errors caused by form.

2. To rebuke all longing for sound involves music, male and female

voices and songs which can cause the worldlings who hear them to cling to them, thereby committing evil karmic deeds. For instance, the five hundred seers (ṛṣi) who succumbed to the melodious songs of a kinnara[1] maiden which disturbed their minds so that they failed to realize dhyāna. This shows the mistakes and errors caused by sound.

3. To rebuke all desire for smell involves the odours of male and female bodies and all fragrances of worldly drinks and food as well as all kinds of perfume. The ignorant who are not clear about the (evil effects of) smells, like them and cling to them, thereby opening wide the door to the 'instigator of passions'.[2] For instance, once when a bhikṣu came to a lotus pond and liked its fragrance, its spirit guardian reprimanded him for stealing the perfume that belonged to him. Thus by clinging to smell, all the dormant instigators of passions wake up (ready for mischief). This shows the mistakes and errors caused by smell.

4. To rebuke all desire for taste involves all the flavours of drink, food and delicacies which can stain the minds of worldlings and cause them to commit evil karmic actions. For instance, once a novice who was very fond of sour milk was reincarnated as a worm in sour milk. This shows the mistakes and errors caused by taste.

5. To rebuke all desire for touch involves discrimination between the bodies of both sexes; the illusion that they are soft, smooth, warm in winter and cool in summer and other pleasant sensations of touch. The ignorant, who do not understand all this, are immersed in touch and are thereby hindered in their practice of Tao. For instance, Ekaśṛṅga ṛṣi[3] lost his supernatural power because he was ensnared by a prostitute and allowed her to ride on his neck. This shows the mistakes and errors caused by touch.

The methods of rebuking desires are taught in the Mahāyāna śāstra which says: 'It is a great pity that living beings are constantly disturbed by the five desires for which they unceasingly look.' These five desires are thus like additional faggots that make a fire bigger. They do not give joy and are like (hungry) dogs biting a dry bone. They incite disputes like birds struggling for a piece of meat. They burn men like torches held in a contrary wind. They are as harmful as poisonous snakes. They are unreal, like things seen in a dream. They are not permanent and are like sparks seen when flint is struck. So the sages regard them as their bitter enemies (but) worldlings are ignorant and seek for and keep them until their death, thereby suffering from boundless miseries. Animals also possess these five

1. Kinnara: heavenly musicians noted for their songs and dances.

2. Lit. 'a binding messenger', a Buddhist term meaning an inciting agent that urges the meditator to discriminate and so disturbs the stillness of mind.

3. Lit. 'unicorn seer', an ascetic born of a deer, who was seduced by a woman, lost his supernatural power and became a high minister; he was one of the previous incarnations of the Buddha.

desires. All living beings act according to their desires of which they are the willing slaves. He who clings to desires is bound to fall into the three lower realms of miseries. When we practise dhyāna, we are handicapped by these bandits and so should avoid them, as taught in the following gāthā of the Dhyāna-pāramitā Sūtra:

Continuity of births and deaths
Comes from craving for (the sense of) taste.
When wrong doing is carried to the grave
All miseries are uselessly endured.
The human body is like a stinking corpse
With nine openings to discharge its filthiness.
Like a worm enjoying dung in a latrine
Is the body of a man who's ignorant.
A sage should meditate upon his flesh and bones
Renouncing attachment to all earthly pleasures.
Freedom from craving and from
Bondage is True Nirvāṇa.
As taught by all the Buddhas, the practice
Of singleness of thought and mind by counting
Breaths while sitting in dhyāna is called
Performance of ascetical (dhūta) conduct.

3. REMOVAL OF SCREENS

There are five kinds of screen to be removed:

1. The screening desire. We have already dealt with the five desires arising from the five sense data and here 'desire' originates in the intellect (manas). This means that, when sitting in meditation, if we give rise to a desire for enlightenment, unending thoughts will result which will hinder our self-mind and prevent it from manifesting. As soon as we are aware of this, we should give up this desire. For instance, Śubhakara,[1] who stirred up sexual thoughts, was burnt up by his inner desire; how much more so will the fire of desire, aroused in our minds, destroy all our goodness. The greedy stray far from the Tao because their desires are the cause of all passions and troubles. If the mind clings to desire, it can never come near to the Tao, as said in the following gāthā of The Destruction of Screens:

A man who humbly enters on the path
Holds a begging bowl to help all beings.[2]

1. Śubhakara: a fisherman who was burnt by his sexual love.

2. So that all living beings can give him food thereby sowing in the field of blessedness.

How can he crave for those sense data
Through which he falls into five passions?
He has rejected five desires
On which he now has turned his back.
Why should he then revive them
Like one who eats his vomit?
Hardship is caused by seeking objects of
Desire which are a source of dread when won;
When lost, they create grief and resentment,
None of them ever can bring happiness;
This is the trouble which desires confer.
The problem is to cast them all away
So that real bliss in dhyāna-samādhi can be
Enjoyed whilst deception disappears for evermore.

2. The screening hatred which is at the root of our loss of the Buddha Dharma is the cause of our fall into the realms of miseries, an obstacle to our quest for joy in the Dharma, a great robber of all morality and the prime mover of evil speech. Therefore, a student should, when sitting in meditation, give rise to this thought: 'My opponent now irritates me and my dear ones and delights in wronging me: he did so in the past and will continue to do so in the future. These are the nine kinds of irritations which cause anger, and anger leads to resentment which incites to retaliation. Thus hatred veils my mind and is called its screen. Consequently, I should remove this screen so that it cannot thicken.' Hence, when Śakra[1] asked the Buddha:

What is that which destroys happiness
And kills freedom from anxiety?
What is the root of that poison
Which wipes out moral excellence?

the Buddha replied:

To root out hatred brings happiness
And gives freedom from anxiety.
Hatred is poison's root, to destroy
It brings moral excellence.

When we know the evil of hatred, we should practise compassionate endurance to root it out, thereby purifying our minds.

3. Screening sleep and drowsiness. When the mind is inactive and dull, and when the five passions[2] are gloomy and confused, one feels inclined to

1. Ruler of the thirty-three heavens, considered as a protector of the Buddha Dharma.

2. Stirred by the five senses.

relax by drowsing. This is the causal sleep and drowsiness that can damage our true joy (found) in the Dharma in present and future transmigrations, our happiness in our rebirth in the heavens or the bliss in nirvāṇa attainable in a coming incarnation. It is the worst evil because while all other screens can be destroyed as soon as one is aware of them, sleep and drowsiness are like a dead man who is unconscious. For lack of consciousness of this evil, it is very difficult to root it out. It is described in the following gāthā which reprimands all sleepy disciples:

Embrace not a stinking corpse in sleep for it contains
Impurities and is miscalled a human being.
Like one gravely ill wounded by an arrow
How can you sleep peacefully with all this pain?
Like one tied up about to die, how can
You sleep when calamity befalls?
While the binding robber is not killed and harm still prevails,
You are like one who shares his home with poisonous snakes.
If you lie between crossed swords
How can you sleep serenely?
Drowsiness is like great darkness that hides everything,
Ever deceiving you and robbing you of perception.
With mind screened by drowsiness that keeps you blind,
How, mindless of your own ruin, can you sleep?

Thus with all these causal warnings about screens, you should waken to impermanence and reduce your drowsiness to avoid dullness of mind. If fondness for drowsiness is great, a Ch'an staff should be used to dispel it.

4. Screening by restlessness and grief. There are three kinds of restlessness: (1) that of the body which is responsible for fondness of walking and strolling and for uneasiness in sitting; (2) that of speech which gives rise to delight in humming, arguing about right and wrong, aimless sophistry and worldly talk; and (3) that of the mind which clings to externals and indulges in worldly arts and skills as well as wrong views. Restlessness damages the state of mind of those who have joined the Saṅgha. It is difficult enough to realize dhyāna by controlling the mind; how much more so if restlessness is indulged in during self-cultivation. Restlessness is like a mad unbridled elephant, rabbit or camel which cannot be checked. A warning is given in the following gāthā:

With shaven head and with dyed robes
You take earthen bowls to beg for food.
How can you delight in restlessness by giving
Rein to passions, losing all Dharma's benefits?

After losing all benefits of the Dharma and all worldly happiness, you should realize your errors and eliminate restlessness. However, if you grieve about your faults, this grief will act as a screen (to your minds). If restlessness is not followed by grief, there will be no screen. Why so? Because no cause was formed during your restlessness, but if afterwards, during your meditation, you realize your restlessness and are grieved at it, your worry will hinder your minds; hence an (additional) screen.

There are two kinds of grief: one is that felt after noticing your restlessness as already dealt with, and the other is grief after breaking a grave prohibition of which you are in awe and fear. In the latter case, the arrow of grief has entered your mind and cannot be extracted, as explained in the following gāthā:

To do what you should not,
To do not what you should,
Cause bitter grief that burns like fire,
You then fall into evil realms.
If you repent of wrong already done
Worry not after your repentance.
With heart thus set at rest
You should not cling to grief.
If with two kinds of grief for former sins
You once more abstain from doing what you should
And do what should be avoided,
You are indeed a stupid man.
If there be no thought of repentance,
You can repeat what you should avoid.
Once an evil has been wrought
It can never be undone.

5. The screening doubt. Once doubt veils the mind, no faith in the various Dharma (doors) is possible. For lack of faith, no advantages can derive from the Buddha Dharma. For instance, if a handless man enters a mountain of precious gems, he cannot carry away any treasure. There are, however, many kinds of doubt and not all of them[1] hinder (the practice of) dhyāna. Those that do so are these:

1. Doubt about the self, when the practiser thinks: 'Am I a man of dull roots and with great sins?' If he harbours this doubt, he can never achieve dhyāna. For he who meditates, should not slight himself, as no one knows if he has planted good roots in former lives.

2. Doubt about the teacher, of whom the student may think: 'If his

1. For instance the i ching is also a doubt which does not hinder dhyāna but causes it to manifest in Zen meditation.

appearance and deportment are such and such and if he has not acquired the Tao himself, how can he teach me?' If he harbours this doubt and contempt, they will hinder his (practice of) dhyāna. The way to eliminate (doubt and contempt) is taught in the Mahāyāna Śāstra which says: 'Like a stinking skin bag containing gold pieces, it should not be thrown away, if its gold is wanted.' Likewise, although a teacher may not be perfect, the student should regard him as a Buddha (when learning the Dharma through him).

3. Doubt about the Dharma. Most worldlings grasp their minds and have no faith in the Dharma which has been taught to them and which they cannot receive and practise with reverence. If they doubt about it, the Dharma will not penetrate their minds. Why so? Because of the obstructing doubt as explained in the following gāthā:

As when a man arrives at some cross-road
His hesitation leads him to no place;
So in the Reality by Dharma
Taught, doubt also to negation leads
For it remissness causes.
When seeking the Reality in
Dharmas, ignorance produces doubt;
This is the worst of evils.
Amongst good Dharmas and their opposites,
As 'twixt nirvāṇa and saṁsāra,
In truth there is but one true Dharma
About which you should never doubt.
But if you still suspect it,
You will be bound by Yama,[1]
Like a deer caught by a lion
Never can you hope to escape.
Though in this life you may have doubts,
You should rejoice in perfect Dharma,
Like one who at the cross-roads chooses
The way that is most profitable.

Faith alone can enable one to enter the Buddha Dharma and without faith, no benefit can derive from it. Therefore, when doubt is known as wrong, it should be cast away.

Question: Since there are so many kinds of evil, why do you urge the removal of only five of them?

Answer: These five screens comprise the three poisons and represent a group of four main troubles (kleśa) involving all the 84,000 defilements.

1. Lit. 'You will be bound by the god of the dead and hell-keepers'.

This group of four main troubles consists of desire that hinders; anger and resentment; drowsiness and doubt caused by stupidity; and restlessness and grief. Each main kleśa comprises 21,000 evils[1] and the four together involve 84,000. Therefore, the removal of these five screens destroys all (the 84,000) evils. He who accomplishes it is like a debtor who is rid of all his debts, a sick man freed from illness, a starving man who arrives in a country full of food and a man who escapes from bandits and is out of danger. Likewise, he who is rid of all five screens enjoys rest and happiness. When the sun and moon are veiled by the five screens of smoke, dust, cloud, fog and eclipse, they lose their brightness. Likewise, the mind of man is in the dark when it is hidden by the five screens.

4. REGULATING FOOD, SLEEP, BODY, BREATH AND MIND

Before sitting in meditation to practise the Dharmas of all Buddhas of the past, present and future in the ten directions, a beginner should take the great vow of liberating all living beings and of seeking the Supreme Buddha stage with a mind firm as a diamond, set on perfecting all Buddha Dharmas without the least backsliding. Then while sitting in dhyāna, he should give rise to the right thought about the true reality underlying all dharmas, that is about all good, evil and neutral (lit. unrecordable) things; about the internal sense organs, external sense data and false consciousnesses; about all earthly troubles and afflictions; and all causes and effects of births and deaths in the three realms of existence which are created by the mind. Hence, the Daśabhūmi Sūtra says:

The three worlds are not elsewhere,
They're created by One Mind.
If the mind is known as being without nature,
The unreality of all things is exposed.

If the mind is free from pollution and attachment, all saṁsāra producing karmic actions will come to an end. It is only after this meditation that the next practice of regulating (food, sleep, body, breath and mind) can be started.

What does 'regulating' mean? As illustrations, a potter who wants to make earthenware should first prepare proper clay that should be neither too hard nor too soft so that it can be cast in a mould; and a lute player

1. 21,000 evils = 250 × 4 × 3 × 7: i.e. 250 precepts for a monk, multiplied by the four states of walking, standing, sitting and reclining; then by the three propensities of those decided for the Dharma, those for heresy and the undecided; and then by the seven deeds, namely: killing, stealing, unchastity, lying, double-tongue, coarse talk and filthy language.

should first tune the strings if he is to create melody. Likewise, in the control of mind (the following) five things should be regulated so that unperturbed stillness can be realized as otherwise the inner excellent roots (qualities) cannot manifest.

1. Regulating food. Food is to nourish the body so that it becomes fit to enter the Tao. If too much is taken, the stomach will be full and will keep one out of breath, with the result that the inner psychic centres will be blocked and the mind obstructed, thereby interfering with the meditation. If insufficient food is taken the stomach is not full enough and the mind and its cognition will be unsteady. These two conditions do not help one to realize dhyāna. Impure food causes confusion of the mind and its cognition. Unsuitable food causes a relapse into sickness and keeps the four elements in disharmony. A student therefore should be very careful about all this when beginning to practise meditation. Hence the sūtra says: 'If the body is at ease, the Tao will prosper. If food and drink are properly regulated, happiness will be enjoyed in quiet and the still mind will make a great show of zeal. This is the teaching of all the Buddhas.'

2. Regulating sleep. Sleep results from ignorance that screens (the mind) and should never be encouraged. He who sleeps too much will not only cast aside the practice of holy Dharma but will also lose the ability to practise so that his mind becomes confused and all good roots disappear. Therefore, one should awaken to the impermanence (of life) and regulate one's sleep in order to keep one's spirit high and one's mind clear, for the purpose of abiding in the holy state which leads to the manifestation of imperturbable stillness. Hence, the sütra says: 'Self-cultivation should not be given up before or after midnight (and the habit of) sleeping should not be allowed to cause one's life to pass aimlessly without gaining anything from it.' One should think of the (destructive) fire of impermanence that scorches the whole world and strive to be liberated from it as soon as possible instead of indulging in sleep.

3, 4 and 5. Regulating body, breath and mind. These three practices should not be separate but concurrent. However, the preliminary, intermediate and final methods differ; hence, the difference between entering and coming out of a state of meditation.

Now about the method of regulating the body at the beginning of meditation. If the meditator wishes properly to control his body for its entry into the state of imperturbable stillness, he should, even before sitting, examine closely to find out whether or not his acts of walking, standing, moving or staying are rough. If they are, his breathing will be coarse so that his mind will be unsettled and unrecordable, and when he sits, it will be perplexed and uneasy. Therefore, before sitting, he should expediently visualize his body as relaxed so that it is at ease during the meditation.

When going to his meditation in bed,[1] he should arrange his cushions so that they are fit for a long sitting. Then he should know how to sit cross-legged. In a half lotus posture, the left leg should be placed on the right one and drawn close to the belly so that the toes of the left foot are parallel to the right thigh and those of the right foot to the left thigh. If a full lotus posture (padmāsana) is desired, he should also place the right leg upon the left one. The next thing to do is to loosen his belt but just enough to prevent it from slipping. Then his left hand should be laid upon the right one, both being placed on the legs and drawn close to the belly. After this, the body should be adjusted by keeping it straight and by shaking it and the limbs seven to eight times to relax them. Thus the body will be erect with the backbone being neither bent nor raised. After that, the neck and head should be held in the proper position, so that the tip of the nose and the navel are in line. The head should neither slant nor incline to one side, and neither bow nor raise, but should be perfectly level. Next he should exhale all impure air through his mouth, not in haste, but slowly and continuously, visualizing at the same time all obstructions to the psychic centres in the body as following the breath and being thereby ejected. Then he should shut his mouth to inhale fresh air through the nostrils. This should be repeated once or twice more, but if his body and breath can be regulated after doing so once, that will suffice. When he closes his mouth, the upper lip and teeth should touch the lower ones, and the tongue the palate. Then he should close his eyes to shut out the light.

Thus he should sit erect like an inanimate boulder without allowing his body, head and limbs to shake. This is the proper way of regulating the body at the start of meditation and is essential to avoid both strain and slackness.

4. Regulating the breath at the beginning of meditation. There are four kinds of breath: audible, gasping, coarse and restful. The first three are improper and the fourth is correct. What is audible breath? When one sits in meditation, if the breath is perceptible to the ear, it is audible. What is gasping breath? When one sits in meditation, although the breath is not audible, if it is not free and is obstructed, it is gasping. What is coarse breath? When one sits in meditation, although the breath is not heard and is free, if it is not fine, it is coarse. What is restful breath? When it is neither audible nor obstructed nor coarse, but is continuous, being barely perceptible and so fine that it is almost imperceptible, with the resultant comfort and easiness, it is restful.

An audible breath scatters (your composure); a gasping breath ties you up; a coarse breath tires you; and a restful breath quiets your mind. If the first three are present, they show that your breathing is not regulated, and if

1. Lit. 'rope-bed' formerly used to sleep on at night in China.

you use your mind to stop them, it will be upset and it will be very difficult to quiet it. If you wish to regulate them, you should follow three methods: calming the mind by concentrating it below (in the body), relaxing the body and visualizing the breath coming in and going out through all your pores freely and unobstructedly. If you concentrate your mind on a fine breath, it will be properly regulated and all the troubles will be avoided; then it will be easy for you to quiet the mind.

This is how to regulate your breath at the start of meditation for it is essential that it should be neither rough (i.e. obstructive) nor smooth (i.e. elusive).

5. Regulating the mind at the beginning of meditátion. This involves three phases: entry into, stay in and coming out (of the state of meditation).

(1) Entry into the state of meditation implies control of confused thinking to prevent the mind from wandering outside, and adjustment of the sinking, floating, strained or loose mind to normalize it.

What is a sinking mind? If during the meditation the mind is dull, confused and unrecordable, while the head drops, this shows a sinking mind. In such a case, it should be fixed on the tip of the nose to nail it there and to prevent it from wandering elsewhere. This is the way to regulate a sinking mind.

What is a floating mind? If during the meditation, it drifts about and the body is uneasy, while thoughts follow externals, this shows a floating mind. In such a case, it should be pushed down and fixed on the navel to prevent thoughts from rising; thus the mind will be stabilized and will be easily quieted. Therefore, the absence of the sinking or floating state shows a regulated mind.

A stabilized mind may be either strained or loose. It is strained when, during the meditation, all thoughts are turned on regulating it to ensure its stabilization; thereby bringing (the vital principle or prāṇa) up to the chest in which pain is felt. In this case, you should relax the mind by visualizing the prāṇa as descending and the trouble will disappear at once.

If the mind is loose, it either jumps about while the body sways and the mouth waters or it becomes gloomy. In this case, the meditator should compose his body and fix his mind as aforesaid, using the body as its support. It can thus be deduced that the mind is either rough or slippery.

The above are methods of regulating the mind at the beginning of meditation. Entry into its stillness is from a coarse state to a fine one. Since the body is coarser when the breathing process is functioning inside it, while the mind is finer, the preliminary step of entering the state of dhyāna consists of adjusting the coarser to the finer for the purpose of quieting the mind.

(2) During his 'stay' in the state of meditation, the practiser should

regulate three things. Whether the meditation is long or short, lasting either for twenty-four, or just one, two or three hours, the practiser, while controlling his thoughts to master his mind, should be well aware whether his body, breath and mind are properly regulated.

If, after having regulated his body, he notices that it is either strained or loose, is inclined to one side, bent, drooping, raised, or not erect, he should adjust it at once to stabilize it.

It may happen that, although the body is regulated, the breath is not. We have already dealt with various unregulated aspects of the breath which may be either audible, gasping or coarse, so that the body is inflated. In such a case, he should use the methods mentioned earlier to adjust the breath so that it will become continuous and so fine that it is half perceptible and half imperceptible.

It may happen that though the body and breath are regulated, the mind is either floating, sinking, loose, strained or unsettled. In such a case, the methods earlier mentioned should be employed to regulate and normalize the mind.

The above three ways of regulating body, breath and mind are not to be employed successively one after the other; either one or all of them should be used when necessary so that body, breath and mind will be all well adjusted, will not hinder each other and can be brought into perfect harmony during the meditation. Thus all previous troubles will be eliminated and all obstructions removed, ensuring the realization of the state of dhyāna.

(3) When coming out of the state of meditation, body, breath and mind should also be regulated beforehand. Before the meditation is ended, the practiser should lay down his mind to release it from this state and open his mouth to let out the breath, visualizing the air as leaving the psychic centres. Then the trunk followed by the shoulders, arms, hands, head and neck should be shaken gently. Next the two feet should be moved to relax them. Then the meditator should rub his body with his two hands, chafe his palms and place them over his eyes before opening them. He should wait until his body has cooled before leaving his seat. If he does not follow this method, although his mind may have been stabilized while in the state of meditation, his abrupt coming out of that state may leave in his body an impure element which can cause headache and rheumatism in the joints. In his next meditation, he will feel agitated and his mind will be impatient to end it as soon as possible. You should pay attention to all this. This is the method of regulating body, breath and mind before coming out of the state of meditation, which means returning from the finer to the coarser (state).

The above are the perfect ways of entering, staying in and coming out of the state of stillness as explained in the following gāthā:

Entry and exit should both be orderly for then
The states of coarse and fine do not impair each other.
This is like a horse that's tamed
At your will to stay or go.

The Lotus Sūtra says: 'All the Bodhisattvas in this assembly have, for countless thousands, tens of thousands and hundreds of thousands of aeons, diligently practised zeal and devotion which have enabled them to enter, stay in and come out of countless hundreds, thousands, tens of thousands and hundreds of thousands of states of samādhi, thus winning all the great transcendental powers; all this is possible because of their unflinching pure living and their skilful practice of all excellent methods (Dharmas) in good order.'

5. EXPEDIENT LINES OF CONDUCT

The practice of chih-kuan is conditional upon five expedients:

1. A vow to keep from all worldly wrong thinking to realize all Dharma doors by means of dhyāna and wisdom (prajñā). This is also called (right) determination, (right) vow and delight or fondness (for the Dharma). This means the practiser's 'determination' in his 'vow' to take 'delight' in his 'fondness' for all profound Dharma doors; hence a vow. As the Buddha said, a vow is essential for all excellent Dharmas.

2. Unremitting zeal in the strict observance of all prohibitions so as always to avoid the five screens without backsliding.[1] Unremitting zeal is likened to the friction (of two pieces of) wood which must be continued until fire is obtained. This is unremitting zeal in the practice of excellent Dharma.

3. Remembrance that the world is deceitful and despicable whereas dhyāna and wisdom are two precious things worthy of reverence. If dhyāna-samādhi is attained, the practiser will be able to develop transcendental wisdom, to acquire all supramundane powers, to achieve universal enlightenment and to liberate living beings. This is the most excellent thing, hence (right) remembrance.

4. Skilful discernment which distinguishes worldly happiness from the bliss in dhyāna-wisdom with the resultant loss or gain. It enables the practiser to realize that there is more suffering than happiness on the worldly plane which is deceitful and unreal, hence the loss; and that the bliss in dhyāna-wisdom, which is beyond the earthly stream, is non-active, still and boundless; is above birth and death; and is free from all miseries for ever;

1. Lit. 'without backsliding before and after midnight'.

hence the gain. This ability to distinguish between the two planes is called skilful discernment.

5. Lucid single-mindedness by means of which the practiser can see clearly that the world is harmful and abhorrent and that merits derived from dhyāna and wisdom are precious and exalted. Therefore, he should determine to practise chih-kuan with a single mind as indestructible as a diamond (vajra), a mind which cannot be deterred by either heretics or heavenly demons and which will refuse to backslide even when no result seems to be obtained. This is single-mindedness.

For instance, a traveller should know first if the road is open or closed before developing a single mind to make a long journey. Hence, skilful discernment and lucid single-mindedness, the meaning of which is found in the sūtra's words: 'Without wisdom, there is no dhyāna and without dhyāna, there is no wisdom.'

6. THE MAIN PRACTICE

The chih-kuan method can be practised either while sitting in meditation, or when involved in causal activities and facing phenomena.

I. Practice of chih-kuan while sitting in meditation

Although the chih-kuan method can be practised while walking, standing, sitting or reclining, the sitting position is the most appropriate for students of the Tao and is now dealt with to explain this method of meditation which aims at the following five objectives:

(a) mastering the coarse and disturbed mind of a beginner;
(b) checking the sinking and floating mind;
(c) (stabilizing the mind) as occasion requires;
(d) normalizing the fine mind;
(e) equalizing dhyāna and wisdom with each other.

(a) Practice of chih-kuan to master the coarse and disturbed mind of a beginner

When a beginner sits in meditation, his mind is usually coarse and unsettled. To put an end to these two states, he should practise chih, and if he fails, he should (immediately) practise kuan. Hence, it is said that chih and kuan are practised to regulate the coarse and unsettled mind of a beginner. Let us see how this is done.

First, the practice of chih, of which there are three methods:

(i) Fixing attention on an object, that is fixing the mind on the tip of the nose or on the navel so that the mind cannot wander elsewhere. The sūtra says: 'A fixed mind that cannot stray is like a bound monkey.'

(ii) Restraining the mind, that is subduing it as soon as it moves in order to stop it from wandering. The sūtra says: 'The five sense organs are all controlled by the mind; therefore, you should put a stop to your (wandering) mind.'

The above (i) and (ii) pertain to the phenomenal and need not be differentiated.[1]

(iii) Stopping all rising causes to ensure the embodiment of (absolute) reality by realizing that all things (dharma) arise from the mind, due to direct and circumstantial causes, and are devoid of any nature of their own. (If this is understood), the mind will not grasp them and its stirred condition will come to an end. Hence (chih or) stopping. The sūtra says:

Causes that are ownerless and empty
Create phenomena. Whoever calms
His mind the fundamental
To attain a true monk is called.

During his meditation, a beginner will find that not even one of the thoughts arising in his mind stays for an instant. If his use of the above chih method (iii) of stopping all rising causes fails to stem the flow of false thoughts, he should employ the kuan method and look into the mind from which they arise. He will find that the past mind has gone, the present mind does not stay and the future mind has not yet come. He will discover that it cannot be found anywhere after an exhaustive search for it in the three times. As it cannot be found, it follows that it is non-existent and that all things (dharma) are so as well. Although his introspection (kuan) proves that the mind does not stay and is consequently non-existent, there is, however, the thought of his awareness that rises of itself. He should then look (kuan) into this thought and will find that the contact of the six inner sense organs with the six outer sense data creates the intermediary consciousness which fundamentally does not arise without this contact. As creation has been thus looked into, so is now annihilation in the same manner. Therefore, creation and annihilation are but arbitrary inventions. When the creating and annihilating mind vanishes, the nirvāṇic condition of voidness and extinction (of passions) becomes manifest, wherein not a thing (dharma) obtains. This is the principle of immaterial and still nirvāṇa and (when it is realized), the mind will come to a stop (chih). The Awakening of Faith says: 'If the mind wanders outside, it should be brought under control and fixed on right thought. By right thought is meant the mind outside of which there are no phenomena. Even this mind is devoid of

1. The phenomenal, or external activity, as contrasted with the noumenal, or undamental principle.

entity[1] and cannot be found in a moment of thought.' This means that it is difficult for a beginner to stabilize his mind at the start of meditation, while if it is unduly repressed, derangement may result. This is like archery which can be mastered only after long training.

Second, the practice of kuan of which there are two methods:

(i) Contemplation of the opposite, for instance, of filthiness to eliminate desire and love; of a compassionate heart (mind) to eradicate anger and resentment; of limitation in the realms of existence[2] to wipe out attachment to the ego; and of counted breaths to put an end to flowing thoughts. All this excludes discrimination.

(ii) The right contemplation which consists in looking into all things that have no reality of their own but are creations due to direct and circumstantial causes. Since causes also have no nature, they are identical with the (underlying) reality (from which they arise). As the objects thus contemplated are unreal, it follows that the mind which contemplates them will cease to arise. This doctrine is frequently discussed in the text and readers should be clear about it. Hence the following gāthā in the sūtra:

All things are unstable
But in our thoughts appear.
When perceived as unreal
No thoughts of them remain.

(b) Practice of chih-kuan to check the sinking and floating mind

When a practiser sits in meditation, his mind may be either dull and blocked; unrecordable, obscure and torpid; or drowsy. In such cases, he should practise kuan to shine upon (i.e. waken) it. If during the meditation, his mind is drifting, restless and uneasy, he should practise chih to check it.

This is the usual way of checking a sinking and floating mind by means of chih-kuan practice, but the meditator should know how to take the right medicine appropriate for the moment and to guard against using the wrong one.

(c) Expedient practice of chih and kuan as occasion requires

When a practiser sits in meditation, although he uses the kuan method to adjust his sinking mind and awaken it, it may not become bright and clear. In this case, he should try the chih method (to put an end to this state). If,

1. Svalakṣaṇa, or individuality.

2. i.e. limited regions divided into realms of desire, of form and beyond form, as contrasted with the pure, universal and boundless region of the Buddhas which is beyond these three limitations.

after the chih method has been used, he feels that his body and mind are at ease, this shows that chih is appropriate and should be practised to calm his mind.

If during his meditation, although chih has been employed to adjust his floating mind, the latter may remain unsteady. This proves that chih is not appropriate and, in this case, he should try the kuan method. If, after using kuan, he feels that his mind becomes bright, clear, still and stabilized, this shows that kuan is appropriate and should be practised to calm his mind.

The above is the expedient use of chih and kuan which should be properly practised as occasion requires, to ensure stabilization of mind and eradication of troubles (kleśa) for realizing the various Dharma doors (to enlightenment).

(d) Practice of chih and kuan to normalize the fine mind

Previously the practiser has employed the chih-kuan method to master the coarse and unsettled mind, and after its stabilization he enters the state of stillness (dhyāna). As his mind is now refined, he feels that his body is void and still, filled with joy and happiness. Or, due to this refined mind, he may be tempted to slip into heterodoxy. If he does not know that the purpose of quieting the mind is to put an end to all deceptive falsehood, he may become fond of the latter and grasp it as the real. On the other hand, if he knows that all deceptive falsehood is unreal, he will avoid both kinds of trouble (kleśa), (false) love (of the unreal) and wrong views (about it). This is the practice of chih.

If, after practising chih, his mind still grasps these two kinds of kleśa, thereby creating more karma and being unable to rest, he should practise kuan by contemplating his refined mind in this state of stillness. If he cannot find it, he will cease clinging to the idea of stillness, and if this idea of stillness is not grasped, the two kinds of kleśa will vanish. This is the practice of kuan.

The above are the usual ways of practising chih and kuan to normalize the refined mind. They are similar to those previously taught, except that the notion of stillness is discussed here.

(e) Practice of chih and kuan to equalize stillness with wisdom

When a practiser sits in meditation, he may realize dhyāna by either chih or kuan. Although he has achieved this state of stillness, he may not realize the contemplating wisdom. This is a dull dhyāna which cannot help him to untie bonds. Or it may be that he has realized too little wisdom to undo his bonds to understand the various Dharma doors. In such cases, he should practise kuan to break this stalemate so that dhyāna and wisdom will be in equal proportions for these purposes.

If in his meditation, because of his practice of kuan, he is suddenly awakened with his wisdom clearly manifest but with his dhyāna disproportionately dim, his mind will move like a candle in the wind which cannot illumine surrounding objects; he will be unable to escape from birth and death. In such a case, he should practise chih to still his mind which will then be like a candle in his own room that can destroy darkness and illumine all objects inside. The above are the usual ways of practising chih and kuan to equalize dhyāna with wisdom.

If a practiser while sitting in meditation can make proper use of the above five modes ((a) to (e)) of practising chih and kuan, he will be able correctly to practise the Buddha Dharma, and because of his right practice, he will not pass his life in vain.

II. Practice of chih-kuan when involved in causal activities and facing phenomena

Although the above method of sitting cross-legged is the most appropriate one, a practiser is burdened with a physical body which cannot avoid being involved in all causal activities. If he follows them and thereby faces external objects, without continuing to practise chih-kuan, his training will be intermittent, and he will thereby form new karma; how then can he awaken to the Buddha Dharma as speedily as he wishes? If he can continue at all times (and under all circumstances) to practise the expedient method of achieving dhyāna and wisdom, he will thoroughly understand all Buddha Dharmas.

How should one practise chih-kuan when involved in causal activities of which there are six kinds: walking, staying, sitting, reclining, working and speaking? How should one practise chih-kuan when facing external objects? There are six kinds of objects to be faced by the sense organs, namely form that confronts the eyes: sound, the ears; smell, the nose; taste, the tongue; touch, the body; and things (dharma), the intellect (manas). If the meditator while being involved in these twelve (common acts of daily life) practises the chih-kuan method, this is practice while in the state of causal activity and when facing external objects (as explainedbelow).

(1) While walking

The practiser while walking should give rise to this thought: 'Why am I now walking? Is it because I am pushed by kleśa or because of my desire to do evil or unrecordable (neutral) things? If so, I should not walk. If not so and if it is for the benefit of the Dharma, then I should walk.'

How should one practise chih while walking? If the practiser clearly knows that because he is walking, all kleśa as well as good and evil things are created, and if he perfectly understands that his mind set on walking and on all things arising therefrom cannot be found anywhere, his wrong thoughts will come to an end. This is the practice of chih.

How should one practise kuan while walking? The practiser should give rise to this thought: 'As the mind causes the body to move, there is advancing which is called walking. Because of this walking, all kleśa as well as good and evil things are created.' He should then turn inwards his contemplation to look into his mind set on walking, which has neither form nor shape. He will thus realize that that which walks and all things arising therefrom are fundamentally immaterial.[1] This is the practice of kuan.

(2) While staying

The practiser while staying should give rise to this thought: 'Why am I now staying? Is it because of my desire to create kleśa as well as evil or neutral things? If so, I should not keep on staying. If it is for some profitable objective, then I should continue so doing.'

How should one practise chih while in the staying state? If the practiser knows that because of his staying, all sorts of trouble (kleśa) as well as good and evil things will result and if he clearly knows that his mind set on staying and that all things arising therefrom cannot be found anywhere, his perverted thoughts will come to an end. This is the practice of chih.

How should one practise kuan while in the staying state? The practiser should give rise to this thought: 'As the mind halts the body, there is staying. Because of this staying, all kleśa as well as good and evil things will result.' He should then turn inwards his contemplation (kuan) to look into the staying mind which has neither form nor shape. He will thus realize that that which stays and all things arising therefrom are fundamentally immaterial. This is the practice of kuan.

(3) While sitting

The practiser while sitting should give rise to this thought: 'Why am I now sitting? Is it because of my desire to create kleśa or to do evil or unrecordable things? If so, I should not sit. If it is for some profitable objective, then I should sit.'

How should one practise chih while sitting? If the practiser clearly knows that, though it can create kleśa and good and evil things, there is not a single thing (dharma) that can be found anywhere, his perverted thoughts will not arise. This is the practice of chih.

How should one practise kuan while sitting? The practiser should give rise to this thought: 'As my mind thinks of resting, I am sitting with my legs placed upon one another to keep my body at ease, and because of this, all kinds of good and evil things will result; hence this is called sitting.' If

1. A void and still condition beyond all disturbance, the condition of nirvāṇa.

he turns inwards his contemplation (kuan) to look into his mind set on sitting, he will not discover its form and shape. Thus he will realize that that which sits and all things arising therefrom are fundamentally immaterial. This is the practice of kuan.

(4) While reclining

The practiser while reclining should give rise to this thought: 'Why am I now reclining? If it is because of my delight in evil things or in self-indulgence, I should not continue to recline. If it is to harmonize the four elements (earth, water, fire and air), I should continue to recline like the lion king.[1]

How should one practise chih while reclining? If the practiser clearly knows that when he reclines, although all good or evil dharmas arise therefrom, there is in reality not a single thing (dharma) that can be found anywhere; his false thoughts will cease to arise. This is the practice of chih.

How should one practise kuan while reclining? The practiser should give rise to this thought: 'Because I am tired, I feel gloomy and give rein to the six passions,[2] thereby creating all kinds of kleśa as well as good and evil things.' If he turns inwards his contemplation (kuan) to look into the mind set on reclining, he will find that it has neither form nor shape. Thus he will realize that that which reclines as well as all things arising therefrom are fundamentally immaterial. This is the practice of kuan.

(5) While working

The practiser while working should give rise to this thought: 'Why am I now working? If it is for evil or unrecordable purposes, I should refrain. If it is for some profitable reason, I should keep on working.'

How should one practise chih while working? If the practiser clearly knows that while he is working, although good and evil things arise therefrom, there is in reality not a single one that can be found anywhere, his false thoughts will then cease arising. This is the practice of chih.

How should one practise kuan while working? The practiser should give rise to this thought: 'Because my mind causes my hands to move and work, good or evil things will result; hence I am working.' If he turns inwards his contemplation (kuan) to look into this mind set on working, he will perceive neither its form nor its shape. Thus he will realize that that which works and all things arising therefrom are fundamentally immaterial. This is the practice of kuan.

(6) While speaking

When he is about to speak, the practiser should give rise to this thought: 'Why am I now talking? If I delight in kleśa and speak of things that are of

1. i.e. the Buddha who reclined on his right side.
2. Arising from the six sense organs.

evil or neutral effect, I should stop talking. If my speech is for some profitable purpose, I should speak.'

How should one practise chih while speaking? If the practiser knows that when he talks, kleśa as well as good or evil dharmas arise therefrom, he will clearly know that the mind set on speaking and all the above effects cannot be found anywhere; his false mind will come to an end. This is the practice of chih.

How should one practise kuan while speaking? The practiser should give rise to this thought: 'Because the mind discriminates and causes the inner air to rise and the throat, tongue, palate, teeth and lips to produce sound and voice, there is speech which will result in good or evil effects.' If he turns inwards his contemplation (kuan) to look into the mind set on speaking, he will find that it has neither form nor shape. Thus he will realize that that which speaks as well as all things arising therefrom are fundamentally immaterial. This is the practice of kuan.

The above six methods of practising chih and kuan are to be employed as occasion arises. Each of them involves all the five objectives ((a) to (e)) of the Main Practice (See p. 129). Now the (control of the) six sense organs will be dealt with (in (7) to (12)).

(7) While seeing

When the eyes see a form, for instance the moon (reflected) in water, the practice of chih consists in looking into the unreal reflection. If the eyes meet a pleasant form, the practiser should not give rise to feelings of like and when they meet an unpleasant one, he should refrain from feelings of dislike. If the form seen is neither pleasant nor unpleasant, he should abstain from stupid and confusing thoughts. This is the practice of chih.

How should one practise kuan when the eyes see a form? The practiser should give rise to this thought: 'When a form is seen, its nature is immaterial. Why is it so? Because in the clear emptiness between the organ of sight and form, there is nothing to be seen and discerned, but when circumstantial causes intervene and unite them, perception of sight (i.e. the first consciousness) will result, followed by the faculty of mind (i.e. the intellect) which then distinguishes all forms. Hence, the creation of all kinds of kleśa as well as good and evil things (dharma).' The practiser should then turn inwards his contemplation (kuan) to look into the mind that perceives forms and will find that it has neither form nor shape. He will thus realize that that which sees and all things seen are fundamentally immaterial. This is the practice of kuan.

(8) While hearing

When the ears hear a sound, the practice of chih consists in abstaining from like when a pleasant one is heard, from dislike when an unpleasant one is heard and from differentiation when a sound that is neither pleasant nor unpleasant is heard.

How should one practise kuan when a sound is heard? The practiser should give rise to this thought: 'The sound heard is void and unreal by itself but when the organ of hearing and the sound unite, the perception of sound (i.e. the second consciousness) will result, followed by the faculty of mind which arbitrarily differentiates. Hence all kinds of kleśa as well as good and evil dharmas are created.' The practiser should then turn inwards the contemplation (kuan) to look into the mind that hears the sound and will find that it has neither form nor shape. He will thus realize that that which hears and all sounds heard are fundamentally immaterial. This is the practice of kuan.

(9) While smelling

When the nose perceives a smell, the practice of chih consists in looking into the smell which is unreal like a flame. The practiser should abstain from liking a smell that is fragrant, from disliking one that is offensive and from confusing thoughts when it is neither pleasant nor unpleasant. This is the practice of chih.

How should one practise kuan when a smell is perceived? The practiser should give rise to this thought: 'As I am smelling an odour, it is deceitful and unreal. Why? Because of the union of the organ of smell and the odour smelt the perception of smell (i.e. the third consciousness) will result, followed by the faculty of mind which arbitrarily grasps the odour; hence the creation of all kinds of kleśa as well as good and evil dharmas.' He should then turn inwards his contemplation (kuan) to look into the mind that smells and will find that it has neither form nor shape. He will thus realize that the perception of smell and all odours are fundamentally immaterial.

(10) While tasting

When the tongue perceives a taste, the practice of chih consists in looking into the taste which is like a thing existing only in a dream or an illusion. He should abstain from liking a taste that is pleasant, from disliking one that is unpleasant and from differentiating thoughts when it is neither pleasant nor unpleasant. This is the practice of chih.

How should one practise kuan when the tongue perceives a taste? The practiser should give rise to this thought: 'The taste I am perceiving cannot be found. Why? Because the (underlying) nature of the six tastes[1] does not differentiate and because the union between tongue and taste begets the perception of taste (i.e. the fourth consciousness): followed by the faculty of mind which arbitrarily grasps taste, thus creating all kinds of kleśa as well

1. i.e. bitter, sour, sweet, acrid, salt and insipid.

as good and evil things.' He should then turn inwards his contemplation (kuan) to look into that which perceives taste and will find that it has neither form nor shape. He will thus realize that that which tastes and the taste itself are fundamentally immaterial. This is the practice of kuan.

(11) While touching

When the body is touched, the practice of chih consists in looking into this touch which is but a shadow that is illusory and unreal. He should abstain from liking this touch when it is pleasant, from disliking it when it is unpleasant and from thinking of it when it is neither pleasant nor unpleasant. This is the practice of chih.

How should one practise kuan when the body is touched? The practiser should give rise to this thought: 'Physical sensations such as lightness, heaviness, coldness, warmth, roughness and smoothness are felt when touch is experienced by the body which comprises the head, trunk and four limbs. The nature of touch is non-existent and the body also is unreal. When touch and body are united by causal circumstances, consciousness of the object of touch (i.e. the fifth consciousness) will result, followed by the faculty of mind which remembers and distinguishes all pleasant and unpleasant sensations.' The practiser should then turn inwards his contemplation (kuan) to look into the mind which feels this touch and he will find that it has neither form nor shape. He will thus realize that that which feels physical sensations and these sensations themselves are fundamentally immaterial. This is the practice of kuan.

(12) While being conscious of things

When the faculty of mind is conscious of things (dharma), the practice of chih is the same as that taught before to beginners when sitting in meditation.

The above six methods ((7) to (12)) of chih and kuan in respect of the six sense organs are to be employed as occasion arises. Each method involves all the five objectives ((a) to (e)) of the Main Practice (see p. 129).

He who practises chih and kuan while walking, staying, sitting, reclining seeing, hearing, feeling and discerning, really treads the Mahāyāna Path. This is dealt with in the following passage quoted from the long chapter (of the Mahāprajñāpāramitā Sūtra):

'The Buddha said to Subhūti: "If a Bodhisattva while walking is aware of his act of walking; while sitting is aware of his act of sitting; and while wearing a robe keeps an eye on his One Mind that enters and comes out of his state of stillness, he is a true Mahāyāna Bodhisattva. He who can practise Mahāyāna in this manner under all circumstances is the unsurpassed and most excellent man without equal in the world.'

In his Commentary on the Mahāprajñāpāramitā Sūtra, Nāgārjuna wrote the following gāthā:

To sit carefree in a grove (of trees)
For silent removal of all evils
And attainment of a mind that's still
Earns bliss that is above the heavens.
All men seek only worldly weal
Caused by good clothes and bedding,
But such happiness is insecure
For desire can ne'er be satisfied.
To wear the saṅgha robe frees one from all cares and brings
One-mindedness in stillness and disturbance.
With wisdom clear and bright one contemplates
Reality that underlies all things.
Thus all the vast variety of things
Impartially can be looked into.
With wisdom realized, the mind is still;
In the three worlds there's no comparison.[1]

7. MANIFESTATION OF GOOD ROOTS (QUALITIES)

If the meditator can thus practise properly the chih-kuan method in his contemplation of the seeming to enter the void (the real), he will, while sitting, perceive the purity and brightness of his body and mind. At the same time his excellent roots (dormant qualities) will manifest themselves; he should know how to recognize them. There are two kinds of these manifest qualities which differ from each other:

1. The external manifestation of (dormant) qualities which causes the meditator to practise charity (dāna), discipline and morality (śīla) and filial piety; to respect his superiors and make offerings to the Three Precious Ones[2] and to followers of the Teaching. These are outer manifestations but if his practice is not proper, he will fall into the realm of demons; this will be explained later.

2. The internal manifestation of (dormant) qualities in the state of dhyāna, which should be interpreted in three ways as follows:

(a) manifestation of excellent roots;
(b) genuine and false manifestation; and
(c) practice of chih-kuan to preserve and develop these excellent qualities.

1. Worlds of desire, form and beyond form.
2. Buddha, Dharma and Saṅgha.

(a) Manifestation of excellent roots

There are five kinds of excellent qualities which are:

(i) The manifestation of excellent qualities due to the (effective) control of breathing. Because of his proper practice of chih-kuan, the meditator succeeds in regulating his body and mind, thus stopping the flow of thoughts, and so causing his mind gradually to enter the state of dhyāna which still pertains to the realm of desire before he has achieved the (dhyāna) stages of Bodhisattva development. In this stillness, both his body and mind (seem to) vanish and become immaterial. His stabilized mind is now at ease, and in this dhyāna condition, the form and shape of his body and mind cannot be perceived. Thus after one or two meditations, or in one or two days or months, his breath (seems to be) imperceptible. This dhyāna condition will not disperse but will last, and suddenly, his body and mind will react to it with (involuntary) movements producing eight physical sensations such as pain, itching, coldness, warmth, lightness (or weightlessness), heaviness, roughness, and smoothness.[1] When these sensations are felt, his body and mind are incomparably easy, calm, void, subtle, joyful, blissful, pure and clean. This is the manifestation of excellent qualities due to basic dhyāna produced by restful breathing.

The practiser may also, while still in the realm of desire and before attaining the stages of Bodhisattva development, suddenly be conscious of the length, either long or short, of each in and out breath and feel that all the pores of his body are open and unobstructed, so that in his mind's eye he sees clearly everything inside his body as if he had opened a warehouse to see distinctly all the hemp, cereals, etc., stored therein. He will be startled and overjoyed and his mind will be calm and happy. This is the manifestation of excellent roots caused by the stabilization of breathing.

(ii) The manifestation of excellent qualities due to the contemplation of filthiness. The practiser may, while still in the realm of desire and before attaining the dhyāna stages of Bodhisattva development, perceive the immateriality of his body and mind in their still condition, seeing suddenly the swollen and decaying corpses of men which discharge worms and pus and expose a mess of white bones. With grief and joy intermingled, he will now detest all that he previously treasured. This is the manifestation of excellent roots due to the ninefold meditation (on corpses).[2]

The meditator may also, while in this still condition, suddenly see filth in his body and messy swellings on it, and become aware of how his white

1. See Chapter 6 for detailed explanation.

2. Navasaṁjñā, one of the meditations on filthiness, or the ninefold meditation on a dead body: (1) its tumefaction; (2) its blue, mottled colour; (3) its decay; (4) its mess of blood, etc.; (5) its rotting flesh and discharges; (6) its being devoured by birds and beasts; (7) its dismembering; (8) its white bones; and (9) their cremation and return to dust.

bones support each other from his head to his feet. After this vision, while his mind is stabilized, he will be startled and awaken to impermanence and so hate the five harmful desires and discard the notion of self and others. This is the manifestation of excellent roots as a result of renunciation.

Or, he may, while in this stillness of mind, see that the inside and outside of his own body; all birds and beasts; food, drink and clothing; and houses, huts, hills and groves are all unclean. This is the manifestation of excellent roots due to (total rejection of) all impurities.

(iii) The manifestation of excellent qualities due to (inherent) kindness (maitrī).[1] Because of his (successful) practice of chih-kuan, the meditator realizes the condition of stillness in the realm of desire, prior to achieving the dhyāna stages of Bodhisattva development. While dwelling in this state, he may suddenly give rise to kind thoughts of living beings, or because of the happiness of some relative, he will achieve a profound dhyāna, thereby experiencing joy, bliss, purity and cleanness which are incomparable. Likewise he will achieve the same attainment in the case of the happiness of a neutral,[2] an opponent, or any living being in the five worlds of existence. After his meditation, his mind will be joyful and happy, and when he meets others, his mien will always be friendly and sympathetic. This is the manifestation of excellent roots due to the practiser's (inherent) kindness of heart.

Likewise, the same excellent roots also manifest because of the practiser's (inherent) compassion (karuṇā), joy (muditā) and renunciation (upekṣā).

(iv) The manifestation of excellent qualities as a result of awakening to (the twelve links in the chain of) causality.[3] Because of his (effective) practice of the chih-kuan method, the meditator achieves the condition of stillness in the realm of desire, prior to his realization of the dhyāna of body and mind in the stages of Bodhisattva development. While in this state, he (may) awaken suddenly and, by looking into the (twelve links in the chain of existence such as:) ignorance (avidyā), activity (saṁskāra), etc., of the past, present and future, he will fail to perceive the existence of self and others; he thus succeeds in avoiding mortality and immortality, in relinquishing all bigoted views, in becoming stabilized and at ease, in developing correct understanding through wisdom, in experiencing joy in the

1. The first of the four immeasurables, four universals, or four infinite Buddha states of mind: boundless kindness, maitrī; boundless compassion, karuṇā; boundless joy, muditā, on seeing others delivered from suffering; and boundless indifference, or renunciation, upekṣā.

2. A person who is neither friendly nor hostile.

3. Nidāna, causes or links in the chain of existence: (1) ignorance or unenlightenment; (2) action, activity, conception or disposition; (3) consciousness; (4) name and form; (5) the six sense organs, i.e. eye, ear, nose, tongue, body and mind; (6) contact or touch; (7) sensation or feeling; (8) desire or craving; (9) grasping; (10) being or existing; (11) birth; and (12) old age and death.

Dharma and in being unconcerned about the worldly. He (may) come to the same result by looking into the five aggregates,[1] the twelve entrances,[2] and the eighteen realms of sense.[3] This is the manifestation of excellent roots through the twelve nidānas.

(v) The manifestation of excellent qualities due to remembrance of Buddha. Because of his (effective) practice of the chih-kuan method, the meditator realizes the (worldly) dhyāna in the realm of desire but not yet that of the stages of Bodhisattva development. While his body and mind are in this state of still immateriality, he suddenly remembers the inconceivable merits, physical marks and excellent aspects of all Buddhas; their unfathomable (ten) powers, (four kinds of) fearlessness, (eighteen) unsurpassed characteristics, samādhis and liberation; and their mysterious powers of transformation and unobstructed widespread preaching for the benefit of living beings. While recollecting these, he gives rise to feelings of reverence and devotion; thereby developing his own state of samādhi which causes his body and mind to be joyful, happy, easy, stabilized and free from all evils. When he comes out of this condition of stillness, he feels comfortable and light (weightless), and is aware of his imposing merits which command the admiration and respect of others. This is the manifestation of excellent roots due to the realization of the samādhi of remembrance of Buddhas.[4]

Furthermore, if a meditator, because of his (effective) practice of the chih-kuan method, realizes the state of purity and cleanness of both body and mind, he may awaken to the Dharma doors such as (the doctrines of) impermanence, suffering, unreality and non-existence of ego; of filthiness and the repulsive and unclean (way in which) the worldly feed; of (what follows when) mortality ends; of the constant recollection of Buddha, Dharma, Saṅgha, precepts, renunciation and heavenly (blessings); of the (four) subjects of reflection (or fourfold objectivity of thoughts), the (four) proper lines of exertion, the (four) advanced steps to powers of ubiquity, the (five) positive agents, the (five) powers intensifying the (five) positive agents and the (seven) degrees of enlightenment;[5] of voidness, immateriality and inactivity; of the six perfections and other pāramitās; and of supernatural

1. The five aggregates, or skandha, are: form (rūpa), reception (vedanā), discerning (sañjñā), discrimination (saṁskāra) and consciousness (vijñāna).

2. The twelve entrances, or āyatana, are: the six organs and six sense data that lead to discrimination.

3. The eighteen realms of sense or dhātu are: the six sense organs, their objects and their perceptions.

4. A samādhi realized by a meditator who concentrates his attention solely on the Buddha by calling his name endlessly. (See Chapter 3, the Pure Land School.)

5. See *Ch'an and Zen Teaching*, Third Series, the Sūtra of Complete Enlighten ment, p. 193, note 2, for detailed explanations.

powers and transcendental transformations, etc., which should be distinguished properly from one another. Hence the sūtra says: 'When the mind is brought under complete control, all things are possible.'

(b) Genuine and false manifestations

There are two ways of distinguishing between false and genuine manifestations:

1. An evil manifestation can be recognized when the meditator, while experiencing the above state of dhyāna, feels that his body is either restless or seems to be laden with a heavy burden, is so light that it is inclined to fly, seems to be tied up, or sways to fall into a sound sleep, or when he senses bitter cold or intense heat. At times, he sees strange visions, or his mind is dim and stupid: he gives rise to evil feelings, or mixed and confused thoughts of good actions. At times, he is filled with joy and is thereby agitated or he gives way to sadness and depression. At times he experiences evil sensations that cause all his hair to stand on end or he is muddled through rapture. Such manifestations in the state of stillness are false and come from evil dhyāna. If the meditator delights in and clings to them, he will be responsive to the ninety-five ways of ghosts and spirits, and may contract an illness of mind and so become insane. Or he may come under the evil influence of ghosts and spirits who know of his clinging to their heresies and will increase their power to hold him fast to compel him to realize evil dhyāna and evil knowledge, thereby acquiring the power of (evil) speech that impresses worldlings. The ignorant will regard this as attainment of the Tao and will believe and submit to him. However, his inner mind is already perverted and he will tread the ways of ghosts to deceive and disturb worldly men. At his death, he will not meet the Buddha but will fall into the realm of hungry ghosts. If he practises heresies when meditating, he will fall into the realm of hells.

If a practiser of the chih-kuan method experiences these states of evil dhyāna, he should drive them away. How? If they are known as deceitful, he should correct his mind by not accepting and clinging to them and they will vanish of themselves. He should then contemplate (kuan) properly to break up this evil dhyāna which will disappear.

2. A genuine manifestation is recognizable by the practiser if his state of dhyāna is free from the above experiences. In the right dhyāna, each of its successive manifestations accords well with the state itself which is immaterial, bright, pure and clean, and in which his inner mind is joyful with feelings of ease and bliss; freedom from hindrance; emergence of good-heartedness; increase in faith and devotion; clear perception and insight; and his body and mind being mild and in the condition of immateriality and stillness. He has an aversion to the worldly, being inactive

with no desire, and able to enter or leave this state of dhyāna at will. These are the manifestations of genuine dhyāna. As an illustration, when you work with an evil man, he will irritate you but if you work with a good man, his excellent behaviour will satisfy you. Distinction between an evil and a genuine dhyāna is made in the same way.

(c) The practice of chih-kuan for preserving manifestly excellent roots

When his inner excellent qualities manifest during meditation, the practiser should employ the chih-kuan method to advance further. He should practise chih or kuan as the case requires, as taught above.

8. DISCERNING MĀRA'S HARMFUL INTERFERENCE

The Sanskrit word 'māra' means 'murderer' in Chinese. Māra robs the practiser of his wealth of merits and destroys the life of his wisdom,[1] hence the aims of evil demons. The Buddha's aim is to lead, by means of merits and wisdom, all living beings to nirvāṇa, but māra's target is to destroy their good roots so as to condemn them to drift in the stream of birth and death. If we can quiet the mind to practise the right Tao, we will find out that māra grows fiercely as our Tao progresses higher; hence the need to discern māra's aim.

There are four kinds of māra: the demon of trouble (kleśa), the demon of the five aggregates, the demon of death and demoniac spirits. The first three are common being created by the self-mind and should be eradicated by it. They are (well known and are, therefore) not dealt with here. As to demoniac spirits, they should be known and are now discussed. There are three kinds:

1. The mischievous māras who are typified by the twelve animals which stand for the twelve hours of day and night and which take various bodily forms, either as girls or elderly men and various frightening appearances to deceive and trouble the meditator. These demons choose their characteristic times to come and annoy him and should be recognized. If a demon comes between 3 and 5 a.m., he stands for a tiger; between 5 and 7, a rabbit: between 7 and 9, a dragon: between 9 and 11, a snake: between 11 a.m. and 1 p.m., a horse: between 1 and 3 p.m., a sheep: between 3 and 5, a monkey: between 5 and 7, a chicken: between 7 and 9, a dog: between 9 and 11, a pig: between 11 p.m. and 1 a.m. a rat and between 1 and 3, a buffalo.[2] If the

1. Wisdom life, a Buddhist term, means wisdom as life, being the basis of spiritual character.

2. These twelve symbolic animals can be likened to the twelve signs of the zodiac: aries, taurus, gemini, cancer, leo, virgo, libra, scorpio, sagittarius, capricorn, aquarius and pisces.

practiser regularly sees them coming at specific hours, he will know that they are animal spirits. He should name and shout at them and they will disappear at once.

2. The harassing māras who aim to trouble the meditator and who appear as worms and grubs that sting his head, tickle him under the arms, clutch at him, make a disturbing noise or appear as beasts or in other strange forms to annoy him. He should recognize them, close his eyes, concentrate on his single mind and scold them, saying: 'I know you; you are the fire-eating, incense-smelling and offerings-stealing demons of this world, who hold evil views and delight in breaking the precepts. I keep the commandments and am not afraid of you.' If the practiser is a monk, he should read the śīla text, and if he is a layman, he should recite the three formulas of refuge and the five prohibitions, whereat these demons will crawl away. There are many ways of getting rid of them which are taught in the sūtra.

3. The confusing māras who create conditions of sense data to destroy the meditator's mental progress, such as: (1) an adverse surrounding of five fearful sense data to scare him; (2) a favourable surrounding of five pleasant sense data to incite him to cling to them; and (3) a surrounding of ordinary sense data, which is neither favourable nor adverse, to confuse him. Hence, they are called murderers, flowery (i.e. attractive) arrows, or the five arrows that hit a man's five senses.

They produce all kinds of states to deceive and mislead the meditator, such as: friendly states in which his parents, his brothers, Buddhas and respectable men and women appear to arouse his attachment to them; hostile states in which wild beasts such as tigers, wolves, lions and malignant spirits (rākṣasas) come in frightful forms to terrify him; and ordinary states that are neither friendly nor hostile to divert and confuse his mind, causing his failure to realize dhyāna; hence they are called māras. Sometimes they make pleasant or unpleasant speeches or sounds, give off fragrant or offensive smells, produce good or bad flavours and create happy and unhappy situations that affect his body; these are demonic influences which are too many to be counted. To sum up, they assail the senses in all kinds of ways to annoy and upset the meditator, causing him to deviate from all good Dharmas and to get involved in all sorts of kleśa. They all belong to māra armies that aim to destroy the universal Buddha Dharma and to obstruct the Tao by causing desire, sadness, hatred, sleep, etc., as said in the following gāthā:

Desire is the first of your armies;
Worry and sadness is the second;
The third is thirst and hunger;
Craving for love's the fourth:

The fifth is sleep and drowsiness;
While awe and fright compose the sixth;
Doubt and repentance are the seventh;
Anger and resentment make the eighth;
Gain and preservation form the ninth;
While pride and self-importance are the tenth.
With so many troops you aim
To destroy the Saṅgha.
I use strong dhyāna wisdom
To break up all your strength
And when I am a Buddha
To free all living beings.

When the practiser is aware of these māra disturbances, he should avoid them. There are two ways of so doing:

(i) By the practice of chih. When encountering these external māra states, he should know that they are all unreal and should never worry or be frightened. Neither should he accept or reject them and give rise to discrimination. Directly he stops all the activities of his mind and sets it at rest, they will disappear of themselves.

(ii) By the practice of kuan. When these māra states appear, if he fails to avoid them by means of chih, he should look into the subjective mind that beholds them. He will find that since his mind leaves no traces,[1] no demon can trouble it. By so practising kuan, these states will vanish.

If they do not disappear, he should set his mind aright and avoid giving rise to fear. He should, even at the sacrifice of his own life, remain unperturbed in his right thought. For he should know that the (fundamental) condition of suchness of the māra realm is identical with that of the region of Buddhas. Since both conditions are of the same absoluteness, they are but one and are, therefore, non-dual. Thus he will understand that while the māra realm should not be rejected, the region of Buddhas should not be grasped and, as a result, the Buddha Dharma will manifest itself before him, with all māra states vanishing of themselves.

If these māra states do not disappear, he should not worry and if they vanish, he should not be delighted. Why? Because, up to now, no meditator has actually seen a demon take the form of a tiger or a wolf to come and devour him. Neither has a meditator actually seen a demon take a human form of the opposite sex to come and live with him (or her) as wife or husband. An ignorant man who does not know that these transformations are illusory is scared or gives rise to attachment, thereby upsetting his own mind and becoming insane (in the worst case). Thus he harms himself

1. Lit. has no whereabouts.

because of his ignorance and his troubles are certainly not caused by demons.

If these māra states last for months or even a whole year without any likelihood of their disappearance, the meditator should set his mind aright and firmly abide in the right thought, even at the peril of his body and life, without giving way to worry and fear. He should recite the Mahāyāna and Vaipulya sūtras, silently repeat the māra-repulsing mantras and fix his mind on the Three Gems. After his meditation, he should repeat the mantras for self-protection, observe the rules of repentance and reform and read the pratimokṣa.[1] Since wickedness is no match for righteousness, these māra states will sooner or later disappear of themselves. They are too numerous to be listed, but they should be recognized by beginners who should call on learned masters for guidance. These difficult situations show that māras have entered the mind of the practiser to deceive and disturb him and to cause him to be either happy or sad, thereby bringing harm or even death to the victim. Sometimes they mislead him so that he realizes evil dhyāna, evil knowledge, evil spiritual power and evil dhāraṇīs (i.e. black magic), preaches wrongly and leads others to evil ways. He then believes in and submits to them and they encourage him to break the saṅgha's rules of conduct and to destroy the right Dharma. There are so many of these states that they cannot be given in full. I have mentioned only the important ones so that students sitting in dhyāna can know how to avoid them. To sum up, the avoidance of depravity in order to return to righteousness consists in looking into the (underlying) reality of all things (dharma) in the practice of chih and kuan which will destroy all depravity. Hence, Nāgārjuna said in his Commentary on the Mahāprajñāpāramitā Sūtra: 'Besides the reality underlying all dharmas (i.e. the Bhūtatathatā), there is not a thing that does not pertain to māra.' This is explained in the following gāthā:

Discrimination, thought and recollection
Are the net of Māra.
Imperturbability and non-differentiation
Are the seal of Dharma.

9. THE HEALING OF AILMENTS

During his practice of self-cultivation, the meditator may fall ill because of either his (wrong) contemplation of mind and counting of breaths which may bring into play disharmony between the four elements or because of his

1. The 250 precepts for monks in the vinaya; they are read in assembly twice a month.

(improper) control of body, breath and mind, thereby affecting his health. If the mind is properly controlled during the meditation, all the 404 ailments[1] will be eliminated, but if it is wrongly regulated, they will manifest. Therefore, during his own practice or when teaching others, the meditator should know the origins of ailments and the method of healing them by means of mind (control) while sitting in dhyāna, because not only do illnesses hinder his self-cultivation but also (in the worst case) they may endanger his life.

To heal ailments requires the knowledge of diagnosis and treatment.

(a) Diagnosis of ailments

In spite of a great number of illnesses, diagnosis does not exceed the following two modes: the condition of the four elements and of the five viscera.

Chih I here details in turn the ailments due to an excess in the body of the elements of earth, water, fire and air and those which are caused by some irregularity in the heart, liver, lungs, stomach or kidneys. He then continues:

Furthermore, there are three different causes of ailments: excessive or deficient conditions of the four elements and five viscera, as already explained; harmful interference by ghosts and spirits; and karmic influences.

Ailments are easy to eliminate if they are treated at the very beginning, but if they are allowed to worsen with the passing of time, when the body is greatly affected and becomes emaciated, it is very difficult to cure them.

(b) Treatment of ailments

After diagnosis has determined the origin of an ailment, a method should be employed to cure it. There are many ways of treating illnesses, but essentially only two are expedient, chih and kuan.

(i) Treatment by chih. How should one employ chih to cure ailments? A master said: 'Just fix the mind on the affected spot and the ailment will be cured.' Why so? Because mind is mainly responsible for the rewards and punishments in a lifetime.[2] It is like a king from whom, when he comes to a place, bandits flee in all directions.

Another master said: 'Within an inch below the navel is the udāna,

1. Each of the four elements (earth, water, fire, wind) is responsible for 101 ailments; thus 101 × 4 = 404 ailments in all.

2. Lit. is the chief in a retributive lifetime.

called tan. 'ien in Chinese.[1] If the mind is definitely fixed there, all ailments can be cured in time.'

A (third) master said: 'If, while walking, standing, reclining and sleeping, the mind is fixed on the soles of the feet, one will cure all ailments.' Why so? Because illnesses are caused by the four elements being out of order. This is due to the mind and its cognition that float up to follow external causes and so upset the four elements. If the mind is brought down, the four elements will not be affected and will be in their proper working condition, with the elimination of all ailments.

A (fourth) master said: 'If all things (dharma) are perceived as unreal and non-existent and if no ailments are thought of (all stirring) will cease in the state of stillness; many ailments are thereby eradicated.' Why so? Because of the stirring mind that rouses the four elements and so produces illnesses. If the mind is at rest and in a happy state, all ailments will disappear. Hence, the Vimalakīrti Nirdeśa Sūtra says: 'Where do ailments originate? From attachment to (external) causes. How is this cut off? By realizing that the mind does not gain anything therefrom.'

The above are different methods of curing illnesses by means of chih. Therefore, we know that if chih is properly practised, all ailments can be eradicated.

(ii) Treatment by kuan. A master said: 'Just visualize your thinking mind as defeating ailments by either of the six kinds of breath.' This is cure by kuan. The six breaths are the puffing,[2] expelling,[3] shouting,[4] sighing,[5] soothing[6] and restful[7] breaths which are expediently imagined as coming from the mouth and thrown out continuously to drive away all illness. Hence, this stanza:

All sages know that a sigh heals the heart; a puff, the kidneys;
Breathing out will cure the stomach and a restful breath, the lungs;
A soothing breath cools heat in the liver,
While indigestion is stopped by a shout.

Chih I here quotes at length from another master who listed twelve other types of breathing and the respective ailments which each could cure.

1. Tan t'ien: a reservoir of the vital principle that can be transmuted into the Elixir of Life according to the Taoists.

2. A puffing breath: a short quick blast of cold breath to blow ailments away.

3. An expelling breath: an audible exhalation, expressive of discharge.

4. A shouting breath: an audible exhalation, expressive of driving away.

5. A sighing breath: an audible expiration of warm breath, expressive of relief.

6. A soothing breath: a slow expiration of warm breath to soothe.

7. A restful breath: a fine breath to harmonize body and mind and so to ensure recovery.

A (third) master said: 'If visualization is effective, it can cure all illnesses.' For instance, when a man suffers from a shivering fever, he should (mentally) visualize a rising fire in his body and so get rid of the chill. This is taught in the Saṁyuktāgama Sūtra[1] which lists seventy-two secret methods (of visualization).

A (fourth) master said: 'Just employ the chih-kuan method to examine and analyse all illnesses due to the four elements (because these) ailments cannot be found in either body or mind, and you are on your way to recovery.'

These are different methods of treating illnesses and if they are well understood (and properly employed), they can all cure ailments. So we know that with the efficient use of chih-kuan, there is not a single illness that cannot be healed. Nowadays, however, man's roots are very shallow and so these methods are not practised properly; hence they have been forgotten. Since people do not follow (the Taoist) method of developing the vital principle (prāṇa) and of abstaining from cereals, lest they fall into heresy,[2] they use medicinal herbs and minerals which can also cure illnesses.

If illnesses are caused by the harmful influences of demons, one's mind should be strengthened by repeating mantras to overcome them. If they are due to karmic influence, one should repent, reform and cultivate one's field of blessedness (with moral actions), thereby rooting them all out. If we understand only one of these two courses, we can practise it effectively for our own benefit and can also teach it to others; how much more so if both courses are well understood and followed? If we do not know them, we will be unable to cure our illnesses; and then, not only will we be compelled to give up the right Dharma, but our lives may even be in danger. How then can we practise the Dharma and teach it to others? Therefore, in our practice of chih-kuan, we should understand perfectly the methods of treating diseases by means of our inner minds. These methods are many and comprehension of them depends on individual (responsiveness); how can they be handed down by writing?

Furthermore, the mental treatment of illness during meditation should include ten beneficial essentials which are: faith, practice, exertion, non-deviation, discernment of the causes of illness, expediency, long endurance, ability to retain or drop, taking care and awareness of hindrances.

What is faith? Faith in this method which can heal illnesses. What is practice? Practice of the method as occasion requires. What is exertion?

1. A miscellaneous treatise on abstract meditation, one of the four Āgamas.

2. The Taoist practice referred to is not that taught by Lao-tzu but was known before him.

Exertion in the correct practice until recovery. What is non-deviation? The mind in close conformity with this method without deviating from it for even an instant. What is discernment of the causes of illness? Discernment as explained in the earlier paragraph on the diagnosis. What is expediency? Expediency in proper breathing and in skilful visualization for recovery. What is long endurance? If the practice does not give an immediate result, it should be continued unremittingly, without taking into account the number of days or months required for success. What is ability to retain or drop? This means that in the subtle state of the mind concentrated on the cure of illness, whatever proves beneficial to ultimate recovery should be retained whereas whatever proves harmful should be dropped. What is taking care? It is the skilful discernment (and avoidance) of all discordant causes. What is awareness of hindrances? Whatever is profitable should not be (lightly) disclosed to others; before (a method) is proved harmful, there should be neither distrust nor criticism (of it). If these ten essentials are fulfilled, recovery from the illness is assured.

10. THE FINAL REALIZATION

If the meditator so practises the chih-kuan method, he will be able clearly to realize that all things are created by the mind and are void because all the direct and circumstantial causes of their creation are unreal. As they are void, their names and terms are also unreal.[1] This is the stopping (chih) of all rising causes for apprehension of Reality.[2] He who achieves this stage will perceive neither the Buddha fruit, high above, that can be realized, nor living beings, here below, who can be liberated. This is meditation on the unreal resulting in realization of the void, which is also called meditation on the void, or wisdom's eye, or all-knowledge.[3] If you stay in this meditation, you will fall into the śrāvaka and pratyeka-buddha stages. Hence the sūtra says: 'The śrāvakas declared: "If we hear about (the teaching which consists in) purifying Buddha lands and in teaching and converting living beings, we are not happy. Why? Because all things are in the nirvāṇic condition which is beyond creation and destruction, which is neither large nor small and which is above the worldly plane and in the transcendental

1. Lit. 'their names and designations cannot be found anywhere', because they do not show anything that really exists. We live in the world of illusions because we cling to names and terms which have no substance of their own.

2. See also p. 130, paragraph (iii).

3. The first of the three kinds of wisdoms which are: (1) śrāvaka and pratyeka-buddha knowledge that all things are void and unreal; (2) Bodhisattva knowledge of all things in their proper discrimination and (3) perfect Buddha knowledge of all things in their every aspect and relationship past, present and future; omniscience.

(wu wei) state. Thinking thus, we are unhappy." You should know that he who perceives the wu wei state and thereby reachs the right position, will never be able to develop the saṁbodhi mind.[1] This is due to excess of dhyāna (i.e. stillness over wisdom), hence inability to perceive the Buddha nature.

If, for the benefit of all living beings, a Bodhisattva achieves all Buddha Dharmas, he should not grasp the wu wei state for self-attainment of nirvāṇa. He should shift his contemplation of the void to that of the seeming and thereby realize that although the nature of his mind[2] is void, it can, when encountering external causes, create all phenomena which are like illusions and transformations, and, though not in a fixed and real state, can perform the various functions of seeing, hearing, feeling and knowing. In such a meditation, although he knows that fundamentally all things are in the void state of nirvāṇa, in this voidness, he is able to do everything perfectly, like someone planting trees in the emptiness (of space), and to discern the different roots (propensities) of all living beings because of the countless desires that arise in their natures. He will expound (to them) countless Dharmas and if he realizes the unhindered power of speech, he will be able to look after the welfare of living being in the six realms of existence.

This is the expedient method of following external causes in the practice of chih meditation, which consists in shifting the contemplation of the void to that of the seeming, called universal meditation, or Dharma mind or wisdom of the Tao seed.[3] While staying in this meditation, because of excess of wisdom (over dhyāna), although a Bodhisattvas perceives the Buddha nature, he does not see it distinctly.

Although the practiser achieves these two kinds of meditation, they are only expedients and are not the right insight. Hence the sūtra says that they are two expedient paths and that contemplation of the emptiness of both leads to right insight into the 'Mean' which is inclusive of both and wherein the mind in its nirvāṇic condition will of itself flow into the sarvajña ocean (omniscience). If a Bodhisattva wishes to achieve in the flash of a thought the wholeness of all Buddha Dharmas, he should practise laying down (chih) the two extremes to achieve right insight into the Mean. What does the practice of right insight mean? If the nature of mind is cognized as being neither real nor unreal, the mind that ceases to grasp both the real and the false is right. Insight into the nature of mind which is neither void nor false, free from the annihilation of both the void and the seeming, will ensure

1. As he clings to the wu wei state, this attachment hinders his realization of saṁbodhi, or universal enlightenment which is free from all differentiation. The right position is the Buddha stage or Buddhahood which should not be grasped.

2. The self-existing fundamental pure mind, or Tathāgata-garbha.

3. Or Bodhisattva knowledge, the second of the three kinds of knowledge. See also p. 151, note 3.

attainment of the Mean that includes both. If the Mean inclusive of both the void and the seeming is perceived within the self-mind, it is also perceived within all things (dharma), but should not be grasped for its fixed nature is undiscoverable. This is called right insight into the Mean as explained in the following gāthā of the Mādhyamika śāstra:

All things causally produced
I say are void,
Are but false names
And also indicate the Mean.

Ponder over the deep meaning of this gāthā which not only fully defines the Mean but also the aims of the other two expedient meditations (on the void and the unreal). You should know that right contemplation of the Mean is the Buddha's eye or omniscience (sarvajña). He who stays in this meditative stage will equalize dhyāna with wisdom, will clearly perceive the Buddha nature, will abide comfortably in (the state of) Mahāyāna, will tread the Path evenly and correctly and, advancing like the wind, will automatically flow into the sarvajña ocean (where) he will act like the Tathāgata (by) entering the Tathāgata abode, wearing the Tathāgata robe and sitting on the Tathāgata throne.[1] Thus he will adorn himself with the Tathāgata majesty, purify his six sense organs, enter the Buddha realm and free himself from defilement in the midst of all phenomena (dharma). Since he is now well versed in all Buddha Dharmas,[2] he will achieve the samādhi of the Remembrance of Buddha[3] and will abide in the Śūraṅgama Samādhi. Thus he will (be able to) appear in bodily forms in all Buddha lands in the ten directions to teach and convert living beings, embellish all Buddha realms, make offerings to all Buddhas in the ten directions, receive and uphold the Teachings of all Buddhas, achieve all perfections (pāramitā) and awaken to and enter upon the great Bodhisattva (Mahāsattva) stage where he will keep company with Samantabhadra and Mañjuśrī, will not stray from the Dharmakāya, will receive praise from all the Buddhas who will foretell his future attainments, that is his embellishment of the Tuṣita heaven (with his saving work), his coming birth from the sacred womb of a mother, his retirement from the world, his sitting at a holy site (bodhimaṇḍala), his overcoming of all demons, his realization of Universal Enlightenment, his turning of the Wheel of Dharma, his entry into Nirvāṇa, his

1. A quotation from the Lotus Sūtra. Tathāgata abode stands for universal compassion for all living beings; Tathāgata robe, for kindness and forbearance; and Tathāgata throne, for immutability within the voidness of all things.

2. Lit. 'Since all Buddha Dharmas now appear in front of him'.

3. A samādhi realized by contemplating the Buddha and by repeating his name. See Chapter 3, The Pure Land School.

accomplishment of all Buddha works in all lands in the ten directions and his acquisition of the two bodies.[1] Therefore, he is a Bodhisattva whose mind is newly initiated (into the Mean).

The Avataṁsaka Sūtra says: 'At the time of his mind's initiation (to the Mean, a Bodhisattva) realizes the right bodhi, clearly perceives the true nature of all things and understands that his body of wisdom[2] is self-begotten.' It also says: 'A newly initiated Bodhisattva who realizes one Tathāgatakāya[3] can transform it into countless Nirmāṇakayas.'[4] It further says: 'A newly initiated Bodhisattva is but Buddha.' The Mahāparinirvāṇa Sūtra says: 'The newly initiated mind and the ultimate mind do not differ from each other; of the two, the former is difficult (to realize).' The Sūtra of the Long Chapter[5] says: 'Subhūti, there are Bodhisattvas and Mahāsattvas who, from the moment their minds are initiated (to the Mean), sit in the bodhimaṇḍala and turn the Wheel of Right Dharma;[6] you should know that they act like the Buddha.' As said in the Lotus Sūtra, Nāgakanyā[7] presented her gem to the Buddha to bear witness to her speedy realization. These sūtras clearly show that a newly initiated mind is complete with all Buddha Dharmas. This is but the first letter Ā[8] mentioned in the Sūtra of the Long Chapter; the opening up of Buddha knowledge inherent in all living beings, in the Lotus Sūtra; and the perception of Buddha nature for abiding in Final Nirvāṇa, in the Mahāparinirvāṇa Sūtra.

We have explained briefly the realization of (bodhi) fruit as a result of the practice of chih-kuan by Bodhisattvas whose minds are newly initiated

1. Real body comprising the Dharmakāya, Sambhogakāya and Nirmāṇakāya or transformation body.

2. The first of the five kinds of Dharmakāya: (1) the spiritual body of existent wisdom, (2) of all meritorious achievements, (3) of incarnation, (4) of unlimited power of transformation and (5) of boundless space. The first and second are defined as Sambhogakāya, the third and fourth as Nirmāṇakāya, and the fifth as Dharmakāya which possesses all the others.

3. Body of suchness, or absolute body.

4. Transformation body.

5. Kumārajīva translated into Chinese two chapters of the Mahāprajñāpāramitā Sūtra (600 chuan or rolls) and edited them separately: the long one is called Ta Pin Ching or the Sūtra of the Long Chapter (27 chuan) and the short one, called Hsiao Pin Ching or the Sūtra of the Short Chapter (10 chuan).

6. In contrast with worldlings who are turned upside down by the wheel of birth and death.

7. A nāga maiden who, according to the Lotus Sūtra, presented her precious gem to the Buddha who immediately accepted it in the presence of His disciples to bear witness to her realization of enlightenment in the time that it took for the gem to pass from her hands to those of the World Honoured One.

8. Ā is the first letter of the Siddham alphabet and stands for the uncreate. It has seven meanings: (1) Bodhi mind, (2) Dharma, (3) Non-duality, (4) Dharmadhātu or realm of dharma, (5) Dharmatā, or Dharma nature, (6) Sovereignty and (7) Dharmakāya, or essential body.

(to the Mean). We will now deal with their realization of Ultimate Mind.

The stage attained by the Ultimate Mind cannot be known, but one can deduce from the Teaching that it does not stray from the twin method of chih and kuan. Why so? Because the Lotus Sūtra says: 'Persistent glorification of the wisdom of all Buddhas is what kuan (vipaśyanā) means.' This is kuan, a term used to describe the fruit realized. The Mahāparinirvāna Sūtra makes an extensive use of terms and expressions conveying the meaning of liberation to explain the Final Nirvāṇa, and by nirvāṇa[1] is meant chih (śamatha) which is a term employed to describe the fruit attained. Hence, this sūtra says: 'Mahāparinirvāṇa is called the eternally still samādhi.' By samādhi is meant chih.

Although the Lotus Sūtra uses the word kuan to describe the fruit realized that word also includes chih. Hence, this sūtra says: 'Even the eternal stillness and extinction (of passions) of Ultimate Nirvāṇa finally revert to the void.' Although the Mahāparinirvāṇa Sūtra uses the word chih to describe the fruit attained, that word also includes kuan. Hence, this sūtra defines Mahāparinirvāṇa as possessing all three of the (meritorous) virtues.[2] Although the explanations in these two great sūtras differ, both use the two methods of chih and kuan to discuss the Ultimate and both depend on ting (dhyāna-samādhi) and hui (prajñā) to describe the Supreme Fruit. You should know that the initial, intermediate and final attainments are all inconceivable. Hence, the Suvarṇa-prabhāsa-uttamarāja Sūtra[3] says: 'The past Tathāgata was inconceivable, the present Tathāgata is adorned with all forms of majesty and the future Tathāgata will be eternal, being free from decay.' Thus the two chih and kuan states of mind are used to distinguish the (Supreme) Fruit.

A gāthā in the Pratyutpanna-samādhi Sūtra says:[4]

All Buddhas won liberation through the Mind
Which, when pure and clean, is also undefiled.[5]
The five worlds,[6] *when spotless, are devoid of form:*
He who studies this will realize great Tao.

1. The nirvāṇic state of stillness and extinction of all passions.

2. The virtue of (1) the Buddha's Dharmakāya, (2) of his wisdom and (3) of his liberation from all bonds, i.e. Sovereignty.

3. Called Chin Kuang Ming Ching, or Golden Light Sūtra, translated in the sixth century and twice later, and used by the founder of the T'ien T'ai school.

4. A sūtra teaching the samādhi in which all the Buddhas in the ten directions are seen clearly like the stars at night. Its practice requires ninety days during which the practiser does not rest but persistently thinks of Amitābha Buddha and calls his name.

5. The stage of undefilement is the final one before attaining Buddhahood.

6. The five worlds of existence of (1) the hells, (2) hungry ghosts, (3) animals, (4) men and (5) asuras and devas.

Those who vow to tread this Path should eliminate the three obstructions[1] and the five screens[2] and if they fail to do so, all their efforts will be in vain.

When studying the above comprehensive treatise, we should not allow ourselves to be misled by the words 'For Beginners' in the title and think that it is ordinary and simple, for the practice of the Teaching is far from easy for beginners. Master Chih I warned his disciples against 'slighting the seeming shallowness of the text', for as he said, they 'would blush when finding its practice very difficult'. To make the text more clear, we divided the chapter into sections and subsections marked with numbers and letters. This important treatise of the T'ien T'ai school should be studied with the greatest care and attention so that it is thoroughly understood before one begins to practise it.

When I was young, I practised this T'ien T'ai meditation but failed miserably because of impatience for quick results which has always been my great weakness. Impatience is a very great obstacle in our spiritual training and should be overcome at all costs in the practice of any Dharma door. Once this obstruction has been removed and when the mind is free from all impediments, the various states described in the text will unfold of themselves, with the meditator as an unconcerned spectator. Only then can the training be effective.

After we have disengaged ourselves from all worldly feelings and passions, the excellent roots or qualities which lie dormant within us will manifest as described in section 7 (p. 139). The involuntary movements producing eight physical sensations will be described in full in Chapter 6 and show that the practiser, at this stage, is well on the right path. These experiences come automatically and unexpectedly to the practiser who should never intentionally wait for the outcome of his training in order to set his mind at rest. It is like flowing water which forms a channel of itself without outside help.

1. Self-importance, jealousy and desire.
2. See p. 118, Removal of Screens

Hence the ancients' repeated warnings against adding a second head to one's own, for if the mind is set on results, the practice will be handicapped and will lead nowhere.

For the benefit of practisers of T'ien T'ai meditation, we quote below some passages from the book *Yin Shih Tsu's Experimental Meditation for the Promotion of Health* (Yin Shih Tsu Ching Tso Wei Sheng Shih Yen T'an) by the late upāsaka Chiang Wei Ch'iao who was well known for the three books that he wrote after his successful practice of meditation according to the Taoist, T'ien T'ai and Tibetan schools. The above volume is his third book, under his usual *nom de plume* of Yin Shih Tsu, published in Taiwan and Hong Kong after his death on the Chinese mainland a few years ago.

THE CHIH-KUAN DHARMA DOOR

When a practiser sits in meditation, he should keep his body and limbs in the proper position and regulate his breath because his mind is very difficult to control. As man's mind is always accustomed to wander out in search of externals, it is really not easy to collect and hold it. Therefore, he should be very patient in his practice of the chih-kuan Dharma door. After he has made some progress in regulating his body, breath and mind, his training should be complemented with the chih-kuan method. Even if he fails to regulate his body, breath and mind, he can always practise chih-kuan.

Chih is stopping, that is halting the false (and misleading) mind. The mind is like a monkey and does not stop for an instant. What then should we do? We should prevent this monkey from moving by tying it to a stake and it will cease jumping about aimlessly. In the practice of chih, the first step is to fix the mind on an object (hsi yuan chih). When the false mind moves, it looks for something that is called its object. When all of a sudden it thinks of one object, then of another, and then of a third and a fourth; this is its clinging to objects. The purpose of the chih method is to fix the wandering mind to a post in the same way that a monkey is tethered to a stake; this stops it wandering. There are several ways of stopping (chih) the mind but the two usual ones are:

(1) By fixing it on the tip of the nose where the meditator does not see his breath coming in and out, nor its whence and whither; thus his mind will be gradually brought under control, and

(2) By fixing it on the spot just below the navel. As the body's centre of

gravity is in the belly, it is the most appropriate place in which to fix the mind. Then the practiser should visualize each in and out breath as passing in a vertical line from the nostrils down to the belly and vice versa, and as time passes, his wandering mind will be brought automatically to a stop. This exercise also helps to regulate the breath.

When the meditator is familiar with either of these two exercises of fixing the mind on objects, he should practise the (chih) method of restraining it (chih hsin chih). What is this restraining method? We have dealt with the method of tying the mind to (external) objects but the present one consists in grasping at the mind itself. This means that we should look into it to find out where a thought arises, thereby stopping it and preventing it from following externals. This method is much more subtle than the previous one of fixing the mind on an object: this is a shift from a coarse to a subtle exercise.

As a further step, the meditator should practise the (chih) method of embodying the real (t'i chen chih) which is much more advanced than restraining the mind. The first two methods are preliminary and the third one is the real method of stoppage (chih). What is this method of embodying the real? 'Embodying' means understanding or realizing, and 'the real' is but reality. It means close understanding that all passing thoughts belong already to the past as soon as they arise in the mind and are, therefore, unreal and devoid of reality. By not clinging to them, the mind will be void and thus there is no need to stop falsehood which will vanish by itself. When there is no more falsehood, that is reality. As the mind is in this state, this is 'embodying reality'.

The training according to the method of embodying the real consists, while sitting in meditation, in closing the eyes and in turning backward the contemplation to ponder over this human body which grows from childhood to manhood and then to old age and ends in death, and over each of its cells which changes and is replaced by a new one every second, without interruption, and which is, therefore, totally unreal: this shows that there is no reality of an existing ego that can be evidenced.

Then the practiser should turn inwards the contemplation to look into the thoughts that arise in his mind and flow without interruption; he will find that past thoughts have gone, that present ones do not stay and that future ones have not yet come. Then he should ask himself: 'Which of these thoughts is my mind?' Thus he will realize that his false mind which so rises and falls is also unreal and devoid of reality. Gradually, he will become familiar (with this unreality) and his false mind will then come to an end by itself. Where the false mind stops, reality appears.

At the beginning of his meditation, his mind is unsettled and cannot be easily controlled; this is the unsettled mind which always tends to soar. The way to set it at rest is by means of stoppage (chih). If it is stopped again and again, the thinking process will gradually come to an end. A little later, he will be unaware that he is already inclined to drowsiness; this is the sinking mind. The way to awaken it is by contemplation (kuan). Contemplation does not mean looking outwardly; it consists in closing the eyes and turning inwards the contemplation to look into the self-mind. There are three kinds of contemplation (kuan):

(1) Contemplation of the void, which consists in looking into all things within the universe, from the largest including the great earth, mountains and rivers, to the smallest, including his own body and mind; he will perceive that all of them change every instant and are thus non-existent and void. So when his mind looks into this voidness, this is called contemplation of the void.

(2) When he is familiar with this contemplation of the void, he should look into his mind from which thoughts arise and he will find that each thought has its object which is either one thing or another. He will thus realize that all phenomena owe their existence to a union of inner direct cause and outer concurring circumstance.

For instance, a grain of rice sprouts because of a union of inner direct cause which is the seed, with outer concurring condition in the form of the water and mud that moisten and nourish it. If the grain is not sown and is left in the warehouse, it will never sprout because there is only an inner direct cause without an outer concurring condition and for lack of a union of both. If there are only water and mud without the seed being sown, they alone cannot produce the sprout because there is only an outer concurring circumstance without an inner direct cause and for lack of their union. Every phenomenon in the world is created by the union of direct and circumstantial causes and vanishes as soon as they disunite, Likewise, thoughts that rise and fall in the mind cannot be grasped. Contemplation in this manner is called looking into the unreal.

(3) Thus viewed from opposite positions, contemplation of the void pertains to one side and that of the unreal to another. When this stage is reached, the achievement is still incomplete, and the meditator should take a step further with zeal and diligence. When he achieves contemplation of the void, he should not cling to the void and when he achieves contemplation of the unreal, he should not grasp the unreal. When he succeeds in keeping from both extremes, the void and the unreal, his non-relying and non-clinging mind will be really bright; this is called contemplation of the 'mean'.

At first glance, the above chih-kuan Dharma door seems to imply different successive stages. In practice, the employment of either chih or kuan depends solely on the inclination of the mind during the meditation.

As a matter of fact, the purpose of chih is to return all thoughts to one (mind) and that of kuan is clear insight (into the truth for riddance of illusion). When stoppage (chih) is practised, it should not stray from contemplation (kuan) and when contemplation is practised, it should not stray from chih. Readers should not grasp at printed words but should practise the method intelligently according to circumstances.

(II) THE SIX PROFOUND DHARMA DOORS (LU MIAO FA MENG)

(taught by Master Chih I, or Chih Che, at Wa Kuan monastery)

Instead of translating this treatise, which is full of Buddhist terms and may not be very clear to readers unfamiliar with the Mahāyāna, we give below Chapter 6 of *Yin Shih Tsu's Experimental Meditation for the Promotion of Health* (Yin Shih Tsu Ching Tsu Wei Sheng Shih Yen Y'an) which explains clearly the Six Profound Dharma Doors as taught by Master Chih I.

Breath is the source of life. When breath stops, the body is just an (inanimate) corpse, and since the nervous system no longer works, the mind vanishes and life comes to an end. Life (therefore), is preserved by breath which links body with mind and thus ensures its existence.

Though imperceptible to the eyes, the air is actually inhaled and exhaled through the nostrils by the function of breathing. Thus we know that a human being is made of body, breath and mind and that breath plays the important role of uniting the other two components.

The six Profound Dharma Doors centre on breath and are a thorough method of meditation. It can be practised after training in the chih-kuan method as taught in the T'ung Meng Chih Kuan (p. 111), or alone without previous chih-kuan meditation.

This method consists of (1) counting, (2) following, (3) stopping (chih), (4) contemplating (kuan), (5) returning and (6) purifying.

(1) What is counting? This is the counting of breaths, of which there are two phases:

(a) Practice by counting. After a meditator has regulated his breath so that it is neither tight nor loose, he should count slowly, from one to ten, either his inspiration or expiration, choosing whichever he likes, but on no account both. He should fix his attention on this counting so that his mind will not wander elsewhere. If before coming to the number ten, his mind suddenly thinks of something else, he should turn it back and start counting again from one. This is practice by counting.

(b) Realization by counting. As times passes, the meditator becomes familiar with this counting from one to ten which will be orderly, until his breath is so fine that it becomes uncountable. This is realization by counting.

(2) Then he should stop counting and practise the method of following (the breath) of which there are two phases:

(a) Practice by following (the breath). After stopping to count his breath, he should concentrate his mind on following each in and out breath. Thus his mind will accompany his breathing which also follows it until both mind and breath become mutually dependent closely and continuously. This is practice by following (the breath).

(b) Realization by following (the breath). As his mind gradually becomes refined and subtle, the meditator will notice the length of his breath, either long or short, and then will feel as if his breath passes through all the pores of his body. His intellect (or sixth consciousness) is now frozen, quiet and still. This is realization by following the breath.

(3) Gradually the meditator will notice that this method of following the breath is still coarse and should be given up and substituted with the practice of chih (stopping) of which there are two phases:

(a) Practice of chih. After ceasing to follow the breath, the meditator should, as if intentionally yet unintentionally, fix his mind on the tip of his nose. This is the practice of chih (stopping).

(b) In the course of this exercise, the meditator will suddenly perceive that his body and mind seem to vanish completely and he will thereby enter a state of stillness (dhyāna). This is realization by the practice of chih.

(4) At this stage, the meditator should know that though the state of dhyāna is good, he ought to turn back the light of his mind upon itself so that he can be clear about it and will not remain caught in this stillness. Thus he should practise contemplation of which there are two phases:

(a) Practice by contemplation (kuan). In this still state, he should look closely into his refined and subtle inspiration and expiration which are like wind in the void and have no reality of their own. This is the practice of contemplation.

(b) As time passes, little by little, the eye of his mind will open and he will clearly feel as if his breath enters and leaves his body through all its pores. This is realization by contemplation (kuan).

Although the two words chih and kuan are the same here and in the

Śamatha-vipaśyanā for Beginners, there is a slight difference in their meaning, because in that treatise they indicate the control of mind whereas here they concern the regulation of breath.

(5) After a long practice of contemplation, it should be followed by the method of returning, of which there are two phases:

(a) Practice of the returning method. When the mind is set on contemplating the breath, there are created the subjective mind that contemplates and the objective breath that is contemplated, which are the two extremes of a duality and are not in the absolute state; they should, therefore, be returned to the fundamental mind. This is the practice of the returning method.

(b) Since this knower that contemplates (the breath) rises from the mind, it will also follow the mind in its fall. Since rise and fall are fundamentally illusory and unreal, the rising and falling mind is like water that rises in waves; waves are not the water whose fundamental face can be seen only after they have subsided. Therefore, the mind that rises and falls like waves is not the true self-mind. We should look into this true self-mind which is uncreated. As it is uncreated, it is beyond 'is' and is, therefore, void. Since it is void, it follows that there is no subjective mind that contemplates. Since there is no contemplating mind, it also follows that there is no object contemplated. Since knowledge and its object vanish, this is the realization of the returning method.

(6) After this realization, there remains the idea of returning which should be wiped out by meditation on purity of which there are two phases:

(a) Practice of the purifying method. When the mind is pure and clean and ceases discriminating, this is the practice.

(b) Realizing the state of purity. When the mind is still like calm water, with complete absence of false thinking, followed by the manifestation of the real mind which does not exist apart from this false thinking, the return of the false to the real is like subsiding waves that reveal water. This is the realization of purity.

Of the above six Profound Dharma Doors, the counting and following methods are the preliminary practice, the stopping (chih) and contemplating (kuan) methods are the main practice and the returning and purifying methods are the concluding practice. Hence, stopping (chih) is the chief meditation with contemplating (kuan) as its support until clear perception is realized. Only then can returning and purifying bring about the ultimate result.

5

SELF-CULTIVATION ACCORDING TO THE TAOIST SCHOOL

We cannot deal with this subject without mentioning Lao Tsu's *Tao Teh Ching* which is regarded as the most important book of the Taoist school, but which for lack of space we cannot translate here. However, he who understands the first paragraph of the *Tao Teh Ching* has a general idea of the whole teaching in the book which contains more than 5,000 Chinese characters. Its first paragraph reads:

The Tao that can be expressed in words is not the eternal Tao (and) the name (given to it) is not (that of the) eternal. That which cannot be named is the beginning of heaven and earth. That which can be named is the mother of all things. I always look into that which 'is not' (the immaterial) to contemplate (the Tao's) wonders, and into that which 'is' (the material) to contemplate its boundaries. Both 'is not' and 'is' are one and the same, from which all things, with different names, arise. This sameness is wonderful, more than wonderful—the door to all wonders.

Lao Tsu was born in 604 B.C. Named Li Erh and also called Li Po Yang, he was a native of K'u district in Ch'u state (now Hupeh province). He was for a long time a censor under the Chou dynasty, but seeing that it began to decline, he left the country for an unknown destination. At the request of the official defending the pass at the frontier, he wrote the *Tao Teh Ching*. According to the legend then current, he was already old at birth, hence he was called Lao Tsu, or 'Old Son'.

The profound meaning of the first paragraph of the *Tao Teh Ching* is as follows:

The eternal Tao is inexpressible and since it has neither form nor shape, it cannot be called by any name. If a name is arbitrarily given to the eternal Tao, it will be a false one for the eternal is indescribable. *This is the substance of immaterial Tao.*

Though this eternal Tao is immaterial, heaven and earth, that is the material universe, arise from it by transformation, with the creation of all phenomena with different names. *This is the function of immaterial Tao.*

Thus Lao Tsu deals with both the substance and function of eternal Tao. Then he teaches the method of practice for realizing this Tao, saying: 'In practice, I always look into the immaterial aspect of the Tao to contemplate its profundity and wonderfulness, and into phenomena to contemplate their boundaries or manifestations. In other words, I also look into both the substance and function of eternal Tao. Since the immaterial substance of the Tao creates all phenomena which are material and can be called by names, they are all contained in its substance.' Consequently he who looks into its activities can trace them back to their source, or substance: hence, the Tao is all embracing and prevails everywhere. For this reason, Chuang Tsu says: 'The Tao is in grass; it is in excrement and urine.' If contemplation is made in this manner, the wonderful Tao will be perceived.

As Lao Tsu is apprehensive that practisers of his doctrine may cling to the two extremes, the immaterial and material, he warns them: 'Both the immaterial and the material are one and the same.' By this he means: 'When I look into the immaterial, I do not contemplate only its imperceptible substance, but also all phenomena created by and contained in it.

When I look into the material, I do not contemplate merely perceptible forms but also the immaterial from which all phenomena arise.' In other words, a simultanous contemplation of both the immaterial and the material which are of one substance.

Being again apprehensive that they may ask why names are invented if the immaterial and the material are the same, he explains that phenomena rising from the Tao have different forms and are, therefore, called by different names to distinguish them.

He is further apprehensive that they may think that if there really exist the immaterial and the material which show the existence of relativities and contraries, there can never be oneness and sameness; if so, how can the Tao be so wonderful? He explains that when heaven, earth and all things are perceived as arising from the same underlying Tao, their sameness is really wonderful. And to wipe out clinging to the idea of the wonderful, he says: 'More than wonderful.' When all clingings have been eradicated, this wonderful Tao is but 'the door to all wonders'.

If we understand the first paragraph of the *Tao Teh Ching*, we will, without difficulty, comprehend the aim of Lao Tsu's profound teaching in the rest of his work. Commenting on the *Tao Teh Ching*, the Ch'an master Han Shan (1546–1623) wrote:

Lao Tsu teaches the immaterial self-existing Tao which the Śūraṅgama Sūtra describes as the non-differentiating that is neither form nor voidness, or the substance of the eighth consciousness (ālaya-vijñāna). This non-discriminating consciousness is very subtle, wonderful and unfathomable and can be looked through only by the Buddha who transmutes it into the Great Mirror Wisdom. . . . This Tao is neither form because it is extensive nor voidness for it creates all things. . . . He who studies the works of Lao Tsu and Chuang Tsu should first understand the Śūraṅgama Sūtra in which the Enlightened One broke up all worldly attachments, and then practise the right dhyāna correctly, before he can be clear about Lao Tsu's great achievement.

The enlightened master also wrote: *The meaning of the Tao Teh Ching can be grasped only after one has had a personal experience of it. . . . When writing a commentary on a sūtra, I would concentrate my mind in order to see into it and be in accord with the Buddha-mind. By so doing, the clue to the correct meaning would jump out instantly and I would write it down on paper. If the thinking process had been involved, it would not have served the purpose.*

Lao Tsu only reached the state of ālaya-vijñāna or store consciousness, an aspect of the self-mind which is deceived by the illusion of voidness and is still free from discrimination. Unfortunately, he did not meet the Buddha and was unable to transmute this state into the Great Mirror Wisdom. According to Han Shan, Lao Tsu was determined to revive the ancient traditions prevalent at the time of emperor Huang Ti (2698–2597 B.C.) and left the country when the dynasty began to decline. Since Huang Ti was the founder of Taoism which Lao Tsu later revived, it is called the doctrine of Huang-Lao. The method of Taoist meditation was, therefore, known in China long before Lao Tsu and was responsible for the high spirituality of the followers of this school. The great Indian masters who foresaw the decline of the Buddha Dharma in their own country, came to the East to spread it in this promised land where Taoism already prospered and where its adherents were mature to awaken to the Mahāyāna and Ch'an Transmission. It is a matter for regret that even today some people still hold the wrong view that Taoism is heretical and should be discarded entirely when studying the Buddha Dharma. They forget that in the practice of the Dharma they should first realize the eighth consciousness in order to transmute it into the Great Mirror Wisdom. The stage of ālaya-vijñāna is, therefore, one through which they must pass to realize Complete Enlightenment. The question is whether they stay in this state and regard it as final achievement or strive to advance further to attain bodhi.

We present below the method of Taoist meditation practised by Yin Shih Tsu as related in his first volume published in 1914.

TAOIST MEDITATION

From Yin Shih Tsu's Method of Meditation
(Yin Shih Tsu Ching Tso Fa)

I. THE MODE OF PRACTICE

There are two important points with regard to the practice of Taoist meditation: regulating the bodily posture and the breath.

A. REGULATING THE BODILY POSTURE

1. Before and after the meditation

(i) Meditation should be made in a quiet place or in the bedroom, the door of which should be closed to avoid interference from outside but its windows should be wide open (to let in more fresh air).

(ii) The meditating cushion should be soft and thick, suitable for a long sitting.

(iii) The meditator should untie his clothes and loosen his belt to avoid restraining his body and limbs.

(iv) The body should be erect and the backbone straight.

(v) After the meditation, the eyes should be opened slowly and the limbs relaxed.

2. The position of the legs

(i) The full lotus posture consists in placing the left leg upon the right one and then the right leg upon the left one. This is the best posture for it presses the (sides of the) knees on the cushion, thereby ensuring a stabilized erect body which does not lean to the right or left and forward or backward. It is, however, not easy for beginners and is very difficult for old people.

(ii) The meditator can, however, take the half lotus posture by placing either the left leg on the right one or the right leg on the left one as he likes.

This posture has its defect, for if the left leg is placed on the right one, the (side of the) left knee cannot rest on the cushion, and it is very easy for the body to lean to the right. If the right leg is placed on the left one, the (side of the) right knee cannot rest on the cushion, and it is easy for the body to lean to the left. If beginners cannot take the full lotus posture, that of the half lotus will fulfil the same purpose provided they keep the body erect and the effectiveness will be the same as in the case of the full lotus posture.

(iii) The two thighs are thus like the (two connecting) sides of a triangle and when they rest comfortably on the cushion, the centre of gravity of the body will automatically be under the navel.

(iv) Beginners usually develop numb legs but if they can endure this numbness, it will finally disappear.

(v) Those who cannot endure the cramp, can change the position of the legs and should they be unable to endure further, they can stop sitting temporarily and sit again after its disappearance.

(vi) If they stubbornly refuse to give way to this unbearable numbness of the legs, they will in time overcome it; after passing through this crucial stage, their legs will never be numb again in subsequent sittings.

3. The chest, buttocks and belly

(i) The chest should bend slightly forward to lower the pit of the stomach, thereby relaxing the diaphragm. Usually when the centre of gravity of the body is unstable, the vital principle (prāṇa) rises to the pit of the stomach which beginners feel to be blocked and not at ease. This shows that the pit of the stomach has not been brought down. In such a case, the meditator should concentrate his mind on the lower belly to relax the diaphragm. As time passes, the pit of the stomach will be lowered automatically, without any effort being made, thus ensuring the stability of the centre of gravity.

(ii) The buttocks should be slightly pushed back to straighten the spine. The backbone is curved like a bow and bends out in the region of the buttocks; its natural position should be maintained during the meditation but force should never be used.

(iii) The lower part of the belly should be stable so as to stabilize the centre of gravity of the body. This is possible by concentrating on the lower belly but without the use of force. To obtain the desired result, the meditator should banish all thoughts from his mind and then fix it on the spot about one and three quarter inches below the navel; the centre of gravity will thus settle down by itself.

4. The two hands

(i) The hands should be placed upon each other, drawn near the lower belly and laid on the lower legs.

(ii) The hand above should be held lightly by the one below, with crossed thumbs.

(iii) Either the left hand lightly holds the right one or vice versa, as the meditator likes.

(iv) The hands can be either drawn against the lower belly or placed on the crossed legs as the meditator likes.

(v) Strain should be avoided so that the hands and fingertips are relaxed and at ease.

5. The face, ears, eyes, mouth and breath

(i) The head and neck should be erect, facing forward.

(ii) The ears should be kept free from hearing voices and sounds.

(iii) The eyes should be lightly shut. Some people urge slightly opened eyes probably to avoid drowsiness, but if the meditator is not inclined to drowse, it is better to close them in order to ensure stillness of mind.

(iv) The mouth should be closed, with the tongue touching the palate to make a bridge (along which prāṇa can move from the nose to the throat).

(v) The meditator should breathe through the nostrils and avoid opening the mouth while breathing.

6. The mental state during meditation

(i) The meditator should lay down everything and abstain from giving rise to thoughts. The field of our intellect is like a play and every thought an actor. Our thoughts rise and fall suddenly just as actors appear and disappear continually on the stage. It is therefore very difficult to put an end to rising thoughts. If we succeed in fixing our attention effectively on some spot (in the body), the thinking process will be kept under control. And so if we concentrate effectively on the centre of gravity in the body, all thinking will gradually come to an end.

(ii) The meditator should introvert so that all false thoughts cease of themselves.

We have mentioned abstention from giving rise to thoughts but the very idea of so abstaining is also a thought. It is, therefore, far better to employ the introverting method which is also called 'looking into the innermost'. In general, when a man sees something, his eyes are directed towards external objects; they therefore cannot be turned inward to look into the internal. Our method consists of closing the eyes for the purpose of turning inward our attention to examine our intellect; first we should be clear about the rise and fall of our thoughts. If a thought rises, it should be looked into to prevent it from clinging to things; thus it will vanish. When a second thought rises, it should also be looked into so that it cannot grasp anything; thus the second one will vanish. When their source is properly cleansed, thoughts will gradually come to an end.

A beginner usually holds the wrong view that before his practice of meditation his thoughts were very few and that after it they become numerous. This is a mistake for these thoughts always rise and fall in his mind; they were not noticed before but are now perceptible during meditation. Awareness of the existence of thoughts is the first step in self-awareness, and with the repeated exercise of this introverting method our thoughts will gradually decrease in number, instead of increasing as we wrongly think.

(iii) Although meditation can cure illness and improve health, the practiser should never give rise to a desire for these results (so as not to disturb his mind).

(iv) He should avoid being impatient for quick results and should always take a natural attitude, like a small boat with neither sail nor paddle which follows leisurely the course of a stream.

(v) During the meditation, though his eyes are closed and cannot see objects, it is not easy for him to abstain from hearing sounds that disturb his mind. He should, therefore, turn inwards both his seeing and hearing and pay no attention to sounds and voices; if he so trains effectively he will, as time passes, be able to remain unperturbed even if a mountain falls down in front of him.

(vi) He should have boundless faith in his meditation, like a devotee in his religion. At the start, he usually does not feel at ease while sitting. He should be very determined in his training and continue it without interruption. As time passes, his meditation will become effective. His success, therefore, depends solely on his faith.

7. The duration of meditation

(i) When the efficiency of the meditation reaches its profound stage, it should be maintained at all times, while walking, standing, sitting or reclining. However, beginners should choose the time for their meditation; the most favourable moments are after getting up in the morning and before going to bed in the evening. The minimum requirement is one meditation a day.

(ii) (In principle) the longer a meditation lasts, the better is its result. However, meditation should be natural and the practiser should avoid straining himself to lengthen its duration. If he can sit for thirty minutes and do so regularly without interruption, he will in time obtain very good results.

(iii) It is advisable for those who are busy to sit for forty minutes; if they can sit for an hour, they will obtain better results.

(iv) Morning and evening are the most favourable times. However, if the practiser (is busy and) can only meditate once a day, it is advisable to do so after getting up in the morning.

(v) Each evening, before going to bed, if he can make another short meditation for fifteen or twenty minutes, he will make quicker progress. Thus his main meditation will be in the morning with a secondary one in the evening.

(vi) Each morning, when the practiser gets up, he should, before leaving his bed, massage the upper and lower parts of his belly and regulate his breath before going to the lavatory; he can then make his morning meditation. It is advisable to begin after easing nature in the morning, but since each man has his own habit, there is no rigid rule.

B. REGULATING THE BREATH

Breathing is the function of life and is most important. Man knows only that food and drink preserve life and that the lack of them causes death. He does not realize that breathing is more important than eating and drinking. He thinks that food and drink are precious because they can be bought with money which can only be earned by hard work. As to breathing, since air is available everywhere, is inexhaustible and is free of charge, it is not regarded as precious. However, if he stops eating, he can still live at least seven days whereas if his nostrils (and mouth) are closed so that he stops breathing, he will die in no time. Breathing is, therefore, more important than eating and drinking.

There are two kinds of breathing: natural and correct which are described below.

1. Natural breathing

An inhalation and an exhalation make a complete breath. The breathing organs consist of the outer nose and inner lungs. These lungs are in the chest and expand and contract when one breathes naturally. Usually man's breath does not expand and contract the lungs to their full capacity; only their upper parts dilate and shrink whereas their lower parts remain intact. Then, since a full supply of oxygen cannot be breathed in nor all the carbon dioxide breathed out, the blood cannot be completely purified, so that all kinds of illness follow. This is the evil effect of unnatural breathing.

Natural breathing, also called abdominal respiration, comprises an inhalation which reaches to and an exhalation (which starts from) the lower belly. When breathing in, the air enters and fills all parts of the lungs, expanding them below and pressing down the diaphragm; the chest will thus be relaxed and the belly will expand. When breathing out, the belly contracts and pushes the diaphragm up to the lungs, thus forcing out all the impure air. It is, therefore, necessary that the respiratory function which expands and contracts the lungs should harmonize with the movements of the belly and diaphragm to accord with the law of nature and to ensure free circulation of the blood. This method of breathing should be followed not only while sitting in meditation, but also at all times, while walking, standing, sitting and reclining.

The breath should be regulated thus:

(i) When breathing out, the lower belly below the navel contracts, pushing up the diaphragm and squeezing the chest, thereby emptying all the impure air from the lungs.

(ii) When breathing in, fresh air enters through the nostrils, slowly filling the lungs and pressing down the diaphragm; the lower part of the belly will then expand.

(iii) Inhalation and exhalation should be gradually deep and continuous, reaching the lower belly which will then be tight and full. Some people advise that the breath be held in the belly for a few seconds but according to my personal experience, beginners should not do so.

(iv) The in and out breaths should be slow, continuous and fine, and this should be practised until the breath becomes imperceptible.

(v) When the above result is achieved, the breath seems to have vanished in spite of the presence of the respiratory organs which seem to be useless; the practiser thus feels as if his breath comes in and out through the pores all over his body. This is the highest attainment in the art of breathing, but beginners should avoid exertion so that their breathing can be natural.

2. Correct breathing

Correct breathing, also called reverse respiration, is deep and fine, reaching also the belly like natural breathing but with contrary expanding and shrinking movements of the lower abdomen and with the diaphragm being pushed up or pressed down for the same purpose. It is called reverse respiration because it is the opposite of natural breathing and is regulated as follows:

(i) The exhalation should be slow and continuous while the lower belly expands; as a result, the latter will be firm and full.

(ii) The region below the navel will be full of the vital principle, the chest will be hollow and relaxed and the diaphragm slack.

(iii) The inspiration should be deep and continuous to fill to its full capacity the chest which will expand, with simultaneous contraction of the lower belly.

(iv) Being pressed down by the air that fills the lungs and pushed up by the contracting belly, the diaphragm will become more active.

(v) While the chest is expanding, the belly, though contracted, is not hollow.

While breathing in and out, the centre of gravity should be in the belly below the navel so that it becomes stable.

(vi) Breath should be still, fine and inaudible even to the meditator himself.

While the ancients postulated a longer duration for inhalation than for exhalation, the modern man urges the opposite, but in my experience, the same duration for both is the most appropriate.

From the above, we can see that in either natural or correct respiration, the purpose is to make the diaphragm more appropriately active. Correct breathing is to make the belly expand and contract by unnatural means so that the diaphragm can tighten and that its movements are easier.

When I began my practice of meditation, I found correct breathing very suitable for me and this is why I mentioned it in the first edition of this book. Since its publication, some readers wrote to me that they were unable to practise it. If it is not suitable for every meditator, I would advise my readers to practise natural breathing which is free from all impediments.

3. The breathing exercise

No matter whether natural or correct breathing is practised, the essentials of the exercise are the same:

(i) The lotus posture should be taken as during a meditation.

(ii) The breath should be short at the start and lengthened gradually.

(iii) It should be slow and fine, inaudible and deep, and gently brought down to reach the lower belly.

(iv) It should come in and out through the nostrils, but never through the mouth.

(v) As soon as the practiser is familiar with the exercise, he will be able without any strain to lengthen his breath gradually until each inhalation and exhalation together last a full minute.

(vi) Every day, fine and inaudible breathing should be practised at all times without interruption.

(vii) During the meditation, all thoughts should be banished for if attention is fixed on breathing, the mind cannot be quieted. It is, therefore, advisable to practise the breathing exercise before and after each meditation.

(viii) This breathing exercise, before and after each meditation, should be made where there is abundance of pure air and should last from five to ten minutes.

4. The lowering of the pit of the stomach in relation to breathing

We have already dealt with the meditative posture in which the pit of the stomach is lowered. In the breathing exercise, the lowering of the pit of the stomach is more important for regulating the breath, thereby ensuring the effectiveness of the meditation itself. Readers should pay attention to the following points:

(i). At the start of the breathing exercise, a beginner usually feels that the pit of his stomach is firm and interferes with his breath which cannot be regulated; this is caused by the diaphragm not being able to move up and down freely. He should overcome this difficulty with determination.

(ii) He should avoid exertion when his breath is so obstructed, and should let it take its natural course by fixing his attention gently on the lower belly.

(iii) He should relax his chest so that the circulation of blood will not bring pressure upon the heart; thus the pit of the stomach will be lowered automatically.

(iv) As time passes, his diaphragm will be relaxed and his breath will be fine and continuous, with every inhalation reaching and exhalation (starting from) the centre of gravity below the navel. This is the proof that the pit of the stomach has been (effectively) lowered.

C. VIBRATION IN THE BELLY

(i) A long practice of meditation usually results in (a kind of) vibration being felt in the lower belly below the navel, this shows that the belly is full of (psychic) force.

(ii) Over ten days before this vibration is felt, the meditator experiences some heat moving in the belly below the navel.

(iii) After this heat has been felt for some times, suddenly the lower belly vibrates and the whole body shakes; the meditator should not be scared but should let this state take its natural course.

(iv) The speed and length of this vibration differs for each individual; it just happens and should neither be sought nor repressed.

(v) When this vibration is felt, the meditator should imagine (but without exertion) that the hot force (goes down and) passes through the coccyx and then rises up the spine until it reaches and passes through the top of the head, thence coming down through the face, the (chest and the) pit of the stomach to return to the belly below the navel. (This channel from the coccyx to the pit of the stomach does not open at once; it may take a few months or even a year after the first vibration. Readers should not be mistaken about this.)

As time passes, this moving heat will go up and down of itself and can, by imagination, be spread to all parts of the body, reaching even the nails and the ends of the hair, with the result that the whole body is warm and unusually comfortable.

The cause of this vibration is very profound and is not easily explainable. Most probably, with free circulation of the blood and an accumulation of (psychic) force in the belly below the navel, this concentration of strength causes the movements which produce the heat. But it is not easy to explain why this force rises up the backbone to the top of the head and then descends to return to the navel. As a matter of fact, I have personally experienced this phenomenon and cannot deny it. (This is what the ancients called 'free passage through the three gates', the first gate in the coccyx, the second in the backbone between the kidneys and the third in the occiput.)

The ancient explanations of this phenomenon are many but the most rational one, though it cannot be called strictly scientific, is this: 'The foetus in the womb does not breathe through the nostrils but its inner vital principle circulates by rising up the backbone to the head and then descending to the navel; this is called foetal breathing. At birth (after the cutting of the navel-cord) this circulation ceases and is replaced by respiration through the nostrils. Therefore, after a long meditation, the practiser can make use of the circulation of the vital principle to restore the foetal breath.'

D. MY PERSONAL EXPERIENCE

1. My childhood

As a child I was always ill, emaciated and bony. At twelve, I foolishly indulged in self-abuse which was later the cause of involuntary emissions, headache, lumbago, dizziness, buzzing in the ears and sweating at night, followed by other illnesses. I was ignorant and did not know the origin of all this. When I was thirteen and fourteen, I began to know a little, but was not at all clear about it. At times I broke off, but then renewed this bad habit, did not tell anyone about it and continued to be ill. We lived only two or three miles from a town, but when I went there with my brothers my legs were so weak that I could not walk. When I returned home, I would perspire profusely six or seven times that night. This was the state of my delicate health as a child.

2. My youth

When I was seventeen my spells of illness became more frequent and I was also troubled by nervousness and palpitation. I can still remember how in the spring I went down every afternoon with fever which vanished the next morning, so that I was always ill and perplexed. In spite of all this, however, I was a diligent scholar, studying my books late into the night as if nothing was wrong. As a result I became weaker and iller.

3. My motive for meditating.

When my illness became serious, I sought its cure by all means. But since we lived in the country, only herbalists were available, whose remedies were useless and I loathed them. Though I did not mention my illness to others, my late father discovered its origin and urged me to read books on spiritual culture. (One day) he showed me the book *I Fang Chi Chiai* (The Ancient Medical Formulas Explained), the last section of which deals with the Taoist technique called 'The Microcosmic Orbit'.[1] (After reading this), unexpectedly I awakened to the teaching, practised it and was relieved from my predicament, but I lacked perseverance. When I fell ill again, I was scared and being frightened, I practised the method again, but after my recovery I was lazy and forgot all about my practice. Nevertheless I had learnt that I should care for my body and never again did anything that could injure it. Since my nineteenth year, though I could not completely rid myself of illness, I felt I was much stronger than in my childhood.

4. Resumption of my practice of meditation

I was married at twenty-two and feeling that my health was stronger I stopped meditating. As I failed to curb my sexual desires, all my former illnesses returned together to harass me. In addition, my intemperate habit of eating and drinking brought on a dilated stomach and inflammation of the gullet which excited me and caused me always to think of eating, but whatever food I brought to my mouth seemed disgusting and was immediately rejected. My friends urged me to rest to take care of my health but seeing no harm in all this, I remained undecided.

In the spring of 1899, my second brother died from consumption. The following year, I suffered from a bad cough and soon after spat blood. I took Chinese medicine but my illness turned serious and continued for three months. I was frightened that I might soon follow my deceased brother. I then threw away all medicines, separated from my family, stayed in a quiet room, retired from the world, remained indifferent to everything and resumed my practice of meditation. I was then twenty-eight.

5. Time-table for my meditation

I fixed a time-table for my daily meditations. Early in the morning, between three and four o'clock, I got up and sat in meditation on my bed for one or two hours. Then I got up, washed, rinsed my mouth, took a little food and went out for a stroll, facing the rising sun. When I reached an open space outside the wall of the town, I stayed there to breathe in fresh air. Between seven and eight, I returned to my room, breakfasted and rested for one or two hours during which I leisurely read the books of Lao Tsu and Chuang Tsu and Buddhist sūtras. After ten I sat in meditation. At midday I took my

1. Explained in full in Chapter 7—Physical and Spiritual Culture according to Chinese Yoga.

lunch after which I paced in my room. At three in the afternoon I played a seven-string lute for amusement or went out for a stroll. At six I again sat in meditation and supped at seven. After eight I again paced my room, sat in meditation at nine and went to bed at ten. I kept strictly to this time-table.

6. Difficulties at the beginning of my practice

As I was impatient to get well, I worked very hard at my practice. Each time I sat in meditation, all kinds of thoughts rose in my mind and the more I strove to stop them, the more numerous they became. I then tried to regulate my breath but soon felt that it became laboured as if there was some obstruction in my chest. Nevertheless I believed firmly that meditation was of great value and I was determined to practise unremittingly. As a result I became very tired and was on the point of giving it all up. But some of my neighbours were elders who knew the art of meditation, so I told them of my difficulties. They all said: 'You are wrong. Your practice should be natural and whether you walk, stand, sit or recline, you should be natural about it. It is useless just to sit like a log.' These words woke me up and since then, each time I sat in meditation, I took a natural attitude. When I felt some uneasiness, I got up slowly from my seat, paced my room and sat again when my body and mind were at ease. Thus three months later, all my difficulties disappeared gradually and were replaced progressively by better (mental) states.

7. The first vibration

Since the 4th of April 1900 when I began my meditation, in spite of difficulties, I practised daily without interruption until it gradually became natural. At the same time, my health improved day by day. Previously when I went out for a stroll, my legs became so weak after walking one or two Chinese miles that I could not go further, but now when I set out, I could do ten miles without feeling tired. Each time, as soon as I sat in meditation, I felt a kind of hot vibration in my lower belly under the navel, I was surprised at this unusual experience. On the evening of the 25th of June of the same year, my lower belly vibrated suddenly and though I sat with crossed legs as usual, I could hardly keep this position as my whole body trembled violently. I felt this hot energy thrust through the coccyx and rise up the backbone until it reached the top of the head. This started some eighty-five days after my first experience on the 4th of April and lasted for six days after which the vibration gradually ceased. I was stunned by it all.

After that, each time I sat in meditation I felt this heat rise to the top of my head, thus following the same path but without vibrating as previously. At the same time I was completely relieved from my old ailments such as nervousness, palpitation, lumbago, headache, buzzing in the ears, dizziness, coughing and spitting blood. Although my stomach was still dilated, it did not worsen.

8. The second and third vibrations

All through 1900 I retired from the world to practise meditation and kept three rules: abstention from (sexual) desires to develop vitality, from speech to invigorate breath and from gazing to raise my spirits. I took note of my daily progress: the preliminary period from April to June was full of difficulty and trouble; June and July were noted for the gradual cure of my illnesses, while from that August my meditation became more effective. I could then sit for three hours at a stretch during which my body and mind seemed to be replaced by the great void free from a single speck of dust and in which I did not even feel the presence of myself; as a result, I experienced very great comfort.

The following year, I had to work for my living and since I could not devote all my time to meditation, I practised it twice a day, in the morning and evening, without interruption.

On the 5th of May 1902, during my morning meditation, I felt the heat vibrating again in my lower belly, exactly as in June 1900 except that, instead of thrusting through the coccyx, it thrust through the upper 'gate' in the back of the head. This lasted for three days, causing my crown to ache. I was not scared and suddenly my crown seemed to split, with the heat winding its way around the spot. Henceforth in every subsequent meditation, I had the same experience but the vibration ceased completely. This was my experience of the second vibration.

On the 4th of November of the same year, in my evening meditation, I again felt vibration in my lower belly, and the heat, after winding round the crown, went down along my face and my chest to return to the lower belly under the navel; thereupon, the vibration came to a stop. This was my experience of the third vibration.

After that, each time I sat in meditation, the heat rose up the backbone to the crown and then descended, passing through the face and chest to return to beneath the navel before repeating the circuit. If I happened to catch cold and felt unwell, I simply directed this heat all over my body until it reached even my fingertips and hairs to produce profuse perspiration, at which the cold vanished. After this all my former ailments disappeared for ever. Each time I climbed the mountain with friends, I did not feel tired even after covering several tens of Chinese miles of mountain paths. What was of real interest to me was that in the summer of the same year, in a walking contest with a friend, we covered ninety Chinese miles from Chiang Yin, which we left in the early morning, to Wu Chin where we arrived at four in the afternoon. I did not feel tired though we walked all the way under a hot sun.

9. Over twenty years' experience.

When I began my meditation at the age of seventeen, I did not believe much in its efficacy; I practised it only because I was very scared of my illnesses. When I read Taoist books, I found they were full of (technical terms such as) yin and yang (the female or negative and the male or positive principles), the five elements (metal, wood, water, fire and earth), the k'an and li diagrams (of the Book of Changes) and the elixir of immortality, which were all beyond my comprehension. For this reason, I did not attach much importance to meditation which I only practised at intervals. When I was twenty-eight it became my regular exercise because of my lung disease. Being a practical man, I thought that this practice was to preserve vitality by preventing its dissipation, thereby uprooting all illnesses. I did not pay much attention to the ancient (method of) invigorating the field of immortality (tan t'ien)[1] and did not believe in the so-called 'free passages through the three gates'. But when I thrice experienced bodily vibrations which were a fact, I realized that the Tao was inexhaustible and that there were many things which our (limited) intelligence could never reach. Thus I came to the conclusion that the ancient teachings should never be rejected as entirely unreliable.

The ancients spoke of 'inner efficiency' (nei kung) as the best method of improving health,[2] but its preliminary steps were not handed down openly (except by word of mouth from teacher to disciple). After the Ch'in (897-295 B.C.) and Han (205 B.C.-A.D. 220) dynasties the Taoists formulated their theory of Immortality, grouping themselves into sects according to their methods of practice, but their aim was similar to Lao Tsu's attainment of stillness and to the Buddha's dhyāna-samādhi. Unfortunately their methods of practice are (now) unknown and are regarded as mysterious.

From 1903 when I came to Shanghai until the publication of (the first edition of) this book (in 1914) when I was forty-two, I practised meditation regularly, twice a day, in the morning and evening. For over ten years, with rare exceptions when I had piles or some external complaint, I would pass each year without suffering from an illness. My recent studies of books on philosophy, psychology, physiology and hygiene have thrown new light on the practice of meditation. I have, therefore, found that the main purpose of meditation is to use the power of mind to guide the body in such a way as to ensure the unhindered circulation of the blood.

As set out in my previous time-table, each morning I walked eastwards

1. In the lower belly under the navel.
2. See Chapter 7—Physical and spiritual culture according to Chinese yoga.

facing the rising sun, to breathe fresh air and absorb solar energy; this accords well with modern hygiene which recommends a sun-bath and open air; moreover sunlight destroys bacteria and is most effective in curing lung diseases. My daily strolls were to relax my legs which had become numb during the meditation; this accords well with modern hygiene which recommends outdoor exercise and sports. Therefore, there is nothing strange or mysterious in the practice of meditation.

There are authentic historical records of Ch'en T'uan (a Taoist) who retired on Hua Shan mountain where he sometimes ceased all mental activities for over a hundred successive days without leaving his (meditation) bed, and of Bodhidharma who faced a wall for nine years. Then in my neighbourhood were elders who practised meditation and were healthy and vigorous in spite of their years. Taoist records show clearly that all immortals began their training with meditation and then achieved spiritual 'metamorphosis'. Therefore, the art of meditation is but the first step (in the training) and, since it enabled me to rid myself so wonderfully of all my ailments, we can conclude that the attainment of immortality as advocated by Taoists is within the bounds of possibility. However, I have not attained this (immortal) state and being a practical man, I do not deal with achievements which I have not realized and every word in this book is well supported by actual facts.

10. The secret of 'forgetfulness'

When I began my practice of meditation, I sought quick results and my time-table was consequently complicated. I would, however, urge readers not to copy it but to practise twice a day, in the morning and evening, in order to avoid unnecessary troubles. As to meditation being 'natural', this is the most important thing and I must deal with it here again. In order to make it natural, nothing can surpass the secret of the word 'forgetfulness'. For instance, if the meditation is aimed at curing an illness, the practiser should forget all about the thought of curing it and if it is for improving health, he should forget all about the idea of improvement, because when mind and objects are forgotten, everything will be void and the result thus achieved will be the proper one. For the efficacy of meditation lies in the gradual transformation of body and mind. If the thoughts of curing an illness and of improving health are clung to, the mind will be stirred and no result can be expected. I made this mistake when I began my practice and now urge readers to avoid it.

11. Avoidance of impatience for quick results

Since my friends knew that I had succeeded in recovering from illness by means of meditation, I received visitors who asked me to teach them, but of the hundreds and thousands of them, only one or two achieved results.

Their failure came from their impatient desire for quick results. They only saw that I had achieved good results but did not realize that my success was due to my perseverance, not to my impatience for quick results. Most students were quite serious at the start of their practice but (abruptly) dropped it when they did not find it as effective as expected; some even thought that I had secrets which I refused to reveal. In general, this impatience ends in negative results. They did not know that meditation is used to cultivate and nourish body and mind. This kind of nourishment is similar to that provided by food. For instance, everybody knows that food nourishes the body but if he wants to obtain quick results and eats more than he can digest, thus impairing his stomach, will he then stop eating altogether? This practice is like a long journey on foot; the traveller, by walking step by step, arrives finally at his destination.

12. Vibration bearing no relation to the effectiveness of meditation

We have dealt with vibrations in the body which manifest long after the meditator has begun his daily practice. Whether they are present or not and quick or slow depends on the physical constitution of each individual. It is wrong to discontinue the meditation if it is thought to be ineffective solely because of the lack of vibrations. It is also wrong to be frustrated when seeing others experiencing vibrations which one does not feel. Because of the difference in bodily constitutions, there are those who feel them only a few months after starting their practice of meditation; others who feel them after a few years of practice; and those who do not feel them even after several years of meditation during which their bodies and minds have been transmuted satisfactorily. Therefore, we know that vibrations bear no relation to the efficiency of meditation.

13. Relation between meditation and sleep

(Chinese) doctors tell us that every man should sleep eight hours a night. They also say that it is wrong for husband and wife to share the same bed because both breathe out carbonic acid which pollutes the air and is the cause of contagion if one of them falls ill. The same rule applies to meditation which should be practised every evening between nine and ten. The practiser should go to bed at ten and get up at six the following morning; it is advisable for him to sleep in a single bed. In 1900 when I began to practise meditation, I achieved very quick results because I abstained from sexual desires for the whole year. Since then, I have always slept alone, although I have not avoided sexual desires completely.

14. Relation between meditation and food

Doctors rightly say that over-eating should be avoided, that meals should be taken at fixed hours and that food should be chewed well and swallowed slowly. We Chinese are good eaters, and an ancient poem said: 'Strive to eat more . . .' Nowadays, when meeting a friend and enquiring after his health, we always ask: 'How many bowls of rice do you take?' The general idea is that the more one eats, the more healthy one is, but we overlook the fact that over-eating causes indigestion which produces other illnesses. Children are encouraged by their parents to take their meals as quickly as possible but they do not realize that food is not properly masticated if eaten quickly. Thus the function of chewing, which should be done by the teeth, is passed on to the stomach and intestines which are overworked and so become ill. The teeth which do not work enough become decayed. If people do not feed at fixed hours, they are always inclined to eat cakes, dumplings, etc., at any time, thus wasting gastric juice and causing stomach trouble. When I was young, I used to eat too much, quickly and at irregular hours, and thereby suffered from a dilated stomach, but once I began my practice of meditation, I gradually realized my error. The meals which I now take represent only a third of what I used to eat. In the morning, I have a glass of milk instead of a full breakfast. Before, though I ate too much, I always felt hungry, but now that I eat much less, I am always satisfied and am much stronger. I now realize that in the old days when I felt hungry, it was not real hunger but an abnormal reaction from my stomach which was accustomed to always being full. It is, therefore, advisable to eat within certain limits, to chew the food well and to swallow it slowly in order to help digestion; this is a rule that cannot be changed.

After the publication of his first book, Yin Shih Tsu received many letters from those who followed and practised his method of meditation. We present below some of their questions and the author's answers which may interest practisers of meditation in the West.

Question. After practising meditation for some time, I have not experienced the inner heat and vibration in the belly but have noticed that my body has been swaying to the right and the left. This happened only a few days after I began my practice; what does it mean?
Answer. This swaying of the body shows that your meditation takes effect, but its effectiveness does not necessarily depend on the inner heat and vibration in the belly. When your meditation is really effective, these will manifest themselves but not after a short period of practice.

Q. Is it true that in each meditation you feel the inner heat that circulates clockwise in your body?
A. Yes.

Q. Can one do hard work after and before each meditation?
A. Yes, but not immediately. After working hard, one should walk about slowly to relax before sitting in meditation at the end of which one should slowly open the eyes and relax the limbs.

Q. Should one close the eyes while sitting in meditation?
A. To close the eyes is to ensure stillness of mind. When one feels tired after a day of hard work, one can open them a little to avoid falling into drowsiness. But it is advisable to close the eyes and direct them inwards to look into one's inner self.

Q. What should I do to rid myself of the pain in my loins after sitting in meditation, which prevents me from continuing my practice?
A. This is because you are not accustomed to sitting in meditation or is most probably due to lumbago. If you do not strain yourself and take a natural attitude, the pain will disappear.

Q. What should I do to get rid of rising thoughts that prevent me from sitting in meditation?
A. Count your breath to control your thinking process.

Q. Is it necessary to concentrate on the lower belly?
A. At the beginning, it is not easy to make this concentration; therefore (the mind) should be brought down gradually until it reaches the lower belly.

Q. I have no time in the morning; may I practise meditation at night?
A. Yes, but after a long day of hard work, you may feel tired and sleepy at night; if so, it is advisable to practise in the morning.

Q. What do you mean by lowering the pit of the stomach? What does it look like?
A. If you concentrate on the lower belly, your chest will be empty and relaxed; this shows that the pit of the stomach has been lowered. Seen from outside, the region immediately below the chest is hollow while the belly bulges.

Q. I began my meditation in March and all my illnesses disappeared gradually in May, so that my health improved and I thought I was rid of all my ailments. But in the middle of June, I suddenly had an involuntary emission which was something new. What is the cause of this and does it show a bad state of health, or does it come from some former illnesses which have recurred with my practice of meditation?
A. It is illogical to attribute involuntary emission to the practice of meditation. Probably your health was poor before, hence the absence of these emissions, but with its improvement, the excess of generative fluid

caused its emission. I can assure you that this is not due to your practice of meditation. You should avoid stirring your mind by banishing all thoughts of sexual desire and then you will get rid of the cause. However, if involuntary emission is not due to self-abuse, it is not harmful.

Q. When I began my practice in early February, my thoughts were very numerous but a few months later, I made some progress and was sometimes entirely free from them for a full minute during which I felt as if I had entered the great emptiness. But now I cannot control myself and am assailed by thoughts; I do not feel at ease and am almost on the point of stopping my practice. What should I do?
A. If while sitting in meditation you can free yourself from thoughts for a full minute, this is a very good sign and you should strive to preserve this state. If you persevere in your practice, you will be able to rid yourself of them. The best way to achieve this is to turn inward your meditation to contemplate the source of these thoughts and when you realize that there is no fixed place where they arise, you will attain the state of thoughtlessness.

Q. My legs are always numb after I have sat in meditation for thirty minutes. I am unable to get rid of this numbness which now seems more unbearable than before. What should I do to be free of it?
A. This numbness is unavoidable. It is like physical exercise which causes one's limbs to ache at the start. There are two ways of getting rid of it: firstly, when it is unbearable, move and stretch your legs to relax them, and secondly, try to bear it until it becomes imperceptible for it will vanish of itself. If you can bear it in this way for a few sittings, your legs will be no more numb and you will then be able to sit for one or two hours without further difficulty.

Q. During meditation, if saliva flows, should I spit or swallow it?
A. This is a very good sign; you should swallow it. According to the ancient (Taoist) method, one should roll the tongue round the mouth to make saliva flow and then swallow it with an audible gulp.[1]

Q. Is it harmful to lengthen the duration of a meditation?
A. You can lengthen it if you can bear with it but you should avoid strain.

Q. During the meditation, the inner heat sometimes goes up and down; what does this mean?
A. This is a very good sign which shows the free circulation of the vital principle.

Q. During the meditation, concentration should be made on the lower belly; afterwards, is it good to concentrate on the soles of the feet?

1. See Chapter 7, Physical and Spiritual Culture according to Chinese Yoga for an explanation.

A. Whether you sit in meditation or not, your concentration should be on the lower belly.

Q. When one is ill, should one concentrate on the part of the body which is affected?
A. The best thing is to forget all about one's illness.

Q. Is it advisable to sit in meditation after a meal?
A. Meditation should be practised twenty to thirty minutes after a meal.

Q. When I sit in meditation, I feel a touch of heat in the lower belly. What does this mean?
A. This shows that your meditation is not really effective; as time passes, this heat will gradually grow in intensity.

Q. Each time I sit in meditation, I feel very impatient and the more I strive to suppress my impatience, the more unbearable it becomes. What should I do?
A. Do not try to suppress it. You should lay down everything by visualizing your body as being dead; this is tantamount to killing it in order to resurrect it.

Q. If the two thighs do not rest comfortably on the cushion, is it advisable to add padding under the buttocks?
A. The buttocks should be raised two to three inches above the knees so that the thighs incline downward and rest on the cushion; thus the legs will also be relieved from numbness.

Q. According to (Taoist) books, the method of turning inwards the contemplation does not mean the forceful stoppage of thoughts, but looking into their rise and fall to clear them away; for instance, returning the first thought to itself, the second thought to itself, and so on. What does 'returning' mean?
A. All false thoughts are but the mind's clingings which succeed one another endlessly. When contemplation is turned inward to look into their rise and fall, the purpose is to isolate these thoughts, thereby cutting off their links and connections. Thus the first thought cannot reach the second one, and this is 'returning' (the first thought to itself without allowing it to be linked with the second one). This is only possible when the rise of every thought is looked into.

Q. Why, when something that is of no real concern enters my mind, cannot I get rid of it?
A. This is because you cling to it. If you look into the unreality of your body which is a union of illusory elements, you will realize that there is

not a thing that is worth your attachment; thus you will be able to lay down everything (and so quiet your mind).

Q. During my meditation, although I practise the counting method, my mind still wanders outside; should I leave it alone?
A. If your mind continues to wander in spite of your practice of the counting method, you should, each time you notice it wandering, bring it back under control so as to 'freeze' it. If you continue so doing, you will prevent it from wandering.

Q. I sometimes feel the vital principle go down and reach the anus; is this a good or bad sign?
A. This is a good sign, but don't be happy about it. Let it take its own course and when there is abundance of vital principle, lead it gently (without exertion) up along the backbone.

Q. You advise us by visualization to lead the breath from the tip of the nose down to the lower belly. Is it the same if concentration is made on the lower belly?
A. My advice is for beginners who are unable to direct their breath to the lower belly at the start of their practice. If you can concentrate on the lower belly, that is much better.

Q. It is said that when one is ill and sits in meditation, one should rid oneself of all thoughts of a cure and it is also said that one should hold on to the thought of being in perfect health. Is there any contradiction in these two methods?
A. There is no contradiction. Fundamentally, there is no illness which is an illusion and is consequently unreal. If you harbour the thought of curing it, you will admit the reality of the illness. Hence you should hold the thought of being in perfect health for the sole purpose of recovering that health, and then your illness will vanish of itself.

Q. During my meditation, I feel vibration in my belly, followed by hiccups and farts. What does all this mean? Moreover, when my mind is still, my cold hands and feet become warm and are wet with perspiration. Is this a symptom of illness or a sign of effective meditation?
A. Vibrations in the belly with hiccuping and breaking wind show the unhindered flow of the vital principle which causes your body and limbs to be hot and to perspire. All these are good signs of effective meditation.

Q. Last night, during my meditation, I gradually felt something quite unusual. It was as if I was in a floating state which was only temporary. As soon as I felt it, my thoughts returned again but I succeeded in stopping them and it reappeared. Thus my thoughts alternated with this state for a few times. At last, while in this state, suddenly the inner heat came down from my nose to my mouth, throat and chest, and the pores all over my body seemed to open up. I was so surprised that I did not notice where this heat stopped. Then I composed myself and felt another inner heat in the backbone between the kidneys which went up to the top of my head. All my body was hot and wet with perspiration. My surprise gave way to fright and then to alarm and I was unable to compose myself. The heat disappeared and the perspiration stopped. My head was wet with sweat and drops of it ran off my cheeks. This experience was very strange to me; what does it mean?

A. These are the best signs of an effective meditation. Your perspiration removes impurities accumulated in your body. Don't be frightened. Let this state take its own course. If the heat is intense, lead it by visualization up the backbone to the top of your head and then down to the lower belly, thus ensuring its continuous flow.

Q. Every morning when I sit in meditation, I feel vibrations in my belly, first in its upper part and then under the navel. The more it vibrates, the more the vital principle flows freely and the more comfortable I feel. In my meditation in the afternoon and in the evening before going to bed, I do not feel vibrations in my belly. It seems that the flowing vital principle reaches the lower belly more easily when it is empty than when it is full. Are vibrations caused by this flow into the lower belly or are they only accidental? What do you mean by settling the lower belly; do you mean expanding it without allowing it to contract?

A. Vibrations show the free passage of the vital principle. As it passes through the stomach and intestines, it vibrates when the belly is empty. But when the belly is full, it ceases to vibrate. The breath reaches the lower belly more easily when the latter is full. Vibrations are not accidental but come from the vital principle circulating in the belly. As times passes, when your meditation is more effective and the vital principle flows freely, then these vibrations will cease.

To settle the belly is to expand it at all times without allowing it to contract. This can be attained only after a long training and cannot be achieved by beginners.

Q. I began to meditate in November last year. Now each evening before going to bed, I practise the counting of breaths and when I come to the fiftieth count, though nothing unusual occurs in my belly, my breathing is regulated with the result that I experience a very comfortable state beyond description.

A. You will experience better states later on.

Q. When I come to the fiftieth count, my head, shoulders and back are wet with perspiration, but as soon as I stop counting, the perspiration ceases. What does this mean?
A. The best way is to continue your counting and stop it only after your perspiration has ceased of itself.

Q. When I was two my health was weak and I suffered from hernia. The physician prescribed medicine to lift up the inner energy, but now when I practise meditation, I feel as if my energy is going down until it reaches the affected spot in my body, thus in contrast with the aim of (Chinese) medical science. Do you think that meditation is harmful in my case?
A. When you concentrate on the lower belly, do not direct the inner energy to go down but leave it alone so that it takes its natural course; thus you will have no trouble. Twenty years ago, I also had hernia and got rid of it by meditation.

Q. Last evening, during my meditation, I suddenly felt that my lower belly was unusually empty with its centre of gravity like a red lump which was perceptible. It was hot and swinging, and the air breathed in went further down (than usual). Then the pores all over my body seemed to open up and I perspired. I was so scared by this unusual experience which lasted three full minutes that I could not continue my meditation. I then lay down and fell into a deep sleep. What does all this mean?
A. This is a very good result of your pointed concentration. You should not be scared; leave it alone and if you feel vibrations in your belly, visualize the vital principle as going up your backbone, but avoid exertion.

Q. At the start of my practice, my breath did not go down and I felt that my chest was stifled, but now with my breath passing freely from my chest down to the belly, the latter expands like a drum with some (silent) vibration in it. However, when a loud voice is heard or a movement felt, there is some slight pain in my chest. What is the cause of this?
A. A loud voice or a movement is not a direct cause of the pain in your chest which is most probably due to strain when breathing. Though your breath goes down, your chest is still not empty and relaxed, and the pain is the reaction of your nerves to external interference. You should avoid exertion and take a natural attitude during your meditation.

Q. My belly vibrates during my morning meditation. Recently I had an unusual experience. An inner heat developed between my eyebrows, reached my eyes and suddenly a bright light appeared in front of me, like the brightness of dawn. The heat then descended to the tip of my nose. Since then, in every morning meditation, my neck and back became very

hot with occasional vibration in my forehead and belly. I still sweat a little but the (above) bright light does not appear any more. Is all this a good sign and what should I do?
A. The appearance of inner heat and a bright light in front of you are good signs, for they show that the vital principle is passing through the two (main) psychic channels in the human body. When concentration on a certain part of the body is effective, it starts the inner heat and vibrations. This heat is bright and is easily perceptible when it passes through your face. But whether this brightness is perceptible or not, you should not cling to it but take a natural (or indifferent) attitude. It is most important for you to continue to concentrate on the lower belly.

Q. After a long sitting in meditation, is some slight deviation from the correct posture harmful?
A. When your meditation is effective and the vital principle flows freely in the psychic channels, it does not matter much whether your posture is correct or not.

Q. My belly has been vibrating for over a month and if I strive to lead the force down, the vibration increases. Should I exert myself to increase the vibration or leave it alone to take its natural course?
A. Vibration is a good sign and should be left alone without making any effort to interfere with it.

Q. After a long vibration, it comes to a stop and although I concentrate on the lower belly, I fail to cause it to vibrate again, but after a few minutes, it starts again. What does this short interruption mean?
A. This is a natural sequence of the free flow of the vital principle for all motion comes to a stop; there is nothing abnormal in all this.

Q. What do you mean by using a single thought to overcome numerous thoughts?
A. When you concentrate on a single thought without loosening your grip of it, you will sooner or later succeed in putting a stop to all thoughts.

Q. What do you mean by turning inwards the contemplation, and by returning every thought to itself?
A. By turning inwards the contemplation is meant closing your eyes to look into the innermost; this can put a stop to false thoughts which will thus be disengaged from one another. This is returning each thought to its origin so that it cannot be linked to the following one, but actually there is no real return to anything.

Q. In my morning meditation, I feel that my chest and belly are empty and relaxed with the free passage of my breath; this state is comfortable, but in the evening meditation, why do I not have the same experience?

A. After a good rest in your sleep at night, your spirits are high the next morning which is always the best time for meditation. Hence the different results.

Q. After my practice of meditation either in the morning after getting up or in the evening before going to bed, I did not feel anything unusual for a whole month. Then, one night, it took effect suddenly and I felt the inner heat and vibration in my lower belly; my head and limbs were also very warm. After a little, the heat reached the coccyx and then went up along the backbone. This happened thrice, each time after a short interruption. However, the heat did not reach the neck. The following morning, I sat again but failed to have the same experience, and nothing happened in three successive days. Since then, although I have practised meditation before going to bed at night, the inner heat has failed to return in the lower belly. What is the reason?

A. The inner heat usually vibrates late at night because the practiser is in high spirits after a restful sleep. It goes up along the backbone, stops and flows again because it is not sufficiently powerful. You should leave it alone and when there is enough of it and it is strong, it will flow further of itself. Don't be impatient.

Q. When the inner heat is present, I do not feel at all tired, but when it is absent, the meditation becomes wearisome. What is the reason?

A. You do not feel tired when there is inner heat in your belly because the vital principle harmonizes with the circulation of blood.

Q. Is it true that some practisers have visions of demons in their meditation?

A. I personally never had any vision of demons during my meditation but a student of mine did. After a few years of practice, he made very good progress, but one evening he suddenly perceived in the still state a group of naked girls who surrounded him clamorously. He was surprised and immediately kept his mind under control, but the girls refused to retreat. He was scared and hastily repeated in silence the Buddha's name. Thereupon, the girls disappeared. He was not a Buddhist devotee but the method he employed was still very effective. This is the best way to deal with demons according to Buddhist sūtras.[1]

1. The meditator was not spiritually strong enough to wipe out the vision created by his own mind and had to rely on the Buddha's power of Samādhi which is effective in similar and other situations. This power of Samādhi is also inherent in his self-nature.

6

AUTHENTIC EXPERIMENTS WITH BUDDHIST AND TAOIST METHODS OF SELF-CULTIVATION

WE MENTIONED in Chapter 4 on Meditation according to the T'ien T'ai school the eight physical sensations experienced by the practiser when his inner excellent qualities, hitherto dormant, manifest themselves after he has achieved stillness of mind, but when he is still in the realm of desire and has not yet attained the stages of Bodhisattva development.[1] As a result of this mental stillness, the vital principle (prāṇa), now sufficiently accumulated in the lower belly, bursts out and flows into the microcosmic orbit[2] or the main psychic channel in the human body and causes involuntary movements, both inner and outer, producing eight physical sensations, such as pain, itching, coldness, warmth, weightlessness, heaviness, roughness and smoothness. There are, besides the main circuit, subsidiary ones linking various psychic centres in the body and moving in sympathy with the main one, hence these involuntary movements of the body and limbs and the eight accompanying physical sensations.

The vital principle stands for the element fire which is hot. When enough has accumulated, it is felt by the meditator and enters the main circuit, spreading its warmth to all parts of the

1. See Chapter 4, pages pp. 139, 140
2. See Chapter 7 for further details.

body, so that he perspires during his meditation. If he succeeds in achieving complete stillness of mind by freeing it from all external disturbances, the prāṇa will become bright and perceptible to him. This brightness will grow in intensity with the effectiveness of the meditation and will become a White Light which only experienced practisers can achieve and which then illuminates everything in a dark room as in broad daylight.

When this vital principle flows into the main subsidiary circuits, it sweeps all obstructions from its path and the meditator feels sensations such as roughness, itching and pain which are sometimes quite unpleasant. For instance, when it forces its way into a small circuit under the skin on the top of the head, he feels as if his hair were being pulled out. Roughness and itching are felt when it flows into subsidiary circuits in front, at the back and on the left and right sides of the head, piercing through the hitherto obstructed psychic centres and muscles. Sometimes as a result of the contraction and expansion of the muscles and psychic nerves in the body, the practiser feels himself as heavy as lead. When prāṇa flows freely without obstruction, he feels smoothness in the body and on the skin. If he achieves pointed concentration, or singleness of mind, he will experience a sensation of intense cold which either descends from the top of his head and goes down his spine and then spreads to all parts of his body, or rises from the coccyx, going up the backbone to the head and pervading the whole body. If this coldness descends from the crown, the resultant state of dhyāna is temporary and cannot be reproduced at will. If it rises from the coccyx, the state of dhyāna is stable and can be regained at will in subsequent meditations. This coldness is sometimes felt before the meditator enters the 'holy stream' in which he will feel as weightless as an astronaut. But there is a difference in that his body and mind disappear completely and are replaced by a great mass of brightness full of bliss while he is free from all worldly troubles and anxieties, whereas the spaceman still worries about his safe landing on earth. The meditator will be one with this brightness wherein his mind alone performs the function of perception.

Yin Shih Tsu, after his successful practice of Taoist meditation which enabled him to get rid of all his illnesses and to improve his health, adopted the chih-kuan method of the T'ien T'ai school and published his second book *A Supplement to Yin Shih Tsu's Method of Meditation* (Yin Shih Tsu Ching Tso Fa Hsu Pien) dealing with the Buddhist meditation of the T'ien T'ai sect.

At the age of eighty-two, he recapitulated his personal experiences in a third book, *Yin Shih Tsu's Experimental Meditation for the Promotion of Health*,[1] from which we quote the following passages:

I went to Peking when I was forty-three after studying the Buddhist Dharma. In the capital, all my friends thought that my first book should be altered because in it my method of meditation was Taoist and was, therefore, heterodox. It happened that the great Master Ti Hsin[2] was expounding the Sūtra of Complete Enlightenment in Peking, so I called on him for instruction in chih-kuan meditation which I then practised. Urged by my friends to write on T'ien T'ai meditation, I wrote and published the *Supplement to Yin Shih Tsu's Method of Meditation* which was based on the teachings in the treatises *T'ung Meng Chih Kuan*[3] and *An Explanation of the Dhyāna-pāramitā's Progressive Stages* (Shih Ch'an Po Lo Mi Tz'u Ti Fa Men). From then on I practised chih-kuan meditation.

When I was fifty-four, I was at Shanghai where over ten of my friends decided to be initiated into the Japanese Shingon sect. I was not interested but since they strongly urged me to join them, I went to the ceremonies, out of curiosity, to see how they were performed. I found the rituals too complicated and since I was already very occupied with my teaching at Kuan Hua University, I had no time for Shingon meditation. I continued, however, with the chih-kuan method without interruption.

According to the T'ung Meng Chih Kuan, when the inner excellent qualities manifest in the practice of dhyāna, the meditator experiences eight physical sensations such as weightlessness, warmth, coldness and heaviness which concern the body, and vibration, itching, roughness and

1. See also pp. 157 and 160.
2. A well-known master of T'ien T'ai school who died in China a few years ago.
3. See also p.111 .

smoothness which pertain to activity. According to my personal experience, these sensations were not all felt at the same time, but one after another. When I was twenty-eight and twenty-nine, I felt only three of them, weightlessness, warmth and vibration. After sitting for a long while, my first sensation was that my body was as weightless as a feather. Later, I felt heat in my lower belly followed by a vibration which rose up the backbone until it reached the crown and then descended down the face (and chest) until it returned to the lower belly, to circulate again and again in the same manner. This is the flow (of the vital principle) joining up the two psychic channels called jen mo and tu mo.[1] According to ancient medical science, there are eight psychic channels;[2] besides the above two, jen mo and tu mo, the other six are: ch'ung mo,[3] tai mo,[4] yang ch'iao,[5] yin ch'iao,[6] yang wei[7] and yin wei.[8]

I practised chih-kuan for over ten years during which I concentrated on the lower belly. One day, I shifted my concentration to the 'central spot' (between the navel and the pit of the stomach) and a few days later, I noticed a profound change in my body, resulting in a free flow (of prāṇa) through the remaining six psychic channels which I describe below.

As I now fixed my concentration on the 'central spot', one evening, at the

1. The jen mo channel rises from the perineum and goes up along the belly, passes through the navel, the pit of the stomach, the chest, throat and upper lip and ends below the eye; it connects twenty-seven psychic centres. The tu mo channel rises from the perineum and passes through the coccyx to go up the backbone to the crown and thence descends along the forehead and nose, ending in the gums; it connects thirty-one psychic centres.

2. As contrasted with twenty-four organic channels according to ancient medical science.

3. Ch'ung mo, or the 'bursting' channel, rises from the perineum, goes up between jen mo and tu mo and ends in the chest; it connects twenty-four psychic centres.

4. Tai mo begins from both sides of the navel forming a belt which circles the belly; it connects eight psychic centres.

5. Yang ch'iao rises from the centre of the sole and turns along the outer side of the ankle and leg, then skirts the back of the body and reaches the shoulder, veering to the neck, the corner of the mouth and the inner corner of the eye, ending behind the brain; it connects twenty-two psychic centres.

6. Yin ch'iao rises from the centre of the sole, turns along the inner side of the ankle and leg, skirts the belly and chest, reaches the shoulder, turns up to the throat and ends in the inner corner of the eye; it connects eight psychic centres.

7. Yang wei rises from the outer side of the foot about one and half inches below the ankle, goes up the outer side of the leg and after skirting the back of the body, enters the upper arm, half way along which it veers to the shoulder, the neck, and then behind the ear ending in the forehead; it connects thirty-two psychic centres.

8. Yin wei rises from the inner side of the calf, about five inches above the ankle, goes up the inner side of the thigh, and after skirting the belly and half of the chest, turns to the throat, ascends along the face and ends in front of the top of the head; it connects fourteen psychic centres.

end of a meditation at midnight, I suddenly felt a vibration in my chest, and my saliva flowed freely.[1] This happened for several evenings. Then the vibration became more intense and thrust up straight to the spot between the eyebrows where I perceived a red brightness. Then pushing up it reached the crown which it circled for a long while. I felt as if an electric shock was pulsing round in my body until it reached my hands and feet after piercing (through my limbs). This lasted a full minute and then stopped abruptly between the eyebrows.

After that, every evening, I experienced the same vibration. It seemed as if there was some mechanism revolving in the 'central spot' and rising slowly until it reached the crown round which it continued to circle. When the vibration became intense, it abruptly stopped between the eyebrows. Then the 'central spot' vibrated again, and there seemed to be an electric shock which pulsed in an oblique oval circuit from my left shoulder to my left leg, so violently that it shook my bed and mosquito-net; when the vibration became more intense, it stopped abruptly. Then I felt another vibration behind the brain, descending along the backbone to stop abruptly in the coccyx. After that, something like another electric shock descended from my right shoulder to my right leg, pulsing in an oblique oval circuit; the vibration became intense and stopped suddenly. These two oblique oval circuits, on the left and right sides of my body, showed that the four psychic channels, ying ch'iao, yang ch'iao, yin wei and yang wei, had joined up. Thus for the first time I understood the inter-relation of the eight psychic channels and the nervous system and realized that there was nothing fictitious and unaccountable in it all.

Up to then, each time the inner vibration took place, it began in (some sort of) change in the 'central spot'. However, one evening, it started in my ears and formed a straight line across my face, swinging from left to right and back again several times before ending abruptly between the eyebrows. (At the same time) another vibration from the forehead to the chin, in a vertical straight line, made, with the horizontal line, a cross and pulsed up and down several times before suddenly ending between the eyebrows. Then another vibration descended in a curve from the crown (along the face) chest and belly to the penis. It pulsed up and down, causing the penis to erect. This showed that the two channels jen mo and ch'ung mo had joined up.

One night, the heat in the 'central spot' vibrated, causing my body to bend forwards and backwards and to the left and right. These bendings were orderly and the same number each time without the least confusion. Then the vibration caused my arms to revolve backwards and forwards quickly

1. This is a very good sign for saliva reduces the scorching effect of the heat of prāṇa which is the cause of a dry and sore throat.

like a wheel with the same number of turns each way. Then it reached my legs so that the left one bent while the right one straightened and vice versa. These movements could not be explained by orthodox science and were involuntary. After them my head (seemed to) swell and the upper part of my body to stretch so that I (seemed) to be over ten feet tall. (The Buddhist Scriptures call this the appearance of the great body.) Suddenly my head bent back and my chest (seemed) as large as the great void. Then with the same suddenness, my head bent forward and my back (seemed) as large as space. As a result I felt (as if) I had only the lower half of my body. Thus with the disappearance of both body and mind, I experienced unusual bliss.

Another evening the vibration in the 'central spot' circled round the spine, then round the chest under the skin, round the belly in the jen mo channel and finally round the waist, in each case first to the left and then to the right for a few tens of turns each way. This final circling of the waist showed that the tai mo channel was clear. Then the vibration descended spirally from the crown down the tai mo channel along the backbone to the coccyx, up and down for a few tens of times. Then it rose from the lower belly, went up the jen mo channel to the top of the head and descended through the occiput and down the spine to the coccyx, up and down for a few tens of times. (The vital principle) after breaking through the jen mo and tai mo channels had risen from the coccyx along the spine to the top of the head and then descended down the face (throat), chest and belly, but now it circled in reverse most probably because these channels were free, so that it could flow either way. Thus the ch'ung mo and tai mo channels were also joined up.

Another night from the 'central spot' and beneath the skin the vibration took the form of a two-inch spiral which circled the body thirty-six times each way. It then circled round the lower belly and (the middle of) the chest, all being orderly and systematic. Next it rose to the head and descended circling the spine to the coccyx, returning up the backbone to the crown, twice each way. Then it rose up along the lower belly first by the left and then by the right ch'ung mo channels to the crown and back, twice by each channel. After that it circled the jen mo channel in the head, descended to the lower belly and returned to the crown. Sometimes it circled round the head, from left to right and then from right to left, stopping in the forehead. Another time it revolved in the left and right shoulder with the same number of turns each way. Suddenly it reached the tips of the fingers which made quick involuntary movements. Finally it descended in a rush from the top of the head, flung out both my legs and moved the toes with the same speed as the fingers.

One evening the vibration began in the centre of the back and spiralled under the skin making thirty-six circles first to the left and then to the right—then again, but starting from between the loins and once more but from between the shoulder blades. All these circuits were orderly and systematic. Before it had moved to the left and right in three circuits beginning from the 'central spot', the middle of the belly and the centre of the chest, but now it started from the middle of the back, between the loins and between the shoulder blades, that is from three spots exactly behind the front ones. These involuntary circular movements were really wonderful and inconceivable. When it reached the tips of the fingers and toes, the latter stretched out to move while the legs bent and straightened alternately and the upper and lower jaws knocked against each other, all making brisk movements. When it reached the nose, suddenly the nostrils contracted and expanded. When it reached the eyes, the eyelids suddenly opened and closed, while the irises moved in sympathy. Finally it caused the ear lobes to move slowly. All these movements to the left and right were natural with the same number of turns in each direction.

One night the vibration in the 'central spot' caused another series of systematic circuits thirty-six times to the left and again to the right, first from between the loins along the tai mo (belt) channel, then from (the middle of) the chest and finally from the middle of the belly. They succeeded each other systematically. Next the vibration made two great ovals by going up and down the left and right sides of the chest, and a second pair by going up to the head and descending first to the left and then to the right side of the back. Each pair of ovals crossed several times.

After that it moved to my limbs so that my arms swung in quick circles to the left and right while my legs bent and straightened and first the toes and then the heel of one foot kept striking those of the other. Suddenly my knees began to swing apart and close; then they bent, forcing up from the floor my buttocks which swung to the left and right. This happened three times, while my jaws, lips, nose and eyes moved more briskly than before.

Another evening the vibration in the 'central spot' spiralled in a large circle round the body sixty times to the left and again to the right and this was followed by similar circuits round the chest and belly. Suddenly each of these three circuits expanded six times in turn, all within them becoming a void for five or six minutes each time.

The vibration then rose from the central spot to the head and made four oblique ovals in turn through which it circled thirty-six times from the top of the head to the left and right sides of the buttocks and back, through the back of the head and along the spine to the coccyx and the left leg and back, and finally to the right leg and back.

Another night . . . when the vibration moved down the face, my shoulders and arms turned: my legs bent and straightened, opened and closed, and then with my feet on the floor and knees bent, my back arched until my shoulders touched the floor. My buttocks and waist swung to the left and right while my whole body shook: it then dropped to the ground. Next my soles rubbed together and each massaged the other leg for the same number of times. When the vibration rose to my shoulders, my hands began to massage each other, my head, neck, shoulders and arms. They then massaged up from my lower belly to my shoulders, then right down my whole body to my toes. Finally my fists clenched and in turn patted, kneaded and rubbed me all over. All this happened systematically and in order, was in: voluntary and quite wonderful.[1]

... These involuntary movements lasted for some six months after which they gradually ceased. This was probably because all the psychic channels had by then opened and been cleared.

Late in my life, I practised Pho-wa,[2] an esoteric Tibetan technique for rebirth in the Pure Land, which had not been introduced in China before. The teaching is based on the principle that when someone who is due to be reborn in the Western Paradise is dying, his consciousness will leave through the Aperture of Brahma (in the top of his skull): thus one is taught to repeat mantras to open this aperture and to practise regularly so that one can follow a similar path at the moment of death. In 1933, when I was sixty-one, I had already received this Dharma from the Tibetan guru No Na[3] who had urged me to practise it at home (which I did) unsuccessfully. In the spring of 1937, when I was sixty-five, I heard that the guru Sheng Lu[3] was teaching this Dharma in Nanking and that all those participating in the four previous meetings had succeeded in opening the Aperture of Brahma. As the fifth and last meeting was soon to take place at the Vairochana temple, I went to Nanking and put my name down to attend it.

I arrived on the first of April to receive the initiation, which was very much more complicated than the one previously given me by the guru No Na. I was taught a vajra mantra as the first step in the practice. It was not a long one but the method of visualization was very elaborate. It had to be repeated one hundred thousand times, but since I had only a few days at my disposal, I did so as many times as I could.

After the first day, I stayed in a lodging house and closed the door of my room to concentrate on repeating the mantra. Before midday on the

1. A detailed description of this patting, kneading and rubbing has been omitted.

2. A tantric practice for opening the Aperture of Brahma on the crown of the head, through which the consciousness leaves the human body for rebirth in the Pure Land. The Taoists employ a different technique which consists in putting the energized vital principle into microcosmic orbits so that consciousness can leave the body through the same opening in the crown.

3. No Na and Sheng Lu are transliterations of Tibetan names. The guru No Na was the chief Hutuktu of Sikang and was my first master.

ninth, I had done so sixty-two thousand times, and in the afternoon I returned to the Vairocana temple where thirty-nine of us assembled. I was told that this was considerably more than at any of the other four gatherings. The guru shaved a small hairless circle in the centre of my crown so that later he could see if the Aperture of Brahma had opened in order to plant a stalk in it.

On the tenth we began to isolate ourselves for meditation. In the main hall an altar was set up with all its majesty, before which the guru led us to practise the Dharma. Every day there were four sessions each lasting two hours.[1] The practice consisted in visualizing Amitāyus Buddha sitting on the top of the head and in imagining in the body a blue psychic tube which was red inside and stretched from the crown of the head to the perineum. Within this tube in the lower belly below the navel was a bright pearl which rose (up it) to the heart (centre). (When the pearl was visualized in that centre) I shouted the mantric syllable HIK, forcing up the pearl which followed the sound and thrust through the Aperture of Brahma to reach the heart of Amitāyus. Then I whispered the syllable GA which caused the pearl to descend from the Buddha's heart and return through the opening to my lower belly. At each session we shouted with such force that we became hoarse and exhausted, and dripped perspiration although it was still very cold. Seeing that we were tired, the guru chanted in Sanskrit and exhorted us to follow his example and relax. This we did four or five times in each two hour session.

Now I was already experienced in (the art of) meditation and had cleared the central psychic passage (in the spine) so that I made remarkable progress on the eleventh. During the first session a red light shone from the crown of my head and (I seemed) to grow taller. In the fourth session, I felt (as if) the Aperture of Brahma was being bored through by a sharp-pointed tool and was repeatedly hit by the ascending pearl. When I went to bed a great white light shone from my head.

On the twelfth I practised as on the previous day. In the second session, I felt (as if) my skull was swelling and cracking and that my cheek-bones were being torn apart. In the third session, my head (seemed to) stretch up, tier upon tier, each (time) seeming to crack.

On the thirteenth in the first session, I felt (as if) my brain was being pierced from all sides by sharp-pointed tools. At first I felt that my skull was very thick, but that the continuous boring had made it thinner. In the third session, I suddenly felt (as if) the upper part of my body was completely void while a great light shone from my head.

On the fourteenth in the first and second seesions, the bright pearl shot

1. From seven to nine in the morning, from ten to twelve, from three to five in the afternoon and from seven to nine in the evening.

up through the cleared passage in the central channel to the foot of the Buddha on my crown. This was different from my previous experience of (my head) swelling and cracking when the channel was not yet quite through my skull. In the fourth session I felt (as if) my neck was splitting to make room for a column which went straight down to my stomach and intestines. This was an actual swelling of the central channel which, untill then, had merely been visualized.

On the fifteenth, in the first session, I felt that there was a hole in the crown of my head. In the second session, the guru moved his seat close to the window where there was abundant sunlight. He then called us to come forward, one after another, so that he (could check whether) the Aperture of Brahma in our heads had opened and could plant in it an auspicious stalk as proof of its opening. If there was a real opening, the stalk was drawn into it without breaking the skin. I was among the first twenty-eight persons whose crowns were opened that day. As to the other eleven the stalk could not be planted. They were consequently required to continue the practice for a few more sessions. As to those who had achieved the opening, they were excused further practice but were asked to enter the hall to use the power of visualization to give (spiritual) aid to the unsuccessful initiates so that they too could achieve the same result speedily.

On the sixteenth, in the first session, nine people had their Apertures of Brahma opened. There remained only a nun and a lay woman whose crowns were still closed. The nun had been in Japan where she had practised (Shingon) meditation and had acquired good experience, yet she had difficulty in opening the Aperture. This shows that in the study of the Dharma, one should bury pride and prejudice which can hinder realization. As to the lay woman, she was of dull potentiality because of her advanced age. The guru ordered them to sit in front of him and used his spiritual power to help them. In the following session, with spiritual help from the whole gathering, they finally succeeded, but not without difficulty, in opening their Apertures of Brahma.

After this, I practised the chih-kuan meditation as my main method, with pho-wa as a complementary one. On the twenty-fourth of May, during a meditation, after I had achieved stillness of mind, my chest emitted a light which gradually expanded to envelop my whole body, forming a bright sphere. Previously either only my head or my chest had shone and been bright, but this radiance had not embraced my whole body. In this experience (of total brightness), I still felt the presence of the Ego.

On the twenty-sixth of the same month, after achieving stillness of mind, my back now emitted a light which soon engulfed all my body. I experienced unusual happiness but still felt my body was there, for I had not yet achieved absolute voidness.

On the twenty-seventh, after achieving stillness of mind, I emitted a light which attained a great height and seemed to reach the clouds in the sky. My consciousness also expanded with this light and then gradually returned (to my body) through the Aperture of Brahma.

On the thirty-first, after stilling my mind, the upper half of my body emitted a light as on the preceding day. Then I felt in my lower belly heat as intense as boiling water; it then emitted light and the lower half of my body became void. This state differed from the previous ones.

On the tenth of June, after calming the mind, all my body radiated and the light was much brighter than before. I felt (as if) I had no head which was replaced by a transparent brightness.

On the fourteenth all my body radiated with both its upper and lower parts being really bright.

On the seventeenth, after entering the state of stillness, my body radiated and I felt (as if) the light illumined my mind's eye and was of a white radiance, engulfing all my surroundings and forming a great sphere.

On the eighteenth, upon entering the state of stillness, all my body radiated and the light was much whiter. All round me was transparent brightness like a searchlight shining upon the four quarters while my consciousness roamed about in the great void. This brightness then shrunk and entered my lower belly; after being subjected to rigid control, it entered my legs and the my arms, finally to return to my head.

These involuntary movements and their number are not the same for all meditators and differ according to the constitution of each. For instance, in my own experience, when the vital principle circulated in my body for the first time, I was stunned by outer movements to the left and the right in sympathy with the inner flow. In other words, the inner circulation of prāṇa was revealed by the outer movements of body and limbs. Their number in either direction was first six, then sixteen and then thirty-six for the first few weeks and later increased to the maximum of one hundred. Every day in my three meditations the total number of these brisk movements was more than nine thousand, but I never felt tired after each sitting.

Although the treatise of Chih I and other Taoist books mention involuntary movements of the body and limbs, they do not give a detailed description of them. I had had only a vague idea of them until I noticed that, in my own case, they were orderly and systematic, without the least confusion. At first, I was very puzzled and thought that I might have been misled into the way of the heretics. One day, I heard of Yin Shih Tsu's third book and bought it to compare his experience with mine. After reading it, all my perplexities vanished and I found nothing wrong in my unexpected experience.

We cannot blame the ancients who taught only a very limited number of chosen disciples by word of mouth, without leaving behind written instructions for posterity, to avoid cheap criticism by sceptics and blasphemers who can never understand the holy teaching. Even nowadays serious Taoists refuse to show outsiders handwritten instructions from past masters in order not to be involved in useless discussion and controversy. For the same reason, my Tibetan guru forbade his disciples to reveal the pho-wa technique to those who are not initiated in his sect and this is why I am unable to present a translation of his teaching in this volume.

It is absolutely wrong to keep the vital principle in the lower belly or to prevent it from flowing freely in the eight psychic channels. When it has accumulated in the belly, it is advisable to shift one's concentration to the 'central spot' so that it can be put into the main orbit. For this reason, in the first volume of our *Ch'an and Zen Teaching* Series—p. 56, note 4—we recommended concentration on the spot between the navel and the pit of the stomach but could not, for lack of space, deal with the subject fully.

It is said that when the vital principle flows freely in all the psychic channels, it permeates first the marrow in the bones, then the nervous system, the flesh and inner organs and finally the skin, thus sublimating the whole body. This perhaps explains the preservation through the ages of the bodies of great masters which were only plastered with a thin layer of rosin mixed with gold powder and dust of sandalwood. This may also explain the presence of relics in the ashes of the cremated bodies of enlightened monks.

The unhindered flow of the vital principle in the eight psychic channels, as explained in Yin Shih Tsu's book, was known to all Taoists whose prime objective was to realize it in their training with a view to attaining immortality. Bodhidharma saw in China a promised land in which to teach his Transmission of the Mind because Taoism already prospered there and because it was easier for anyone who had realized his ālaya-vijñāna to transmute it into the Great Mirror Wisdom. But the greatest obstacle for Taoists to realize the Buddha's Universal Wisdom was their unwillingness to take a step forward from the 'top of a hundred foot pole', a state in which still exist the subjective enjoyer of bliss and the objective bliss which he cannot forsake.

HOW TO ACCUMULATE PRĀṆA AND PUT IT INTO ORBIT

We know now that controlled breathing produces prāṇa which can be accumulated either in the lower belly or in the solar plexus. When enough of this vital principle is stored, it generates heat which produces vibration. According to the Taoist method, the practiser should, at the start of each meditation, massage his loins and the spine between them down to the coccyx until that area is very warm, or visualize the vital principle in the belly as descending to the perineum and breaking through the coccyx, the first of the three psychic gates, the other two being between the kidneys and in the back of the head. If heat is felt in the base of the spine, this shows that the first gate is being forced through, and there will be no great difficulty for it to ascend through the second one and along the backbone to the occiput, through which it is very difficult to pass. If he perseveres in his training, the third gate will be forced open and prāṇa will ascend to the crown of the head, and the rest of the circuit will be completed in due course as explained by Yin Shih Tsu.

A FEW WORDS OF CAUTION

It is advisable for beginners to sit for twenty or thirty minutes, in the morning and evening, and so continue without interruption instead of attempting long meditation at the start. We know by experience that beginners are apt to stop their practice after a few long meditations and their usual pretext is either lack of time or unbearable cramp in the legs. With easy stages of twenty or thirty minutes each, they can continue their meditation throughout the year without difficulty and will certainly find their practice effective. When they have got into the habit of sitting and noticed the progress made, they will be keen to lengthen their meditation.

A practiser at the end of his meditation may feel very hot or may be wet with perspiration. If so, he should relax and wait until the heat has dissipated and his body is completely dry before taking a bath. I mention this because a Western friend of mine recently caught a very bad cold because he bathed immediately after his meditation to get rid of the heat and perspiration which, however, showed the effectiveness of his training.

7

PHYSICAL AND SPIRITUAL CULTURE ACCORDING TO CHINESE YOGA

WE CANNOT speak of spiritual attainment if we disregard physical culture, and the Latin phrase, *mens sana in corpore sano*, expresses the ideal of self-cultivation, for it is impossible to have a sound mind in an unsound body. The practice of physical exercises is, however, beneficial to the body only but not to the mind. It is, therefore, necessary to follow a method that looks after both body and mind at the same time, and, in this respect, nothing can surpass the technique known as the *Microcosmic Orbit* (Hsiao Chou T'ien) followed by Yin Shih Tsu.[1] This ancient method consists in energizing the vital principle, hitherto dormant, to put it into bodily circuits, for the purpose of harmonizing body with mind; in other words, for the integration of both with each other.

We present below the text of the hsiao chou t'ien technique taken from the *I Fang Chi Chiai* which contains many Taoist terms which are quite different from Buddhist idioms.

THE MICROCOSMIC ORBIT TECHNIQUE

First stop your thinking (process). After regulating body and mind, sit facing east, with crossed legs. Adjust your inhalation and exhalation, and place the right hand upon the left one, drawing them close to the lower

1. See page 179.

belly below the navel. Then knock the lower teeth against the upper ones thirty-six times to stabilize both body and spirit. Let the red dragon stir the sea thirty-six times,[1] directing your (closed) eyes to follow its movements. Now let the tongue touch the palate. Calm your mind and count your breath three hundred and sixty times. When your mouth is full of divine water, rinse it a few times and then practise the four acts[2] by drawing up the anus to ensure (for the vital principle) free passage in the jen mo channel through the coccyx and the middle gate (between the loins) and then along the spine up which it moves faster. Close your eyes, turn them up and breathe in slowly through the nose without expiring, until the jade pillow (i.e. the back of the head) is pierced through. Then (the vital principle), as if being forcibly pushed up by the faculty of seeing, rises up the (central channel), circles the Kunlun peak (the top of the head), and descends to the magpie's bridge (the tongue). Now swallow one third of your saliva which should follow (the vital principle) down to the Bright Palace (the heart) before returning to the ocean of prāṇa (the lower belly). Pause for a moment and repeat the same exercise for a second and third time to make three circuits in all. This is called the reverse flowing of the Heavenly Current.

Rest for a little and, with your hands, rub the lower belly one hundred and eighty times. When taking the hands away, put a warm cloth over the navel and lower belly in order not to expose them to cold air. (The ancients said: 'The secret of immortality lies in the preservation of the heat in the Field of the Elixir (in the lower belly).') Then, chafe the backs of the thumbs against each other until they are hot and, with them, rub the eyes fourteen times to quench the 'fire' in the heart, the nose thirty-six times to refresh the lungs, the ears fourteen times to invigorate the kidneys and the face fourteen times to strengthen the spleen. Close the ears with (the palms of) your hands and beat the heavenly drum.[3] Then raise your hands slowly over your head, bringing the two palms together[4] as if to salute the Heavens. Do all this three times and slowly breathe out impure air, inspiring fresh air, four

1. The red dragon is the tongue; roll it round your mouth thirty-six times to make saliva flow, thereby reducing the scorching effect of the heat of rising prāṇa. A quicker way is to roll the tongue back as far as possible.

2. The four acts consist of (a) drawing up, (b) touching, (c) closing and (d) inhaling. Drawing up the anus is to promote free passage of prāṇa through the coccyx; touching the palate with the tongue is to make a bridge connecting the psychic centres in the head with those in the neck and the chest; closing the eyes to look up is to control the mind and to push up the prāṇa; and inhaling without exhaling is to avoid dissipation of the vital energy.

3. Place the palms of the hands on the ears, press the second fingers on the back of the head with the first fingers and snap the latter against the bones above the ears to make sharp sounds.

4. To connect the currents of prāṇa in both arms, thus forming another circuit round the body.

to five times. Then (with crossed arms) hold the shoulders with your hands, shaking them a few times to invigorate your nerves and bones. Conclude by rubbing the jade pillow (the back of the head) twenty-four times, the small of the back 180 times and the middles of the soles 180 times.

Since the above is unintelligible without explanatory notes, this excellent Taoist technique has been largely forgotten in China where people cannot be bothered to investigate it. In my youth, I too was loath to read Taoist books which, like Ch'an texts, seem strange and unintelligible.

SELF-HEALING

I never enjoyed good health before I began meditation and could only obtain temporary relief from modern doctors and herbalists. My heart and stomach were weak and I often fainted, while I also suffered several times a year from bad rheumatism. As I have said in Chapter 4, when I was young I failed miserably in my practice of T'ien T'ai meditation. I continued, however, to concentrate on the lower belly even when I walked in the street and this probably enabled me to accumulate prāṇa. I then practised Hindu breathing exercises to store the vital principle in the solar plexus. The practice of hua t'ou[1] enabled me to forget all about my troubles including the unbearable heat which rose in my apartment to over ninety-five degrees during the summer months. After long hours at my desk translating Chinese texts, I sometimes felt very tired and nearly exhausted. But five minutes of these yogic breathing exercises[2] would renew my strength and enable me to get on with my work. It cured my rheumatism and gave me instant relief not only when I caught cold but when I contracted the dreaded Asian 'flu many years ago.

When prāṇa began to circulate in my body, I felt as if it permeated every organ, bone, nerve and muscle, hence the eight

1. See *Ch'an and Zen Teaching*, Series One, Part I.
2. See *The Science of Breath* by Yogi Ramacharaka, Yogi Publication Society.

physical sensations dealt with earlier. One day, my heart, which was very weak, seemed to be pierced from all sides by what felt like invigorating needles and its weakness vanished like a dream. My appetite grew out of all proportion and each day, besides my three normal meals, I found it necessary to take three extra ones to cope with the involuntary movements which caused profuse perspiration while I was meditating.

A SUBSTITUTE FOR DAILY WALKING

Since I lived more or less in seclusion to control my mind and only went out once or twice a month for a haircut, lack of exercise became a serious problem. I solved it with another Taoist exercise which I describe below.

Two or three times a day, while standing up with the feet some eight inches apart and parallel to each other, I turned my belly and buttocks to the left and the right, one hundred times each way. This simple exercise was equivalent to a short walk in the street, for it worked the lower limbs and was also a necessary complement to my involuntary movements.

INNER ORGAN INVIGORATING YOGA

In order to avoid illness and since prevention is better than cure, I practised twice a day the Taoist Secret of the Six Healing Sounds (Tao Ching Lu Tzu Chueh), the text of which comes after that of the Hsiao Chou T'ien in the *I Fang Chi Chiai* or Ancient Medical Formulas Explained.

THE TAOIST SECRET OF THE SIX HEALING SOUNDS: HO, HU, SZŬ, HSÜ, HSI AND CH'UI

Daily between midnight and midday, a period which stands for the positive (principle yang), sit facing east with crossed legs. Do not close the window but avoid draughts. Knock the lower teeth against the upper ones, roll the tongue round until the mouth is full of saliva, rinse with that saliva a few times and then swallow it all in three audible gulps, visualizing it as reaching the lower belly beneath the navel.

Pucker up your lips slightly and silently make the sound 'Ho!' to eject through the mouth impure air from the heart, then close the mouth to breathe in, through the nostrils, fresh air to invigorate this organ of circulation. Your exhaling should be short and your inhaling long. Do this six times.

After that, follow the same method and make six times each of the five other sounds: 'Hu!' to invigorate the spleen; 'Szŭ!', the lungs; 'Hsü!', the liver; 'Hsi!', the stomach; and 'Ch'ui!', the kidneys. The number thirty-six (six sounds repeated six times each) stands for a microcosmic orbit of 360 degrees.

This method was employed by ancient Taoists to prevent or to cure illnesses when they withdrew from the world to live in the mountains. Before practising it, it is necessary to familiarize oneself with these six sounds in order to harness each of them to the corresponding organ on which it has a psychic influence. For instance, when making the sound 'Ho!', it should actually affect the heart whose impurities are ejected through the mouth, while it is filled with vitality when you breathe in fresh air through the nostrils. During the exercise, it seems as if the heart itself expels its impurities and breathes in energy. One can test its effectiveness by smoking until one's heart is affected, and by then making the sound 'Ho!' to remove the discomfort and by inhaling fresh air to invigorate the heart; one will thus notice the beneficial effect of this sound when made in this way.

ANCIENT MEDICAL SCIENCE

In ancient times, a medical practitioner had to be experienced in the art of self-healing before he could cure others. The art of healing consisted in transferring the physician's own psychic power to his patients to energize their inner prāṇa and to remove all obstructions in their bodies, thereby restoring their health. Even today this healing art is still practised but experienced Taoists are extremely rare and are not easily accessible because they seek neither fame nor fortune and shun sceptics and blasphemers.

ACUPUNCTURE AND CAUTERIZATION

In view of the rareness of experienced Taoist masters and of their reluctance to meet outsiders, the ancients devised a medical science based on the *Nei Ching*, the oldest book on the art of healing, compiled by Ch'i Pai, a minister and noted physician, by order of emperor Huang Ti, also an expert in this science. Its method of treatment is by means of acupuncture and cauterization which remove obstructions in the organic and psychic centres. We know already that the heat of prāṇa sets up vibrations which open psychic channels and dislodge all obstructing impurities in the psychic centres. Since the patients were inexperienced and were unable to accumulate the vital principle to produce the required heat, appropriate means were devised for this end; a silver needle was used to pierce the skin above the obstructed psychic centre or above the psychic channel leading to it, and moxa was burned on the puncture so that the heat reached the affected centre, thereby restoring its vitality and removing its obstructions, the cause of the illness. If the puncture was accurate, the illness would disappear instantly. According to the ancients, silver is soothing and moxa antiseptic. However, the physician had to be well versed in the art of diagnosing illnesses and very familiar with the exact locations of the psychic centres and the channels connecting them. There are books on acupuncture and cauterization and bronze statues of the human body showing the location of the various channels and centres.

SPIRIT OVER MATTER

The ancients advocated the perfecting of spirit for the mastery of matter and great spirit comes from the vital principle being able to flow freely through all the psychic channels. Whoever can so circulate prāṇa is free from all illnesses. The best voice comes from a singer's belly which is full of the vital principle. In boxing, physical force is no match for the hidden strength of prāṇa which enables a little man to defeat a giant. In ancient times, the enlightened masters lived without fear in the mountains infested with wild beasts because powerful psychic waves from their strong minds overcame all hostility. And so when Hsing Ch'ang came with a sword to murder Hui Neng, the patriarch stretched out his neck to receive the fatal blow; the assassin struck thrice but failed to harm him and was so terrified that he fell to the ground. When the late Ch'an master Hsu Yun returned to China from Burma with a jade Buddha carried by porters, they thought it contained precious gems and while passing through an uninhabited region, they put it down and refused to proceed further unless the master gave them a substantial reward. Seeing a large boulder on the roadside, he pointed to it and asked them if it was lighter than the statue. He then moved it with his hands and the porters were so scared that they carried the Buddha to its destination. There was nothing miraculous in this for Hsu Yun merely used the power of prāṇa in his hands to displace the boulder. In her book *With Mystics and Magicians in Tibet*, Mrs. Alexandra David-Neel relates the story of an ascetic who was displeased with her interpreter's disrespectful attitude and who, without rising from his seat, used his psychic power to 'push' violently the latter who staggered and fell back against the wall; she did not see the hermit do anything but the interpreter felt as if he had 'received a terrible blow'.[1]

1. Cf. Mrs. Alexandra David-Neel's book *With Mystics and Magicians in Tibet*, pp. 15–16. Published by Penguin Books Ltd., Middlesex, England.

A friend of mine who began his Taoist meditation when he was only a child, can kick for a few feet a bag of rice weighing about 135 lb. A few years ago, a young Taoist here cured his father's illness by transferring his psychic power to the old man.

REJUVENATION AND IMMORTALITY

Rejuvenation is the first objective of Taoist training and Immortality is its ultimate aim. Taoist practice requires a sound mind in a sound body, for a student should have excellent health to undergo the difficult training. Excellent health comes from perfect harmony of prāṇa, or of the element fire with that of water in the human body. When fire is in excess of water, there will be tears, bad breath, parched throat, thirst, uneasy respiration and dizziness. For this reason, Ch'an practisers drink more tea than most people and sometimes take potions of calming herbs to reduce the effect of the element fire. Taoist students roll their tongues to produce an unusual secretion of saliva which they swallow for the same purpose of reducing the scorching effect of the vital principle. Only when the elements of fire and water are in equilibrium can perfect health be achieved and rejuvenation be possible. When rejuvenation is attained, the span of life easily exceeds the usual limit of three score and ten years. Experienced Taoists know in advance the time of their death and can leave this world when they like. When they meet, they easily recognize each other because of the red glow on their faces which shows their spiritual and physical attainment.

As to Immortality which all Taoists seek, it also has a limit according to the Buddha's Teaching, because immortality and mortality are the two extremes of a duality which has no room in the absolute state. The Śūraṅgama Sūtra lists ten classes of immortals who, though living thousands and tens of thousands of years, are not yet free from the illusion of space and time and are, therefore, unable to escape from the wheel of birth and death. They usually leave their physical bodies in grottoes on high mountains and their consciousnesses roam about in the great void to enjoy freedom and happiness which imply the existence of subject and object.

In the first volume of our *Ch'an and Zen Teaching* Series—pp. 81–3—we presented the story of Lu Tung Pin, an immortal, who threw his sword at Ch'an master Huang Lung. The master pointed his finger at the sword which fell to the ground and could not be picked up by the thrower. This shows the spiritual power of the Ch'an master which was superior to the psychic ability of Lu Tung Pin who, though a famous Taoist, conceded his defeat and vowed to protect the Buddha Dharma.

OMNIPRESENCE AND OMNISCIENCE

The mind expands when it is not stirred by thoughts and is free from bondage. When a meditator wipes out one half of one per cent of his ignorance, he awakens to one half of one per cent of bodhi; this is a minor awakening (Chinese, minor wu; Japanese, minor satori). If he eradicates five or seven per cent of his delusion, he realizes a major awakening or major satori. After achieving several major and minor satoris, there may remain only ten to fifteen per cent of his ignorance which he eliminates at one stroke, this is ultimate awakening or final enlightenment. There are, therefore, many minor and major satoris before his complete enlightenment and the number of these successive awakenings depends on his slow or quick comprehension and realization of the Dharma.

When the late Ch'an master Hsu Yun had a major satori, his mind expanded and embraced his surroundings; he saw everything inside and outside the monastery, and far away, the boats plying on the river and the trees on both its banks. Two nights later, he wiped out all that remained of his delusion and achieved ultimate awakening when he said: 'Mountains, rivers and the great earth are but the Tathāgata.' He perceived his self-nature (Chinese, chien hsing; Japanese, kenshō) which was all embracing. This stage was attained by Hui Neng when he exclaimed: 'Who would have expected that the self-nature is fundamentally pure and clean, beyond birth and death, complete in itself and immutable, and creates all things?'[1] This is omnipresence.

A Taoist practiser, by stilling his mind, also expands it to see and hear those living nearby or in distant places, but his achievement is limited and he cannot reach the 'other shore'.

When the mind of an enlightened master is all embracing, he perceives and knows everything. This is omniscience. Though the knowledge of an experienced Taoist is vast and extensive, it does not go beyond the field of the eighth consciousness for it cannot reach the absolute; hence its limitation as compared with the omniscience or sarvajña of the Buddha.

1. See *Ch'an and Zen Teaching*, Third Series, Sūtra of The Sixth Patriarch, p. 25.

CONCLUSION

CONCLUSION

WE HAVE presented different methods of meditation as practised in China where every student has access to the Chinese texts and can chose the one to his liking. It is true that the Ch'an technique is the best but a student cannot be forced to practise it if he prefers another method. Many Chinese Buddhists have affinity for the Pure Land school and it would be wrong to teach them the Ch'an meditation before they understand it. Moreover the Ch'an teaching is for mature men and only very few people can give rise to the doubt (i ch'ing) without which the hua t'ou technique would fail.[1] We should not forget that karma plays an important role in our decision to practise the Dharma and its obstructing influence ceases only when the student has made real progress in his self-cultivation, that is when his inner excellent qualities, hitherto dormant, manifest themselves as explained by the master Chih I. The practiser will then see clearly and nothing on earth can shake his determination to keep from illusions.

The microcosmic orbit technique employed by ancient Taoists is good for improving the practiser's health which should be strong enough to resist and overcome all hindrances, thereby enabling him to realize stillness of mind. The circulation of the vital principle and the accompanying outer involuntary movements are independent of our will and seem

1. See *Ch'an and Zen Teaching*, First Series, pp. 37–40.

irresistible, but can be stopped as soon as the meditator succeeds in giving rise to the i ch'ing which causes both body and mind to be impenetrable to all illusions, like an impassable wall, as Bodhidharma put it. This shows the superiority of the Ch'an device over all other methods, but the microcosmic orbit technique, by eliminating all obstructions in the psychic centres, forestalls the possibility of contracting the Ch'an illness mentioned in the preface to the second volume of our *Ch'an and Zen Teaching* Series (pp. 22–3). Many Ch'an masters practised Taoism before embracing Buddhism and were well versed in this Taoist technique but they did not mention it lest their disciples clung to it and disregarded the mind Dharma.

Beginners should never be too ambitious at the start of their practice but should commence with short and regular meditations. Yin Shih Tsu rightly suggested two short meditations of twenty minutes each in the morning and evening. If they are regular and without interruption, the result will be very satisfactory and when the practiser is accustomed to sitting and makes real progress, he tends to sit longer.

It is very difficult for beginners to prevent thoughts from arising. Beside the methods dealt with earlier, another effective way to stop thoughts is to concentrate on the third eye, that is the spot between the eyebrows. However, those suffering from hypertension are not advised to try it; they should fix their minds on the lower belly. Another method to stabilize the mind is to bring the two palms together as if to greet a friend in the oriental manner, thereby connecting the psychic centres in both hands and forming a channel through which the vital principle flows. The Taoists place their right palm on and across the left one and grasp their hands to join up the psychic channels in both arms in order to quiet the mind. They get rid of numbness in the legs by placing the palm of one hand on the knee of the numb leg and touching its heel with the other palm; as soon as the vital principle passes through the affected leg, the foot moves a little and the numbness disappears.

It is said that when the pupil is ready, his master will appear to guide him. This teacher will appear only if the student buries his pride and prejudice, cultivates the two great Buddhist virtues which are modesty and humility and vows to practise the holy teaching for self-enlightenment and the enlightenment of others. If he observes the precepts and does not discriminate, his inner excellent qualities will manifest and his inmost teacher will appear to guide him.[1] This master is but his own wisdom now freed from feelings and passions, and no teacher is more reliable than one's self-natured prajñā. For this reason, all serious students will sooner or later discover the profound meaning of the holy Teaching. However, if we rely on our discriminating minds, we remain in the realm of illusions, and this is why the Buddha says that we are the most pitiable of living beings.

It is said that the three worlds (of desire, form and beyond form) are created by the mind and that all phenomena are the product of consciousness. Man's surroundings are conditioned by his discriminating mind and improve or deteriorate according to his good or evil thoughts. His miseries and sufferings come from his spiritual degeneration but his lot can be improved if he strives to better the quality of his own mind. He endures all sorts of troubles and worries about the morrow but we have never heard of enlightened masters dying from starvation or from incurable illnesses. On the contrary, we have only heard of unconcerned monks such as Kuei Shan, Kao Feng, etc., who were penniless and retired to the mountains where monasteries were later built by their followers for the spread of the Dharma. We are now in the Dharma ending period when hatred and harm prevail, with the demon very strong and the Dharma without support. But either demon or Dharma arises from the self-mind and it is up to us to cut down the former for the sake of the latter; only then can we be true Buddhists.

1. See also the Foreword to the Sūtra of Complete Enlightenment in *Ch'an and Zen Teaching*, Third Series, p. 157.

Since we now realize the importance of meditation in our quest of the Truth, it is imperative for us to know that when we achieve the state of dhyāna, no one should be allowed to disturb us by calling or shaking us. This interference by others may have a bad effect on our mental and physical condition. In China, there is a small musical instrument made of stone, called ch'ing, which is held close to the meditator's ear and struck gently to waken him. The Western musical instrument used on board ship to call passengers to meals serves well the same purpose.

GLOSSARY

GLOSSARY

Ā: The first letter of Siddham alphabet which stands for the uncreate. It has seven meanings: (1) Bodhi mind, (2) Dharma, (3) non-duality, (4) Dharmadhātu, or realm of Dharma, (5) Dharmatā, or Dharma-nature, (6) Sovereignty and (7) Dharmakāya, or essential body.

Abhaya: Fearlessness.

Abhimukhī: Appearance of the absolute; the sixth of the ten stages of Mahāyāna Bodhisattva development.

Acalā: State of immutability in the midst of changing phenomena; the eighth of the ten stages of Mahāyāna Bodhisattva development.

Ajātaśatru: A king of Magadha who killed his father to ascend to the throne. At first hostile to the Buddha, later he was converted and became noted for liberality.

Ājñāta: 'Thorough Knowledge', name given by the Buddha to His disciple Kauṇḍinya after his attainment of arhatship.

Ākāśagarbha: 'The Womb of Space', the central Bodhisattva, guardian of the treasury of all wisdom and attainment.

Akṣobhya Buddha: One of the five dhyāni-Buddhas, also called the Immutable Buddha.

Ālaya-vijñāna: The store of consciousness, also called the eighth consciousness.

Amitābha Buddha: The Buddha of Infinite Light of the Western Paradise of Bliss, with Avalokiteśvara on his left and Mahāsthāmaprāpta on his right.

Anāgāmin: A non-coming or non-returning arhat who will not be reborn; the third stage of the path.

Ānanda: A cousin of the Buddha. He was noted as the most learned disciple of the Buddha, and famed for hearing and remembering His teaching. He was a compiler of sūtras and the Second Patriarch of the Ch'an sect.

Anāsrava: No leak, outside the passion-stream as contrasted with āsrava, 'leaking' or worldly cause.

Aniruddha: A disciple of the Buddha, noted for his divine sight.

Antara-kalpa: A small aeon.

Anutpattika-dharma-kṣānti: Rest in the imperturbable reality which is beyond birth and death and requires a very patient endurance. The Prajñāpāramitā-śāstra defines it as the unflinching faith and imperturbed abiding in the underlying reality of all things, which is beyond creation and destruction. It must be realized before attainment of Buddhahood.

Arciṣmatī: 'Glowing Wisdom', the fourth of the ten stages of Mahāyāna Bodhisattva development.

Arhat: A saintly man, the highest type or ideal in Hīnayāna in contrast with a Bodhisattva as the saint in Mahāyāna.

Aśaikṣa: No longer learning, beyond study, the state of arhatship, the fourth of the śrāvaka stages; the preceding three stages requiring study. When an arhat is free from all illusions, he has nothing more to study.

Asaṅkhya: Innumerable kalpas or aeons.

Āsrava: Worldly or 'leaking' cause; inside the passion-stream as contrasted with anāsrava, outside the passion-stream.

Aṣṭavimokṣa: The eight stages of meditation leading to deliverance (1) when there is attachment to form by examination of form and realization of its filthiness; (2) when there is no attachment to form, by examination of form and realization of its filthiness—these two are deliverance by meditation on impurity, the next on purity; (3) by meditation on purity and realization of a state free from desire; (4) by realization of boundless immateriality; (5) by realization of boundless knowledge; (6) by realization of nothingness; (7) by realization of the state wherein there is neither thought nor absence of thought; (8) by realization of the state wherein the two aggregates, feeling (vedanā) and ideation (sañjñā) are entirely eliminated.

Aśvaghoṣa: A Brahmin converted to Buddhism, who became the Twelfth Patriarch of the Ch'an sect; author of *The Awakening of Faith.*

Avalokiteśvara: Kuan Yin or Goddess of Mercy in China, so called because of his appearing as a benevolent lady. He attained enlightenment by means of the faculty of hearing.

Avataṁsaka Sūtra: The first long sūtra expounded by the Buddha after His enlightenment.

Avīci hell: The last and deepest of the eight hells, where sinners suffer, die and are instantly reborn to suffer without interruption.

Avidyā: Ignorance, or unenlightenment.

Āyatana, The Twelve: The twelve entrances, that is the six organs and six sense data that enter for discrimination.

Bhadrapāla: A disciple of the Buddha with an awe-inspiring voice, who realized enlightenment by means of meditation on touch.

Bhaiṣajya-rāja: The elder of the two brothers, who was the first to decide on his career as Bodhisattva of healing, and led his younger brother to adopt the same course.

Bhaiṣajya-samudgata: The Bodhisattva of healing, whose office is to heal the sick; younger brother of Bhaiṣajya-rāja.

Bhikṣu, bhikṣunī: Buddhist monk and nun.

Bhīśma-garjita-ghoṣa-svara-rāja: The King with awe-inspiring voice, the name of countless Buddhas successively appearing during the kalpa or aeon called 'the kalpa free from the calamities of decadence, famine, epidemics, etc'.

Bhūtatathatā: Bhūta is substance, that which exists; tathatā is suchness, thusness, i.e. such is its nature. It means the real, thus always, or eternally so; i.e. reality as contrasted with unreality, or appearance; and the unchanging or immutable as contrasted with form and phenomena.

Bimbisāra: A king of Magadha, converted by the Buddha, to whom he gave the Veṇuvana park; imprisoned and dethroned by his son, Ajātaśatru.

Bodhi: Englightenment.

Bodhidharma: The twenty-eighth Patriarch who came to China in 520 to teach Ch'an; he was the First Patriarch of China and died in 528.

Bodhimaṇḍala: Truth-plot, holy site, place of enlightenment; the place where the Buddha attained enlightenment or where he expounded the Dharma.

Bodhisattva: A Mahāyānist seeking enlightenment to enlighten others; he is devoid of egoism and devoted to helping all living beings.

Buddha: The Enlightened One; the first of the Triple Gem, the second being Dharma, and the third, Saṅgha.

Buddhakāya: Body of Buddha, in the enjoyment of the highest samādhi bliss.

Caṇḍāla: An outcast, a bad and despicable man.

Candraprabha Bodhisattva: A Bodhisattva who attained enlightenment by meditating on the element water.

Candra-sūrya-pradīpa Buddha: Or Candrārkadīpa, the title of 20,000 Buddhas who succeeded each other expounding the Lotus Sūtra.

Catvāriārya-satyāni: The four dogmas: suffering (duḥkha), its cause (samudaya), its ending (nirodha) and the way thereto (mārga). They are the doctrine first preached by the Buddha to his five former ascetic companions, and also those who accepted them in the śrāvaka stage.

Ch'an: Name of mind; Ch'an being name and mind being substance; wrongly interpreted as meditation, abstraction, or dhyāna in Sanskrit (Jap. Zen).

Chan Jan: The ninth Patriarch of the T'ien T'ai school.

Ch'ang Ch'ing: An eminent Ch'an master, Dharma successor to Shueh Feng. Died in 932 in his seventy-ninth year.

Chao Chou: An eminent Ch'an master, Dharma successor to Nan Chuan; noted for his kung an (koan) 'Wu'. Died in 894 in his 120th year.

Ch'eng Yuan: The Third Patriarch of the Lotus sect. Died in 802 at the age of ninety-one.

Chia Shan: An eminent Ch'an master, disciple of the Boat Monk. Died in 881.

Chih Hsin Chih: A method of meditation which consists in grasping at the mind itself by looking into each rising thought, thereby stopping it and preventing it from following externals.

Chih I: Also called Chih Che, the Fourth Patriarch of the T'ien T'ai school. Died in 598 at the age of sixty.

Chih Kuan: Sanskrit, śamatha-vipaśyanā. Chih is quieting the active mind and getting rid of discrimination, and kuan is observing, examining, introspecting. When the mind is at rest, it is called chih and when it is seeing clearly, it is kuan. The chief object is the concentration of mind by special methods for the purpose of clear insight into the truth and to be rid of illusion.

Chin T'u Tsung: The Pure Land school.

Chuan Tsu: A successor to Lao Tsu in the fourth century B.C.

Ch'ung mo: Or 'bursting' channel, a psychic channel which rises from the perineum, goes up between the jen mo and tu mo and ends in the chest; it connects twenty-four psychic centres.

Cintāmaṇi: A fabulous gem, responding to every wish.

Dānapati: An almsgiver; a patron who supports a monk or a monastery.

Daśabala: Or Daśatathāgatabala, the ten powers of a Buddha to know (1) the right and wrong in every situation; (2) the retributive effects of the past, present and future karma of every being; (3) all stages of liberation by means of dhyāna-samādhi; (4) the superior and inferior potentialities of all beings; (5) the ability to know every being's knowledge and understanding; (6) the different worldly conditions of all beings; (7) the ends of all different paths trodden by all beings; (8) all causes of birth and death and all good and evil karmas unobstructedly perceptible to the deva eye; (9) the past lives of all beings and the final nirvāṇa; and (10) the permanent destruction of all worldly habits.

Daśabhūmi: The ten stages of Bodhisattva development into a Buddha: (1) pramuditā, joy at having overcome all hindrances for entering the Buddha path; (2) vimala, freedom from all impurities of kleśa; (3) prabhākarī, appearance of the light of wisdom; (4) arciṣmatī, radiation of full wisdom; (5) sudurjayā, conquest of final hindrances; (6) abhimukhī, appearance of self-nature in its purity; (7) dūraṁgamā, the inconceivable beyond the comprehension of men of Hīnayāna; (8) acalā, imperturbability; (9) sādhumatī, unhindered correct interpretation and expounding of Dharma everywhere; and (10) Dharmamegha, Dharma clouds raining nectar to liberate living beings.

Dengyo Daishi: A Japanese disciple of Tao Sui, the tenth Patriarch of the T'ien T'ai school, who introduced Tendai in Japan in the ninth century.

Devadatta: Brother of Ānanda and cousin of the Buddha of whom he was an enemy and rival.

Dhāraṇī: See Mantra.

Dharaṇiṁdhara: Or 'Ruler of the Earth', a Bodhisattva who realized bodhi by means of meditation on the element earth.

Dharma: Law, truth, religion, thing, anything Buddhist. It connotes Buddhism as the perfect religion; it has the second place in the Triratna or Triple Gem.

Dharmadhātu: (a) A name for things in general, noumenal or phenomenal; for the physical universe, or any part of it. (b) The unifying underlying spiritual reality regarded as the ground or cause of all things, the absolute from which all proceeds. (c) One of the eighteen dhātus or realms of senses. There are categories of three, four, five and ten dharmadhātus. The ten are the realms of (1) Buddhas, (2) Bodhisattvas, (3) pratyeka-buddhas, (4) śrāvakas, (5) devas, (6) men, (7) asuras, or titans, (8) animals, (9) hungry ghosts and (10) hells. The four are: (1) the phenomenal realm, with differentiation; (2) the noumenal realm, with unity, (3) the realm of both the noumenal and phenomenal which are interdependent; and (4) the realm of phenomena which are also interdependent. The three are the above four minus the phenomenal realm, i.e. (1) the noumenal realm, (2) the realm of both noumenal and phenomenal which are interdependent, and (3) the realm of phenomena which are also interdependent. The five are: (1) the worldly, or the above 'phenomenal' realm; (2) the transcendental, or the above 'noumenal'; (3) the realm of both the worldly and transcendental, or the above 'noumenal and phenomenal which are interdependent'; (4) neither the worldly nor the transcendental, or the above 'noumenal and phenomenal which are interdependent'; and (5) the unhindered realm, or the above 'phenomena which are also interdependent'.

Dharmākara: A bhikṣu noted for his forty-eight great vows, who became Amitābha Buddha.

Dharmakāya: Body in its essence nature, or that of the Buddha as such. Only Buddhas can see it.

Dharmamegha: The last of the ten stages of Mahāyāna Bodhisattva development, that of Dharma clouds raining nectar to save living beings.

Dharmarāja: The King of the Law, the Buddha.

Dhātu, The eighteen: Realms of sense, i.e. the six organs, their objects and their perceptions.

Dhūta: An ascetic, a monk engaged in austerities.

Dhyāna: Meditation, abstract contemplation.

Dhyāni-Buddhas, The five: Vairocana in the centre, Akṣobhya in the east, Ratnasaṁbhava in the south, Amitābha in the west and Amoghasiddhi in the north.

Fa Chao: The Fourth Patriarch of the Lotus sect.

Fa Hua: The Sixth Patriarch of the T'ien T'ai (Tendai) school.

Fa Yen sect: The fifth of the five Ch'an sects of China. (See *Ch'an and Zen Teaching*, second series.)

Gāthā: Poems or chants; one of the twelve divisions of the Mahāyāna canon.

Gavāṁpati: A disciple of the Buddha who attained arhatship by means of meditation on the organ of taste.

Gṛdhrakūṭa: The Vulture mountain, near Rājagṛha, where the Buddha sojourned when He expounded the Sūtra of Contemplation of Amitāyus.

Han Shan: 'Silly Mountain', a name adopted by Ch'an master Te Ch'ing (1546–1623) who revived the Ch'an sect in China in the Ming dynasty.

Hīnayāna: 'Small Vehicle', also called 'Half-word', preliminary teaching given by the Buddha to his disciples.

Hsi Yuan Chih: Method of meditation which consists in fixing the mind on an object to stop the thinking process.

Hsing An: The last of the nine Patriarchs of the Lotus sect.

Hsing Ch'ang: The seventh of the nine Patriarchs of the Lotus sect.

Hsu Yun: Also called Te Ch'ing, a Ch'an master regarded as the right Dharma eye of the present generation. 1840–1959.

Huang Po: Ch'an master Hsi Yun of Huang Po mountain; Dharma successor of Pai Chang and teacher of Lin Chi (Rinzai). Died in Ta Chung reign (847–59).

Hui Szu: The Third Patriarch of the T'ien T'ai (Tendai) school. Died in 577.

Hui Wen: The Second Patriarch of the T'ien T'ai (Tendai) school of Pei Ch'i dynasty (550–78).

Hui Yuan: The First Patriarch of the Lotus sect. Died in 416 at the age of eighty-three.

Indra: Or Śakra, the ruler of the thirty-three heavens.

Iśvaradeva: A title of Śiva, king of the devas.

Jambudvīpa: Our earth.

Jen mo: A psychic channel which rises from the perineum, goes up along the belly, passes through the navel, the pit of the stomach, the chest, throat and upper lip and ends below the eye; it connects twenty-seven psychic centres.

Jīva: Or Jīvaka, son of Bimbisāra by the concubine Āmrapālī, noted for his medical skill.

Karma: Moral action causing future retribution, and either good or evil transmigration.

Karuṇā: Pity, compassion; the second of the Four Immeasurables, consisting in saving living beings from suffering.

Kaṣāya: A monk's robe.

Kāśyapa: There were five Kāśyapas, disciples of the Buddha: Mahākāśyapa, Uruvilvākāśyapa, Gayā-kāśyapa, Nadī-kāśyapa and Daśabala-kāśyapa. Uruvilvā, Gayā and Nadī were brothers.

Kauṇḍinya: Also called Ajñāta, the first of the five disciples of the Buddha, who realized arhatship by means of meditation on sound.

Kauṣṭhila: A disciple of the Buddha who, with Sundarananda, attained arhatship by fixing the mind on the tip of the nose.

Kinnara: Heavenly musicians noted for their songs and dances.

Kleśa: Worry, anxiety, affliction, trouble, distress and whatever causes them.

Kṣaṇa: The shortest measure of time; sixty kṣaṇa equal one finger-snap, ninety a thought, 4,500 a minute.

Kṣatriya: A warrior and ruling caste.

Kṣudrapanthaka: A disciple of the Buddha who attained arhatship by means of meditation on the organ of smell.

Kuan: See under chih.

Kuan Ting: The Fifth Patriarch of the T'ien T'ai (Tendai) school.

Kuei Shan: Ch'an master Ling Yu of Kuei Shan mountain; Dharma successor of Pai Chang and teacher of Yang Shan. Kuei Shan and Yang Shan founded the Kuei Yang sect. (Jap. Ikyō Zen), one of the five Ch'an sects of China. Died in 853 at the age of eighty-three.

Kukkuṭa park: A park near Gayā where the Buddha preached the Four Noble Truths after His enlightenment.

Kumāra: A Bodhisattva as son of the Buddha; a son of Buddha.

Kumārajīva: An enlightened Indian master who went to China to translate Siddham sūtras into Chinese and died in Ch'ang An about A.D. 412.

Lao Tsu: Also called Li Erh and Li Po Yang; he was born in 604 B.C. and wrote the Tao Teh Ching.

Lien Ch'ih: Also called Yun Hsi; a Ch'an master of the Ming dynasty who urged his disciples to repeat the Buddha's name and became the Eighth Patriarch of the Lotus sect. Died in 1615 at the age of eighty-one.

Lin Chi: Japanese, Rinzai. Master I Hsuan of Lin Chi, disciple of Huang Po and founder of Lin Chi sect, one of the five Ch'an sects of China. Died in 867.

Lotus samādhi: A state of samādhi wherein the meditator looks into the void (noumenon), the unreal (phenomenon) and the Mean (the absolute) that unites them. It derives from the sixteen samādhis in the Lotus Sūtra, Chapter 24.

Lotus sect: Another name of the Pure Land school.

Lotus Sūtra: Sanskrit, Saddharmapuṇḍarīka Sūtra. Expounded by the Buddha in the eight years of the fifth period of His teaching, in which He revealed the One Buddha vehicle. Its aim consists in 'opening' the treasure of self-possessed Buddha-wisdom, in 'showing' it to His disciples and in guiding them so that they could be 'awakened' to it and finally 'entering' it.

Lu Miao Fa Meng: 'The Six Profound Dharma Doors', a treatise by master Chih I (also called Chih Che) which teaches the six stages of meditation leading to enlightenment.

Madhyamika śāstra: A treatise on the Mean of the Middle School, founded by Nāgārjuna and translated by Kumārajīva.

Mahākāśyapa: A Brahmin of Magadha, disciple of the Buddha, to whom was handed down the mind Dharma, outside of Scriptures; the First Patriarch of the Ch'an sect; accredited with supervising the first compilation of the Buddha's sermons.

Mahā-Maudgalyāyana: Also called Maudgalaputra, one of the ten chief disciples of the Buddha, specially noted for his miraculous powers.

Mahāparinirvāṇa Sūtra: A sermon preached by the Buddha just before His nirvāṇa.

Mahāsattva: A perfect Bodhisattva, greater than any other being except a Buddha.

Mahāsthāma: Or Mahāsthāmaprāpta, a Bodhisattva representing the Buddha wisdom of Amitābha. He is on Amitābha's right with Avalokiteśvara on the left. They are called the Three Holy Ones of the Western Paradise of Bliss.

Mahāyāna: The Great Vehicle which indicates universalism, or salvation for all, for all are Buddhas and will attain enlightenment. (See Hīnayāna.)

Maitreya: The Buddhist Messiah, or next Buddha, now in the Tuṣita heaven, who is to come 5,000 years after the nirvāṇa of Śākyamuni Buddha.

Maitrī: Kindness; the first of the Four Immeasurables, that of bestowing happiness.

Manas: Faculty of thought; the sixth of the eight consciousnesses, or the last of the six means of perception.

Mañjuṣrī: A Bodhisattva who is the symbol of wisdom and is placed on the Buddha's left with Samantabhadra on the right. His bodhimaṇḍala is on W'u T'ai Shan, or the Five-Peaked Mountain in China.

Mantra: An incantation, spell, oath; mystical formulae employed in Yoga. (See Dhāraṇī.)

Māra: A demon.

Mātaṅgī: Name of a low-caste girl who seduced Ānanda.

Mo Ho Chih Kuan: Or Mahā-śamatha-vipaśyanā, a treatise by master Chih I, also called Chih Che, the Fourth Patriarch of the T'ien T'ai school.

Mṛgadāva park: A deer park north-east of Vārāṇaśī, a favourite resort of the Buddha.

Muditā: Joy on seeing others delivered from suffering; the third of the Four Immeasurables.

Nāga: A dragon.

Nāgakanyā: A nāga maiden who, according to the Lotus Sūtra, presented her precious gem to the Buddha who immediately accepted it in the presence of His disciples to bear witness of her realization of enlightenment with the speed of the gem passing from her hands to those of the World Honoured One.

Nāgārjuna: The Fourteenth Patriarch of the Ch'an sect; he founded the Mādhyamika or Middle School and is regarded as the First Patriarch of the T'ien T'ai school.

Navasaṁjñā: One of the meditations on filthiness, or the ninefold meditation on a dead body: (1) its tumefaction; (2) its blue, mottled colour; (3) its decay; (4) its mess of blood, etc.; (5) its rotten flesh and discharges; (6) its being devoured by birds and beasts; (7) its dismembering; (8) its white bones; and (9) their cremation and return to dust.

Nayuta: A numeral, 100,000 or one million, or ten million.

Nidāna, The twelve: The twelve causes or links in the chain of existence: (1) ignorance, or unenlightenment; (2) action, activity, conception or disposition; (3) consciousness; (4) name and form; (5) the six sense organs, i.e. eye, ear, nose, tongue, body and intellect; (6) contact, or touch; (7) sensation, or feeling; (8) desire or craving; (9) grasping; (10) being or existing; (11) birth; and (12) old age and death.

Nirmāṇakāya: Transformation body of a Buddha, that of power to transform himself at will into any form for the omnipresent salvation of those needing him. It is perceptible to men.

Nirvāṇa: Complete extinction of individual existence; cessation of rebirth and entry into bliss.

Niṣad: 'Going to the source of the phenomenal', name given by the Buddha to His disciple Upaniṣad after the latter's attainment of arhatship.

Obstructions, The three: Self-importance, jealousy and desire.

Padma: A red lotus flower.

Padmāsana: A full lotus posture with crossed legs.

Pañca-dharmakāya: The five attributes of the essential body of the Buddha, i.e. that he is above all moral conditions; tranquil and apart from false ideas; wise and omnipresent; free, unlimited, unconditioned which is the state of nirvāṇa; and that he has perfect knowledge of this state.

Pārājikas: Killing, stealing, carnality and deception under the mask of true preaching.

Pāramitā: 'Going to the other shore', or method of attaining enlightenment.

Pilindavatsa: A disciple of the Buddha who realized arhatship by means of meditation on the body.

Prabhākarī: 'Appearance of the light of wisdom'; the third of the ten stages of Mahāyāna Bodhisattva development.

Pramuditā: 'Joy at having overcome all obstructions for present entry upon the path to enlightenment'; the first of the ten stages of Mahāyāna Bodhisattva development.

Prajñā: Fundamental wisdom which is inherent in every man and which manifests itself after the veil of delusion has been destroyed.

Prajñāpāramitā: Realization of enlightenment by means of inherent wisdom.

Prāṇa: The vital principle in the human body which can be energized by means of regulated breath and meditation for the sublimation of body and mind.

Prātimokṣa: the 250 Precepts for monks which are read in assembly twice a month.

Pratyutpanna-samādhi Sūtra: A sūtra teaching the samādhi in which all the Buddhas in the ten directions are seen clearly like the stars at night. Its practice requires ninety days during which the practiser does not rest but persistently thinks of Amitābha Buddha and calls his name.

Puṇḍarīka: A white lotus blossom which stands for pure living.

Pure Land school: Chinese, Chin T'u Tsung, whose chief tenet is salvation by faith in Amitābha Buddha.

Pūrṇamaitrāyaṇīputra: A disciple of the Buddha who realized arhatship by means of meditation on tongue perception.

Rājagṛha: The capital of Magadha, at the foot of the Vulture mountain.

Rākṣasa: A malignant demon.

Ṣaḍabhijñā: The six supernatural powers; (1) divine sight; (2) divine hearing; (3) knowledge of the minds of all other living beings; (4) knowledge of all forms of previous existences of self and others; (5) power to appear at will in any place and to have absolute freedom; and (6) insight into the ending of the stream of birth and death.

Sādhumatī: 'Acquisition of the four unhindered powers of interpretation with ability to expound all Dharma doors everywhere', the ninth of the ten stages of Mahāyāna Bodhisattva development.

Sahā: Our world of birth and death.

Śakra, The vase of: A vase from which come all things required by him.

Samādhi: Internal state of imperturbability, exempt from all external sensation.

Samantabhadra: A Bodhisattva, symbol of the fundamental law, dhyāna and the practice of all Buddhas. He is the right-hand assistant of the Buddha and Mañjuśrī is His left-hand assistant. His region is in the East. Mount O Mei in Szechwan, China, is his bodhimaṇḍala, and devotees go there to see myriad Buddha lamps in the sky at night.

Śamatha: See Chih Kuan.

Sambhogakāya: Reward body of a Buddha, that of bliss or enjoyment of the fruits of his past saving labours. It is perceptible to Bodhisattvas only.

Saṁbodhi: The wisdom or omniscience of the Buddha.

Saṁsāra: The realm of birth and death.

Saṁskāra: The fourth of the five aggregates; functioning of mind in its process regarding like and dislike, good and evil, etc.; discrimination. Also the second of the twelve links in the chain of existence.

Samyak-sambuddha: Universal knowledge of a Buddha, complete enlightenment, omniscience; one of the ten titles of a Buddha.

Samyuktāgama Sūtra: Miscellaneous treatise on abstract meditation, one of the four Āgamas.

Saṅgha: The Buddhist Order; the last of the Triple Gem.

Śāriputra: A disciple of the Buddha, noted for his wisdom.

Sarvajña: All wisdom, Buddha wisdom, perfect knowledge, omniscience.

Śāstra: A treatise, one of the three divisions of the Tripiṭaka.

Shan Tao: The Second Patriarch of the Lotus sect. Died in 681.

Shao K'ang: The Fifth Patriarch of the Lotus sect. Died in 805.

Siddham: The ancient Sanskrit in use at the time of the Buddha. All Chinese sūtras and śāstras are translations from Siddham texts.

Śrāmaṇera: A male novice.

Śrāvaka: A hearer, disciple of Buddha who understands the Four Noble Truths, rids himself of the unreality of the phenomenal and enters the incomplete nirvāṇa.

Śrota-āpanna: One who has entered the stream of holy living, the first stage of the path.

Subhūti: A senior disciple of the Buddha.

Sudurjayā: 'Overcoming of utmost difficulties', the fifth of the ten stages of Mahāyāna Bodhisattva development.

Sundarananda: A disciple of the Buddha who attained arhatship by means of meditation on smell perception.

Śūraṅgama Sūtra: Leng Yen Ching, a sūtra translated by Paramiti in 705, in which the Buddha revealed the causes of illusion leading to the creation of all worlds of existence and the methods of getting out of them.

Sūtra: The Buddha's sermon; one of the twelve divisions of the Mahāyāna canon.

Sūtra of Amitābha: O Mi T'o Ching, a sermon on the Buddha of Infinite Light and his two attendant Bodhisattvas of the Western Paradise of Bliss.

Sūtra of Amitāyus: Wu Liang Shou Ching, a sermon on the Buddha of Boundless Age who was Bhikṣu Dharmākara and his forty-eight great vows.

Sūtra of Complete Enlightenment: Yuan Chueh Ching. See *Ch'an and Zen Teaching*, Third Series, for its English translation.

Sūtra of Contemplation of Amitāyus: Kuan Wu Liang Shou Ching, also called Sūtra of Sixteen Contemplations; a sūtra teaching the methods of meditation for rebirth in the Western Paradise of Bliss.

Suvarṇa-prabhāsa-uttamarāja-sūtra: Chin Kuang Ming Ching, or Golden Light Sūtra, translated in the sixth century and twice later, and used by the founder of T'ien T'ai school.

Svalakṣaṇa: Individuality, personal, as contrasted with general or common.

Ta Ch'eng Chih Kuan: The Mahāyāna's Śamatha-vipaśyanā, a treatise by Hui Szu, the Third Patriarch of T'ien T'ai school in the fifth century.

Ta Chih Tu Lun: A commentary by Nāgārjuna on the 'Long Chapter' of the Mahāprajñāpāramitā-sūtra.

Ta Hui: An eminent Ch'an master in the Sung dynasty; died in 1163 in his seventy-fifth year.

Tai Mo: A psychic channel from both sides of the navel, forming a belt encircling the belly; it connects eight psychic centres.

T'an Lun: The Third Patriarch of the Pure Land school; died in 542 at the age of sixty-seven.

Tan T'ien: Or Udāna, a spot about an inch below the navel where is the reservoir of vital principle which can be transmited unto the Elixir of Immortality according to the Taoists.

Tao: Road, way, path, doctrine, truth, reality, self-nature, the absolute.

Tao Ch'o: The fourth Patriarch of the Pure Land school; died in 645.

Taoism: Doctrine of Lao Tsu. (See also Lao Tsu.)

Tao Sui: The Tenth Patriarch of the T'ien T'ai school in the eighth century.

Tao Teh Ching: A treatise by Lao Tsu.

Tathāgata: He who came as did all Buddhas, who took the absolute way of cause and effect, and attained to perfect wisdom; one of the highest titles of a Buddha.

T'i Chen Chih: The T'ien T'ai method of understanding, realizing and embodying the real.

T'ien Kung: The Seventh Patriarch of the T'ien T'ai school.

T'ien T'ai: Japanese, Tendai. A Buddhist school which bases its tenets on the Lotus Sūtra, Mahāparinirvāṇa Sūtra and Mahāprajñāpāramitā-sūtra and maintains the identity of the absolute and the world of phenomena, thus attempting to unlock the secrets of all phenomena by means of meditation.

Tripiṭaka: The Buddhist canon consisting of three divisions: sūtra (sermons), vinaya (rules of discipline) and śāstra (treatises).

Tri-sahasra-mahā-sahasra-loka-dhātu: A great chiliocosm. Mount Sumeru and its seven surrounding continents, eight seas and ring of iron mountains form one small world; 1,000 of these form a small chiliocosm; 1,000 of these small chiliocosms form a medium chiliocosm; 1,000 of these form a great chiliocosm, which consists of 1,000,000,000 small worlds.

Ts'ao Shan: Ch'an master Pen Chi of Ts'ao Shan mountain, disciple of Tung Shan and co-founder of Ts'ao Tung sect (Jap. Sotō Zen); died in 901.

Ts'ao Tung sect: One of the five Ch'an sects of China, founded by Tung Shan and his disciple Ts'ao Shan.

Tso Ch'i: The eighth Patriarch of the T'ien T'ai sect, died in 742 at the age of eighty-three.

Tu Mo: A psychic channel which rises from the perineum and passes through the coccyx to go up along the backbone to the crown and thence descends along the forehead and nose, ending in the gums; it connects thirty-one psychic centres.

T'ung Meng Chih Kuan: Or 'Chih Kuan for Beginners', a treatise by master Chih I, the Fourth Patriarch of the T'ien T'ai school.

Tung Shan: Ch'an master Liang Chiai of Tung Shan mountain, disciple of Yun Yuen. He and his disciple Ts'ao Shan founded the Ts'ao Tung sect (Jap. Sotō Zen). Died in 869 at the age of sixty-three.

Tuṣita: The fourth heaven in the realm of desire; its inner region is the Pure Land of Maitreya who will descend to earth as a successor of Śākyamuni Buddha.

Ucchuṣma: 'The Fire-head', an arhat who attained enlightenment by meditating on the element fire.

Udāna: See T'an T'ien.

Upāli: A disciple who attained arhatship by means of meditation on perception of object of touch.

Upaniṣad: A disciple who attained arhatship by means of meditation on form.

Upāsaka, upāsikā: A male, female disciple who engages to observe the first five rules of discipline.

Upekṣā: Indifference or renunciation.

Vaidehī: A queen, wife of king Bimbisāra, who was taught by the Buddha to meditate on Buddha Amitāyus for her rebirth in the Western Paradise of Bliss.

Vaipulya: Expanded sūtras; the eleventh of the twelve divisions of the Mahāyāna canon.

Vasubandhu: The twenty-first Indian Patriarch of the Ch'an sect.

Vedas: Brahman Scriptures.

Vimala: State of purity, free from all defilement.

Vimalakīrti Nirdeśa Sūtra: Vimalakīrti, or 'Spotless Reputation', was a native of Vaiśālī and was a Nirmāṇakaya of 'The Golden Grain Tathāgata'; he appeared in the form of a upāsaka to assist the Buddha in converting people to the Mahāyāna doctrine expounded in a sermon called Vimalakīrti Nirdeśa Sūtra.

Vipaśyanā: See Chih Kuan.

Vīra: A strong or mighty man, demigod.

Viśvabhū Buddha: The 1000th Buddha of the Glorious Aeon (Alaṁkāraka-kalpa).

Yakṣa: Demons in the earth, air, or lower heavens.

Yama: A god of the dead, or hell-keeper.

Yamaloka: The realm of Yama.

Yang Ch'iao: A psychic channel which rises from the middle of the sole and turns upward to the outer side of the ankle and leg, then skirts the back of the body and reaches the shoulder, veering to the neck, the corner of the mouth and the inner corner of the eye, ending behind the brain; it connects twenty-two psychic centres.

Yang Shan: Ch'an master Hui Chi of Yang Shan mountain, disciple of Kuei Shan and co-founder of the Kuei Yang sect; died in the ninth century.

Yang Wei: a psychic channel which rises from the outer side of the foot about one and half inches below the ankle, goes up along the outer side of the leg and after skirting the back of the body, enters the upper arm, half way along which it veers to the shoulder, the neck, then behind the ear ending in the forehead; it connects thirty-two psychic centres.

Yen Shou: The Sixth Patriarch of the Lotus sect; died in 975 at the age of seventy-two.

Yin Ch'iao: A psychic channel which rises from the middle of the sole, turns upward to the inner sides of the ankle and leg, skirts the belly and chest, reaches the shoulders, turns upward to the throat and ends in the inner corner of the eye; it connects eight psychic centres.

Yin Wei: A psychic channel which rises from the inner side of the calf about five inches above the ankle, goes upward along the inner side of the thigh and after skirting the belly and half of the chest, turns to the throat, ascends along the face and ends in front of the top of the head; it connects fourteen psychic centres.

Yojana: Distance covered by a royal day's march for the army.

Yun Men sect: One of the five Ch'an sects of China, founded by Wen Yen of Yun Men monastery. Jap. Ummon Zen.

Yung Chia: Ch'an master Hsuan Chueh of Yung Chia, who attained enlightenment the day he called on the Sixth Patriarch for instruction and was called 'The Overnight Enlightened One'. Author of the *Yung Chia's Collection* and of the famous *Song of Enlightenment.* Died in 712. Jap. Yoka Daishi.

INDEX

INDEX